# SPORTS FOR DORKS

# SPORTS
# FOR DORKS
## College Football

EDITED AND BY Mike Leach

*and*

Ferhat Guven

Sports Dorks CFB, LLC

**SPORTS DORKS CFB, LLC**
PO Box 3109 #73200
Houston, TX 77253-3109

www.sportsfordorks.com

Sports Dorks CFB, LLC edition August 2011

Edited by Mike Leach and Ferhat Guven
Cover Design: Pete Garceau
Interior Design, Graphs and Tables: Timm Bryson

ISBN: 978-0615484976

*For Sara, Guy and Coco*

# CONTENTS

# FOREWORD

During the 2010-11 college football season, over a 129-day period beginning September 2, 2010, television networks broadcast 685 live Division I-FBS football games. College football fans across the country had the opportunity to watch an average of 5.3 games per day—roughly equal to sixteen viewing hours per day. Total attendance for Division I-FBS football matchups (including bowl games) exceeded thirty-seven million fans over the same period.[1] In addition to the games themselves, countless television hours were devoted to college football news shows including pregame, halftime, postgame, weekly, daily, recruiting, behind the scenes, behind the lines, reality programs, and so on. If television was not enough to satiate America's demand for college football, there were hundreds of college football radio programs, and thousands of Web sites, blogs, and message boards covering conferences and teams to which a fan could turn. Never in the history of mankind had so much information about college football been available to so many people.

Most fans get their information from watching the game itself. The source of our information comes from the usual suspects: a play-by-play announcer, an "analyst," and a sideline reporter. The content of the broadcasts is predictable. Fans are treated to discussions about the weather, and an acknowledgement of the always loyal, boisterous, knowledgeable fans that come from miles around. The stakes of the game usually have some sort of trancendental significance. In the best case, a team is playing for a shot at the Bowl Championship Series (BCS) crown, an appearance in a BCS bowl game, or at least a bid from a respectable bowl. In the worst case, one of the teams is playing for pride. No game-watching experience is complete without a discussion about the local cuisine, which normally centers on the quality of the local barbecue—invariably considered the best in the country. The broadcasts proceed with the announcers describing their relationship with the head coach. In these discussions, a coach tends to fit into one of three broad archetypes: a winner, a fighter, or a "great guy" who can deliver a witty quote.

The announcers will then discuss what they believe are the three key success factors for each team, which normally include the ever-helpful trinity of playing good defense, limiting turnovers, avoiding special teams' letdowns, or some derivative thereof. If these insights conform to the game's progress, the announcers will trot them out again as the second half is kicking off; otherwise, the keys stay on the shelf. The analyst will often establish his expertise by focusing on some tactical vagary that is ultimately inconsequential to the game's outcome. The sideline reporter will appear three to four times during the telecast to breathlessly update viewers about a player's injury, describe the temperature on the field, or obtain an immediate update from a bewildered head coach prior to or after halftime. While we find something comforting about this ritual, these broadcasts rarely serve as an opportunity to gain a deeper understanding of the game.

If a team wins, the local newspapers will pay homage to its greatness. In this digital age, the local paper remains a stubborn anachronism, and the journalism exhibited reflects that. The tone of the reporting usually ranges between reverential to deferential, or can swing wildly the other way and suddenly become overly critical, depending on the paper's (or the university's) agenda. Most university towns are also one-newspaper towns. Their sports journalists generally cannot afford to bite the hand that feeds. Nevertheless, for many of us, the local newspaper remains a first stop for obtaining information about our teams' fortunes. The local reporters have the best access to the teams, but if hard-nosed investigative reporting is what you are looking for, you might come away disappointed.

Message boards provide catharsis for many of those seeking an outlet to share the joy of victory or anguish over a loss. Generally, message boards will settle on some common denominator of despair or euphoria. Almost all participants are anonymous. Some of the message board participants claim to have unique access to the players, coaches, or school administrators. No one ever really knows. Information is filtered through the rose-colored glasses of the home team. In this setting objectivity more often than not takes a backseat to emotion and the irrationality of the crowd.

Overall, television networks and the various online information providers do a good job catering to the sports information needs of those who see college football as a welcome distraction or a means of staying connected with their favorite teams. The proof is in the numbers. According to the US Department of Education's Office of Postsecondary Education, in 2009, Division I-FBS college football teams combined to generate $2.58 billion in revenues producing $1.1 billion in operating income.[*,2] As those figures suggest, college football is a big business, and there are merits to appealing to the mass market.[†]

In 2003, the book *Moneyball: The Art of Winning an Unfair Game*, written by Michael Lewis, captured the story of how the Oakland Athletics, a team with one of the smallest budgets in Major League Baseball, was able to win more games over a four-year period than any Major League Baseball team, including teams with budgets nearly three times that of the Athletics. *Moneyball* demonstrated how statistics and quantitative analysis could be applied to a sport that had long relied on the collective wisdom of owners and managers based on some useful, albeit not always meaningful, statistics. By penetrating the sea of baseball data and identifying metrics that had essentially been hiding in plain sight, the Oakland A's were able to identify undervalued players who possessed skill sets overlooked by other teams. Since *Moneyball's* publication, other baseball teams have replicated and improved upon the quantitative tactics used by the Athletics. The rise of computing power and quantitative analytics, particularly over the past two decades, has helped to wring out inefficiencies in industry, finance (depending who you ask) and other fields, as well as created new areas of growth and development. The use of quantitative analytics is similarly being applied to other sports.

---

* Because universities receive tax-free status, and college football teams are deemed extensions of these universities, college football teams' earnings are also accorded tax-free status.

† But not quite as big as many make it out to be. Total revenues generated by Division I-FBS schools are 60 percent of those generated by Seaboard Corporation (AMX: SEB), the five-hundredth-ranked U.S. company by revenue according to the 2011 Fortune 500 rankings.

In the context of sports, the practice of innovation encompasses any idea or discipline that seeks to improve the sport. *Moneyball* chronicled the application of quantitative analytics, but innovation can come from a variety of disciplines (the good thing about innovation is that it belies definition by its very nature). Today innovations from disciplines such as economics, psychology, technology, medicine, operational science and even the law are also impacting sports in a number of ways.

For the majority of the viewing public and fans, the impact of these changes is irrelevant to their enjoyment of the game. Life is short. Watching sports is an enjoyable and relaxing diversion. Sports offer quick resolution to a confrontation between good guys and bad guys. It provides fans with likeable heroes and the chance to reinforce their identities by supporting their favorite teams. Popular media tends to cater to the needs of these fans. We would be foolish to challenge the wisdom of market forces in this case. We embrace the joy of watching sports in much the same way.

However, there is another group of fans that is underserved by the popular media. These fans seek to develop a deeper understanding about the game and its intricacies. We affectionately refer to these fans as "sports dorks." In marketing-speak, sports dorks cover a broad demographic swath of eighteen- to sixty-year-old well-educated males. They have good jobs, are usually analytical in nature, and spend a substantial portion of their spare time following sports. While sports dorks are likely to support a particular team or group of teams, what unites them is their desire for more information than can be found in box scores or in the emotional ramblings proclaiming the greatness of their team without specific analysis.

What distinguishes the sports dork from the rest of sports fandom is the sports dork's relentless attempt to understand why or how a particular sport operates the way that it does. Unlike many sports fans who watch games to temporarily escape from the stresses of their daily lives, sports dorks bring their experience and general sense of curiosity with them to the games. For example, some sports dorks believe the same benefits that economic or quantitative analysis provides when trying to solve business or policy problems can be applied to sports. They crunch data provided by sports information Web sites (*for fun!*) in an effort to better understand the sports they are watching.

Other sports dorks spend their time thinking about how teams are managed. They are curious to understand how small market teams, for example, can be successful when competing against richer teams with longer traditions. These sports dorks also think about how dominant teams are able to sustain their success year after year in spite of relentless competition. When there is management failure, they bring their professional experiences to the table. They look beyond the usually shallow analysis offered by most media organizations to understand why the failure happened and how it could have been prevented.

Likewise, software engineers who happen to be sports dorks wonder if game simulation software can be as effective as similar software used in other industries. To satisfy their curiosity, they endeavor to build such models just to see if it is possible. Health care professionals examine controversial health issues like head injuries and performance enhancing drugs, and try to find the underlying cause of the factors driving the debate. The list goes on. It is probably fair to say that sports dorks of all stripes seem to question the legitimacy of the BCS cartel and the byzantine nature of its selection process.

Some of the newest ideas are happening on the field as coaches develop new strategies and tactics to create competitive advantages for their teams. At the tactical level, coaches today rely on sophisticated video and statistics to improve decision making and identify weaknesses in their opponents. At the strategic level, offensive and defensive philosophies are being crafted that are changing the way the game is being played. The two participants in the 2011 BCS championship game, Auburn and Oregon, are testaments to the coaching innovations transforming the sport. Little has been written to explain how two teams from opposite ends of the country with different traditions and identities reached the pinnacle of the sport by following a similar path. Academics and practitioners are developing other types of innovation, yet most of these ideas appear in academic and professional journals, which have limited circulation. Still more ideas are being developed by regular fans in living rooms across the country. Like their academic counterparts, these ideas also receive limited attention, and in the best of cases might be debated within the sports blogs devoted to a particular team with which the innovator happens to be affiliated.

*Sports for Dorks* seeks to consolidate some of the best of these ideas and expose them to a broad group of fellow sports dorks, including coaches, practitioners, fans, and other decision makers who might even act on some the ideas presented in our book. We believe that the ideas of thinkers such as those featured herein will drive the future of college football. The articles are written by a cross section of coaches, academics, journalists, bloggers, and fans. The ideas are well-researched discussions intended to challenge convention and provoke thought. Readers will not find sound bites here.

In the book's first chapter, co-editor *Mike Leach*, the former head football coach of Texas Tech University, provides insights into the ideas that inspired his brand of the Air Raid offense. The chapter, written by co-editor *Ferhat Guven*, also discusses how the most successful football coach in Texas Tech's history, and National Coach of the Year, whose teams graduated football players at a higher rate than any other public university in the country, was unceremoniously dismissed by a coterie of university officials based on nothing more than a poorly conceived fabrication.

*Michael Nemeth*, an information technology professional with over thirty-five years of experience, is also a self-described college football junkie, and former AAU basketball coach who looks after three Yorkies in his spare time. Unlike many sports fans who believe that college football needs a playoff system, Mike is one of the dwindling few who actually believes that the BCS model is a reasonably sound idea. He is critical of the current selection process, and offers a compelling argument for a more sophisticated and rational ranking methodology.

*Caroline Faure* and *Karen Appleby*, professors of Sport Science and Physical Education at Idaho State University in Pocatello, Idaho, and *Cody Sparrow*, a graduate student at Idaho State, explore the growing phenomenon of big schools playing little schools. Fans may hate it when Goliath is paired up against an outmatched David, but it turns out that the small teams actually *want* to play the big teams. It also turns out the big teams like playing the small teams. While the outcomes of these contests might be what you would expect them to be, there are genuine benefits for both sides that go far beyond the results on the field—plus there is always the chance that an FCS team might pull off the inconceivable.

*Neil Reynolds* has been covering the NFL and American football for over twenty years for the BBC and various British sports networks. His article describes how American football, of all things, has become the fastest growing team sport in Great Britain. Reynolds describes a league in which players pay for their own pads, annual program budgets are less than $35,000 a year, and coaches volunteer their time out of sheer love for the game.

*Frank Frigo* and *Charles Bower* are decision theory experts who write for the popular *New York Times' Fifth Down Blog*. Frank is a former world backgammon champion who structures wholesale energy transactions in his day job. Chuck is an astrophysicist whose career has spanned stints at Bell Laboratories, NASA, and Indiana University where he is currently a senior scientist. Frank and Chuck explore decision making on fourth downs. Their research discusses how NFL teams and college football teams can improve their win total by more than one win per season, simply by going for it in (almost all) fourth-down situations.

*Brad Humphreys*, an economics professor at the University of Alberta in Canada where he holds the Chair in the Economics of Gaming; his colleague *Brian Soebbing*, a PhD candidate in Sports Management at the University of Alberta; and *Nicholas Watanbe*, an assistant teaching professor at the University of Missouri, write about the high salaries of FBS head football coaches and explore the factors that account for discrepancies between salaries. They analyze why coaches with losing records at major college football programs earn annual salaries over four to five times higher than their highly successful counterparts from smaller programs. Their research also dispels some of the commonly held beliefs used to justify high salaries. According to these authors, there is a perfectly rational reason why the University of Alabama's head football coach earns forty times more than the governor of Alabama.

*Warren Zola* is the assistant dean for graduate programs in the Carroll School of Management at Boston College. He presents a case study that explores the odyssey of Michael Williams, the former All-American wide-out from USC who unsuccessfully tried to circumvent the NFL's minimum age requirements so that he could participate in the draft following his sophomore year. The case study underscores how the oft-maligned NCAA can actually take a no-nonsense view on the principle of amateurism. Given the recent high-profile scandals involving players receiving illicit payments, Zola argues that properly educating student-athletes, particularly athletes who have the opportunity to play sports professionally, is more of a necessity than ever.

*Mark McElroy* is both the head coach of the Saddleback College Gauchos in Mission Viejo, California and coach of the school's championship surfing program. Mark discusses the rise of the no-huddle offense as one of the least talked about coaching innovations in the past twenty-five years. He argues that the 2011 BCS championship game between Oregon and Auburn marked the crowning achievement of a football strategy that is likely here to stay. He also explains why no-huddle offenses make conventional statistics an antiquated way of measuring a no-huddle team's defensive performance.

Finally, *Dan Hill*, founder and president of Sensory Logic, a marketing consulting firm, explores how facial coding techniques, similar to those used by the FBI and the CIA, can be applied to the high-stakes world of college football recruiting. He describes how facial coding techniques can predict which players are likely to realize their athletic potential during college, and which players probably are not worth the hassle. Dan discusses the power of facial coding as a means of improving recruiting outcomes and providing teams with a crucial advantage over their opponents.

The topics covered in this book are just the tip of the iceberg. There are countless innovations swirling around the world of college football and other sports. We want to make it our business to find out more about those ideas and determine which of those ideas has the greatest potential to impact college football and other sports. We will be exploring this universe of ideas further on our blog, which can be found at *www.sportsfordorks.com*, and invite you to follow the discussion on the *Sports for Dorks* Facebook page and on Twitter *@sportsfordorks*. We encourage you to sign up on these forums to better understand the ideas about which sports dorks around the world are thinking and writing.

If you, like the editors, are unabashed sports dorks, we hope that *Sports for Dorks* can be one medium through which you choose to learn more about the unlimited number of new ideas out there. With thousands of minds spawning ideas, the future of college football will be more exciting than ever. The contributors in this book have stimulated our thinking, which will ultimately generate more ideas about how to build a better mousetrap. We hope you enjoy reading this as much as we enjoyed putting it together.

THE EDITORS
*August 30, 2011*

# INSIDE THE MIND OF MIKE LEACH

## BY FERHAT GUVEN

The author is the co-founder and managing editor of *Sports for Dorks College Football*. A native Texan of Turkish origin, Ferhat is an executive at a global real estate investment firm and has lived in London, England, for over eight years. Mr. Guven is a graduate of Texas Tech University and holds a master's degree in management and finance from the London Business School. He is an unabashed sports dork, and hopes there are many more sports dorks out there like him.

———————

"So pretend this is two tackling dummies and this is your sideline."

It is Friday night in Key West, Florida. We are having dinner with Mike Leach and his wife, Sharon, in a restaurant that serves passable Mexican food.

Mike is, of course, referring to two tortilla chips and the unused butter knife lying on the table.

The two tortilla chips are the tackling dummies. The butter knife is the sideline.

Mike is using these objects as props to explain the "settle and noose" drill. The settle and noose drill has two purposes. The first purpose is to get the players warmed up. The second purpose is to emphasize technique.

Rather than warming up by stretching or doing extensive calisthenics, Mike prefers that his players warm up by performing football activities at half speed. "You don't do jumping jacks in a game," Mike remarks. He pauses. He wants to make sure we're listening. We laugh. He continues.

The settle and noose drill involves the center, the quarterback, and two receivers. The drill teaches receivers how to get off the line of scrimmage, work their way to an area, and settle into an open spot.

Mike initiates what becomes a lengthy description of this basic offensive drill. As he begins his discussion, the cadence of his voice becomes more measured—staccato like. He is slipping into coaching mode. The fact that he is teaching a couple of thirty-somethings about a drill he normally teaches to skinny no-name kids whom he helps transform into record-setting quarterbacks makes no difference.

The whir of the busy restaurant melts around Mike. He settles into his zone. The world has now shrunk to Mike, this drill, and his two newly adopted students. Mike's wife, Sharon, looks on patiently. She has seen all of this before.

Mike's easy-going personality belies an intense focus. He doesn't yell. "Yelling isn't coaching. It's just yelling." On the one hand, he is patient, almost pedantic. He describes every aspect of a drill—in detail. On the other hand, Mike is demanding. "Are you listening? Are you keeping up?" If not, he will slow it down. If he is teaching, he expects you to be paying attention. He expects you to be learning. Even at dinner.

Mike stands up from the table to demonstrate.

Mike begins by explaining the center's objectives. He leans over into a three-quarter stance (Mike started his football career coaching the offensive line).

"The center is focused on executing a snap to the quarterback with his strong hand. As soon as he snaps the ball, he has to simultaneously raise his weak hand to take on the opposing defender."

He demonstrates for our benefit.

Mike continues, moving on to describe the quarterback's objectives. "The quarterback, after receiving the ball, should be focused on getting the ball up to his ear quickly. The fingers on his throwing hand should be lined up over the laces. His non-throwing hand should be placed lightly underneath the ball to reduce the likelihood of the ball slipping out."

The quarterback drops back to make a pass, all the while focused on his footwork.

Mike takes three steps back, unaware of the waitress behind him. She hops out of the way narrowly avoiding what should have been a certain collision.

The quarterback's steps should be parallel with the yard line. The quarterback uses the yard line as a reference to make sure he is dropping straight back. A straight drop back enables the quarterback to see the play unfolding around him better; it ensures that he does not accidently bump into a running back; and it provides the offensive linemen with a sense of where the quarterback is likely to be, given the quarterback is behind them during the play.

The quarterback is also focusing on keeping his shoulders slightly open to the line of scrimmage. If the quarterback's shoulders drift to the left or to the right, the quarterback is essentially losing half of his vision of the field.

Mike asks us to look forward with our shoulders parallel to the table.

We do.

He asks us to turn our shoulders and look forward again.

We do.

He asks us if we can appreciate the difference.

We do.

The idea is simple. The consequence of poor technique is not. Defenders recognize when quarterbacks tend to favor one side of the field. Turned shoulders are an obvious signal. Defenses watch game film and evaluate additional data to confirm their suspicions. Armed with these insights, defenders are better able to focus their attention on one side of the field because of the quarterback's slight mechanical flaw. Secondaries can be much more aggressive because they know in which direction the ball is most likely to be thrown. Consequently, quarterbacks suffer from higher incompletion and interception rates. Quarterbacks who turn their shoulders also reduce the scope of their peripheral vision, surrendering their blind side to fate and the abilities of their offensive tackle. Little things matter in football. Bad habits can turn into big mistakes. This is not just another warm-up drill. This drill is another part of a broader lesson.

Fortunately for the restaurant's wait staff, Mike sits down to explain the lessons he wants to impart to his receivers.

In the settle and noose drill, receivers run crossing routes with tackling dummies acting as defenders. The receivers are required to perform precise movements, even in warm-ups.

At the end of his route, the receiver "settles" into an open spot between the dummies, closer to one of the dummies than the other. "We want the quarterback to throw the ball to the receiver's number that is farthest away from the closest dummy." The receiver's hands should be open toward the quarterback, ready to receive the ball. The quarterback's job is to help direct the receiver based on where the quarterback delivers the ball.

When the receiver catches the ball, his arms should be neither fully extended nor too close to his body, but rather somewhere in between. Once the pass is caught, the receiver should turn immediately up field, tucking the ball tightly into his body to prevent the ball from coming loose while the receiver is making his turn. Leach's receivers are drilled that every catch should be viewed as an opportunity to score a touchdown, whether the catch comes from a five-yard slant or a thirty-yard post route. The goal of the offense is to score. Leach teaches his receivers and quarterbacks that a score can occur at any moment.

And just like that, as suddenly as it had begun, the discussion about the drill is over. Leach goes back to ordering the main course. He bites into one of the tortilla chips, and recommends the chicken fajitas.

———————

The football discussions continue over dinner the following night. This time it's Key West barbecue. The evening's dialogue focuses on a napkin. We ask Mike to describe the common features of rugby and football.

We appear to hit a soft spot. Not only did Leach play rugby as a college student at BYU, he continues to be a fan of the sport, closely following the US and European national teams. He talks about players we've never heard of as if they are household names: Sebastian Chabal, Johnny Wilkinson, Stephen Jones, Scotty Burger, Percy Montgomery, Daniel Carter, and so on. In the sport of rugby, they are indeed superstars.

Mike outlines a basic formation on a napkin to make his points. The similarities to a football formation are obvious. Rugby teams field fifteen players per side. The players are categorized as either forwards or backs. The forwards are the big guys. They look somewhat like a cross between an offensive lineman and a linebacker in build. They tend to be tall, and weigh in around 250 pounds. Because rugby players are in constant motion, even the forwards have to run a full eighty minutes per game.

The formation includes the rugby-equivalent of an offense line made up of eight forwards: three on the front row, two in the middle row, and three more in the back row (see Chart 1.1). Seven additional players spread out behind the back row in what appears to be an overcrowded backfield. Two backs line up off-center behind the forwards, like running backs and fullbacks. The wings, centre backs, and five-eighths spread out from sideline to sideline, like wide receivers—two on one side, and three on the other. In rugby, the ball is "passed" by lateraling the ball. These "receivers" line up to receive the ball well behind the line of scrimmage.

Mike compares the spread offense to rugby by talking about spacing. He explains that spread offenses today, similar to rugby, aim to stretch the field from sideline to sideline. Spread offenses place pressure on a defense to cover more space on the field. The forward pass, which is absent in rugby, makes spreading out the field in football an even more effective tactic.

In rugby, a back must be able to make instant decisions based on how the opposing defense lines up against him. If a player sees a seam in the defense, his job is to attack the seam. If the defender is bearing down on the player, his job is to lateral the ball to a teammate. If the back thinks that his teammate can outrace the defenders to the corner, he is to lateral the ball according to the flow of the defense. If the back sees that the defense has overcommitted in its pursuit, he is to make a pass in the opposite direction.

Mike's enthusiasm mounts as the conversation continues. Mike is passionate about rugby. You can tell. He talks about the ability to physically dominate an opponent, not only as a display of superior athletic ability, but also as a matter of imposing one's will. "Rugby is a combination of fifteen separate parts moving with precision."

Leach comments how he wished his rugby coach in college had allowed him to play the scrum half position because it looked like a lot of fun (he normally played wing). Leach explains that he was pretty fast for a guy his size, and could normally tackle better than players who were bigger. The scrum half position functions somewhat like an option quarterback in football. He is positioned behind the forwards and is the first to receive the ball. The scrum half can start a play by either passing it to one of the backs or running it by himself.

Although Mike does not make the comparison directly, it is easy to see how his rugby background helped attract him to the spread concept instead of, say, a power running game. Rugby, like the spread offense, relies on creating space from constant movement and ball distribution.

In a sport where so many offenses are tightly choreographed affairs, Leach's offense provides its players with an unusual degree of autonomy. His players are expected to make reads and decisions based on what they see right before the snap. We ask Leach if it is difficult to teach football players how to understand and react to a defense intuitively. He looks down at the rugby drawing on his napkin, looks up, and shrugs, as if to say, "Well why shouldn't they be able to?" Mike explains that the fundamental strategies of any team sport are based on taking advantages of mismatches by applying relative strength against an opponent's relative

CHART 1.1    RUGBY UNION TEAM FORMATION

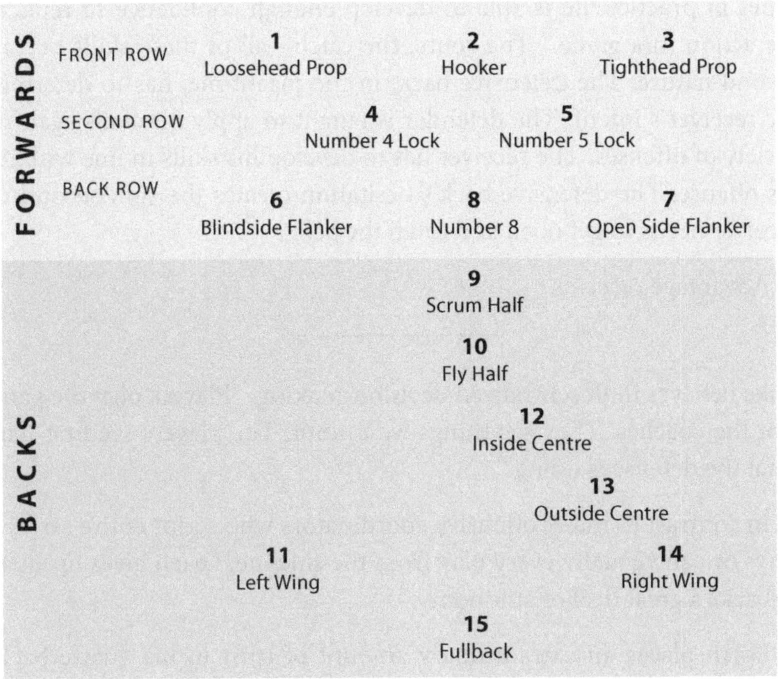

| | | |
|---|---|---|
| **FRONT ROW** | **1** Loosehead Prop | **2** Hooker | **3** Tighthead Prop |

FORWARDS

**SECOND ROW**    **4** Number 4 Lock    **5** Number 5 Lock

**BACK ROW**    **6** Blindside Flanker    **8** Number 8    **7** Open Side Flanker

BACKS

**9** Scrum Half

**10** Fly Half

**12** Inside Centre

**13** Outside Centre

**11** Left Wing      **14** Right Wing

**15** Fullback

weakness. If rugby players can learn to recognize mismatches in real time, then so can football players.

---

Mike is a great believer in the power of simplicity. He does not believe that football needs to be as complex as genomic research. By simplifying concepts, Mike is able instead to spend time on endless repetition, as was captured by Michael Lewis in the *New York Times Magazine* cover story.*

Mike believes that an average receiver who runs the same passing route a thousand times a year will often be able to beat an All-American defensive back. "The receiver knows where he is going. The receiver knows when the ball is coming. The constant repetition helps to reduce

---

* "Coach Leach Goes Deep, Very Deep." By Michael Lewis. *New York Times Magazine.* December 4, 2005.

hesitation. The constant repetition helps to instill confidence. If a receiver catches the same pass running the same route over a thousand times in practice, he is able to develop enough confidence to replicate the action in a game." The route, the catch—all of these skills become second nature. The defensive back, in the meantime, has to determine the receiver's intent. The defender is taught to apply his skills against a variety of offenses. The receiver has to develop his skills in line with just his offense. The defensive back's hesitation creates the split second the receiver needs to get open and catch the ball.

Advantage receiver.

———————

Mike believes in decentralized decision-making. "Players play the game. Not the coaches. They see things we cannot. The players see first-hand what the defense is doing."

In contrast to many offensive coordinators who script entire series of plays or call virtually every play from the sideline, Leach gives his quarterbacks a great deal of autonomy.

Leach places an extraordinary amount of trust in his quarterbacks' abilities to make decisions on the field. "Our quarterbacks are allowed to check from goal line to goal line. They're allowed to check at any time. And if we call a bad play from the sideline, their job is to get us out of it. That is part of the quarterback's responsibility. The quarterback can check in or out of a play anywhere on the field. Theoretically, the quarterback can overrule the coaches on every possession of a game." Leach's quarterbacks are taught to view the field from sideline to sideline in thirty-yard increments, equivalent to about 1,600 square yards of space. "We teach the quarterback to look for multiple opportunities in that type of space."

The two principles that underpin the quarterback's decision-making process are "numbers" and "spatial advantage." "Leverage" is the term that combines the two principles.

"When the quarterback is at the line of scrimmage, he is typically evaluating numbers and leverage. Maybe we're in a pass, and the defense only has four guys up front. In that situation, the better option might be to run the ball. In another instance, we may have called for a running play, and the defense has seven guys up front. In that scenario, the numbers dictate that a pass might be a better alternative.

"We teach our quarterbacks how to evaluate scenarios based on these sorts of odds. The more experience a quarterback has in our system, the better he is able to recognize and take advantage of these mismatches.

"Another aspect of the quarterback's decision making process requires him to evaluate spatial advantage. If a defender is giving a receiver a big cushion to prevent the receiver from running by him, the spatial advantage can be gained by running an underneath route. If the defender is lined head-up on the receiver, the spatial advantage is behind the defender. If the defender is lined up to the outside, the spatial advantage can be inside on a slant or similar route. Sometimes, the defender is lined straight up across the receiver, while another inside defender is blitzing. In that scenario, the spatial advantage is to have the receiver run to an area vacated by the blitzing defender.

"In all of these instances, we provide enough instruction in practice through hundreds if not thousands of repetitions, which teach players to understand leverage as a function of numerical and spatial advantage."

———————

Through that kind of repetition, Leach is able to hone the decision-making abilities of his quarterbacks, running backs, offensive linemen, and receivers. "We teach the receivers and running backs to evaluate leverage opportunities in the same way as the quarterback. If there is a spatial advantage, our quarterbacks and receivers possess enough understanding, gained through repetition in practice, to respond to opportunities based on their ability to read a defensive alignment.

"If the quarterback, receivers, and running backs are utilizing space well, which would be sideline to sideline and up to thirty yards downfield, something should work in the offense's favor. The offense will have gone through those transitions every day in practice so they should be able to execute it effectively."

Leach's offense requires the receivers and backs to attack the whole field, allowing all the skill positions to touch the football. "We feel that every offensive skill position should be contributing to the effort.

"Inside receivers will have more catches, but fewer yards per catch because they're closer to the quarterback. Outside receivers average more yards per catch, but have fewer receptions.

"The running back is going to generate the most overall yards because, generally, he is the best athlete on the field. He also happens to be the closest player to the quarterback. The running back is going to get the ball on runs. He is going to get the ball on passes. If the opposing defense blitzes, the quarterback can get the ball to the running back quickly."

Like his approach with his quarterbacks, Leach applies the concepts of simplicity and decentralized decision making to his offensive line as well. "We try to keep our scheme relatively simple so that we can devote as much time as possible to technique."

Leach favors a man-blocking scheme. "The thing I like about man schemes is that the offensive linemen can immediately decide who is responsible for what. The center's job is to make the call, which defines the other linemen's responsibilities. If a defense twists and stunts, our linemen are taught how to switch the defenders off, but pre-snap, it helps to know which defender they are starting with. It creates accountability."

He is comfortable granting his linemen responsibility to react to what is occurring in front of them. "Generally, once an offensive lineman has time practicing and playing in our system, his decision making capabilities improve immensely. This improvement appears in certain statistics such as sacks allowed per passing attempt. One year, our offensive line allowed one sack per fifty pass attempts, a performance that topped the nation. That performance is a reflection of experience, teamwork, good coaching, talent, and intelligence."

---

While Leach's offenses are known for their prodigious passing statistics, he acknowledges that if defenses would offer more mismatches at the line of scrimmage, he would have few qualms about running the ball every play.

"The reality is that most defenses are generally biased to stop the run. In those circumstances, more spatial advantages can be created by passing the ball than by rushing the ball.

"Defenses can try to disguise their alignments to disrupt the offense's evaluation process, but there are risks to this strategy. Defenses have to be careful about trying to execute too much. Executing the disguise becomes another variable that a defense has to factor on a particular play. If the defensive players do not get out of the disguise quickly enough, they might find themselves out of position. If the defense gets out of the disguise too quickly, then they reveal the disguise and it becomes ineffective."

One way in which offenses can counter a disguised defense is to alternate tempo to keep defenses off balance. "There is always a little bit of a cat and mouse game going on between offensive and defensive co-ordinators. Sometimes it takes a couple of series to get a sense of what a defense is trying to do.

"Defenses that are constantly trying to make adjustments or implement special schemes usually hurt themselves.

"A cover-three defense may not be the best defense to run against our type of offense, but if a defense happens to be really good at cover-three, it may be the best thing for a defense to run anyway.*

"Defenses that work the best are the ones that do not try to do too much, which allow a defense to react to events on the field, regardless of the particular scheme. The truth of the matter is that a good, well-executed defense is the most difficult to prepare for, and defeat."

This conversation is starting to get a little frustrating. "Can everything in football be so simple?"

Mike pauses to respond, and proceeds to ignore the question.

"The best defenses are those that value technique over scheme. Defenses must decide on a scheme that best fits their personnel, and de-vote the rest of their time to technique. A defense with great technique is better than ones that have a whole lot of scheme, but poor technique. A defense with a simple scheme and great technique is tougher than one with a lot of scheme and bad technique.

"There is one thing that has never changed in football. The most important skill on offense is to block and the most important skill on defense is to tackle. And as simple as that sounds, it's easy to lose sight

---

* The term "Cover 3" refers to three-deep defenders, each guarding one-third of the deep zone area. Cover 3 defenses are vulnerable to short, well-timed passes to out-side routes.

of that with all of the bells and whistles that you see in football. If you're not good at blocking, you're not going to be a good football team. If you're not going to tackle, you're not going to be a good football team."

———————————

Mike's approach to the emotional side of football is similar to the way he prepares his team to play. Mike focuses on simple principles, which he emphasizes repeatedly. "We always talk about being a team, being the best at doing your job, taking a lot of pride in your job, but most of all being excited to do your job. Energy matters. Energy matters in practice. Highly motivated players focus the most and develop their skills the fastest. Players who focus tend to make fewer mistakes during games and are better equipped to outperform their opponents late in the game when fatigue starts to set in.

"It is easier to communicate with a player who is focused. Focused players take instruction better. Focused players are better able to assimilate new information that develops over the course of a game. Football is a sport that is played by people, not objects. Part of a coach's job is to evaluate who is up and who has to be settled down. There's no replacement for being excited, but if you're too excited then it takes away from your focus."

———————————

Leach has always remained consistent about what he believes are the essential characteristics of a good quarterback. "You need a guy that's accurate and makes good decisions first and foremost."

There are teams, Mike explains, that fall in love with a quarterback's height or his performance in the forty-yard dash. "Some teams have an almost myopic focus on 'measurables.'"

Mike places far more emphasis on a quarterback's accuracy and decision-making skills. "If a quarterback is not accurate or makes poor decision, the offense is not going anywhere.

"They say 'this guy is this big; he's got an arm that's this strong, and he can run this fast.' Well the quarterback's first job in most cases is to throw the ball. If a quarterback makes bad decisions or is not particularly accurate, then those so-called measurables don't count for very much. At some point the scouts have to ask themselves just what exactly are they seeking to measure.

"By watching a quarterback, you can tell if he is accurate. You can tell if he makes good decisions. One thing we look for is whether a quarterback tends to hit a receiver on the break or waits until a receiver becomes wide open. Quarterbacks who are able to hit receivers just as they are coming open demonstrate a feel for the game, which is important for their success. You can also understand a lot about whether a quarterback has poor decision-making skills based on his tendency to throw into a crowd.

"Another attribute I look at is the quarterback's toughness. Neither his statistics nor his measurables can give you that information. How does he react after he gets hit? How does he play when his team is behind? Does he circle the wagons? Is he afraid of the pressure? How does he play when he's way ahead? Does he keep playing harder or is he a 'coaster'?

"Leadership is the hardest attribute to measure. You want to find a guy that the team really feeds off of. Some quarterbacks are innate leaders. Others are quiet leaders. Others have no ability to inspire their teammates at all.

"Quarterbacks are a funny position. If you look at the NFL, their backgrounds span the entire spectrum. Some come from Division III schools and others come from the most storied programs in the country. A lot of times, they're drafted in places you wouldn't expect, or drafted lower than you would expect. If the quarterback evaluation process was so great in the NFL, then everybody's quarterback should be a first-round draft pick, but there are an awful lot of starting quarterbacks that were not first-round draft picks. Those outcomes suggest that the evaluation process is not an exact science. The evaluation process needs to go beyond measurables.

"Having a good quarterback has a significant impact on coaching. A good quarterback's talent is based on having the intellectual ability to react in a dynamic environment. Good quarterbacks are responsive to coaching. There are a number of fifth-round quarterbacks who are successful, and there are a number of first-round picks who are unproductive. When you ask quarterbacks selected in the fifth round how they were able to become successful, they start by telling you about hard work, absorbing the playbook, improving technique. They don't talk about improving their time in the shuttle run.

"The first-round draft picks who flame out are sometimes the ones who don't spend enough time in practice, struggle to learn the playbook, or have personal problems. People shake their heads when those players don't live up to their 'potential.' In some cases, the only 'potential' they are not living up to is the one a scout or organization bestowed upon them based on their measurables. A player's actual productivity is often different from what is being measured.

"Interestingly enough, the first-round picks who are able to live up to their high draft status talk about their work ethic and football IQ more than they do their physical skills. Too often, the priorities are wrong. Scouts should emphasize a quarterback's intellect, productivity, and his ability to make the players around him better, more than his physical skills. Most quarterbacks begin peaking after they have been in the NFL for several years and have had time to master an offensive system. That also happens to be around the point where their physical skills may start to erode. The reason why so many quarterbacks are still playing well into their mid-thirties is because they have dedicated enough time to master an offense or their position. They have become better game managers.

"Quarterbacks who are drafted for their physical skills in spite of their poor fundamentals and production seldom make it. NBA teams draft unskilled big men year after year for similar reasons. They are enamored by a limited set of physical traits."

---

Thus far, Leach has espoused things that are supposed to be simple and that offensive football execution relies on the interaction between the mental side, numbers and leverage, blocking and tackling, and sound fundamentals. But what metrics are important to Leach? What matters to him?

"The most important statistics in football are wins and losses and whether or not a team can outscore his opponent."

Groan. Another maxim. "Isn't that akin to saying the key to being wealthy is having with the most money?"

Mike cracks a smile and concedes the point.

"The three most important factors that I look at on offense are first downs, number of plays, and converting third downs, because those statistics tell you how well you are controlling the football.

"If you have the most first downs, you're controlling the football. You want to be able to run more plays than your opponents, because more plays generally mean that you have more opportunities to score.

"Third-down conversion rates tie in with first downs and number of plays. Those plays extend drives. While those statistics are important indicators, a coach has to be able to interpret the results.

"Here's the catch. While those statistics are important to us, every single one of them might be meaningless depending on the type of game we happen to be playing. If you're in a game where you can score on three-play drives all the time, those statistics don't really mean very much. As a coach, you have to be flexible about how you interpret them.

"Statistics and analytics have their place in sports. They help to organize data and crystallize tendencies. However, statistics also have their limitations. Football is made up of numerous variables. People who try to define the game through one or two variables underestimate the game's complexity. On the other hand, there is a risk that too much emphasis on statistics can overwhelm a coach's or player's thought process. Statistics inform judgments, but human beings ultimately make decisions. There are countless errors that can occur in a physical contest like football."

Mike argues that advocates of quantitative analysis in sports have to be careful about overstating their case. These proponents look at historical data, and make judgments about coaching decisions, "Coach so-and-so should have done this, because the odds suggest that his probability of success would have been better if he had done x instead of y.

"For some reason, many members of the media have developed a sort of reverence for the power of statistics in football. Few genuinely understand it, and even fewer still have actually applied them to coaching in a football game." Mike raises an amusing observation. It is doubtful that many in the media have ever run a regression analysis.

"I am open minded about the potential benefits that applied statistics might one day provide for the sport. I am someone who appreciates innovation and am always looking for advantages. Right now, it is probably fair to say that some of those innovations are not yet compelling enough for coaches to embrace completely. While there are a number of analytical tools that help to better analyze information, these tools so far are replicating the sorts of things that most coaches have been doing manually for a long time. There is no question that this sort of software has made the process of game analysis more effective. We employ these tools to help us break down an enormous amount of information. For example, we chart plays by down, by distance, by formation, by the receiver's routes, and by the opposing defense's formations.

"We perform a comprehensive evaluation of our play-calling tendencies using these statistics about four times a year. The statistical outputs can tell us which plays are more effective than others are and whether a certain play works better in certain formations. For example, our analysis will show us that our offense is able to gain more yards on a particular play when we send a receiver on a wheel route. We might not complete a single pass to that receiver for an entire game or series of games. However, our analysis can show that our offense is able to generate more yards on those plays, because the wheel route opens up more space for the receiver who catches the ball.

"What the stats proponents tend to forget is that while things like historical data analysis are interesting, most of those analyses are not situational. Going for it on fourth-and-three on the opponent's forty-three-yard line might statistically be a better decision over the course of a thousand games than punting. Keep in mind, I generally try to go for it on fourth down more than most coaches, but we have yet to see data refined to a situational basis, which incorporates time of the game, any injuries, fatigue, weather conditions, personal issues (like did a player break up with his girlfriend before the game), and a host of other factors. Coaches also have to rely on their experience, the team's psychology, and game momentum, when deciding to make a certain call.

"I coached a game two years ago in which my team was leading by five points on the road with about eleven minutes left to go in the game. We were in a fourth-and-one situation from the goal line. We ran a quarterback sneak and the other team managed to prevent our team from scoring. I was roundly criticized for not kicking a field goal and increasing the lead to eight points. I don't exactly recall the statistics crowd jumping to my defense at the time.

"Nevertheless, the decision to 'go for it' was well supported by the statistics. We even had two opportunities to cross the goal line.

"The calculus I employed was straightforward. If we score a touchdown, the game is more than likely over. If we score a field goal, the opposing team still has about eleven minutes to overcome what would be just an eight-point deficit. The opponent has a great quarterback and our defense was struggling in that game. In the worst case, if we fail to score a touchdown, the opponent's offense will get the ball on their one-yard line. In other words, the opposing offense will have to defy the steepest odds in the game to convert the change of possession into a touchdown."

"'Going for it' was statistically the best choice. There were other qualitative factors which went into the decision making process.

"In terms of talent, we had a superior offensive line. Our offensive line had two All-American caliber players. Our offensive line outweighed our opponent's defensive line by fifty pounds per player.

"As it turns out, we run the ball behind our best lineman, who accidently slips as he is blocking the defender. The opponents stop the quarterback and we fail to convert a touchdown. If we ran that play ninety-nine times, we score."

Despite being stopped, the game is not over yet. The opponent's offense now has the unenviable task of marching ninety-nine yards down the field to score the go-ahead touchdown.

"As the statistics would suggest, we managed to stop the ball, in this instance, by intercepting the opposing quarterback's pass. We're still up by five points, there is over seven minutes left on the clock, and we have the advantage of operating with good field position. Our offense, which is ranked among the top five at the time, is facing a defense that is ranked in the bottom quintile of college football. However, on our first set of downs, we punt the ball after just four plays. Still, our punter gets off a great kick, and pins the opponent at their own five-yard line with under six minutes left to play. The opponent's offense takes over, marches ninety-five yards down the field, and scores the go-ahead touchdown."

Murphy's Law reveals itself. Texas Tech loses.

The worst outcome has now happened, defying all likely probabilities. "While we may not have been successful on that occasion, when I review my decision making in that scenario, I have a hard time second-guessing myself. The statistics and the qualitative assessments were overwhelmingly in my team's favor at the time."

---

"In college football, and the Big 12 in particular, we have just completed a decade in which passing offenses dominated the sport. In 2010, the conference saw a return to more run-oriented schemes. Over the past twenty-five years, it is probably fair to say that the spread offense is among the biggest innovations in college football. More teams are recognizing the value of creating and utilizing space.

"Teams are not only able to throw the football out of the spread, but they can also run effectively out of it, as we saw with Oregon and Auburn throughout the 2010 season.

"Those teams' rushing success was based, not only on being able to physically overwhelm their opponent at the line of scrimmage, but by being more effective at exploiting space. Oregon was able to distribute the ball to multiple ball carriers. Oregon also demonstrated the power of operating at a high tempo, which prevented opponents from making adjustments during a game and wore down its opponents' defensive line. The spread offense allowed Auburn's quarterback to feature his athletic skills.

"Right now, many teams are trying to increase tempo. However, it is possible that offenses may slow things down slightly from their current pace. Even if that happens, offenses will probably execute more quickly than they have traditionally.

"When the NCAA changed the offensive play clock, presumably to speed up the game, many teams might have overreacted to the notion that they weren't going to have enough time to call and execute a play. The proliferation of the spread, no-huddle offenses, communication tactics —all of these innovations—were partially a response to this rule change. Now that teams have adapted to the rule change, they realize there is more time to execute a play than they had initially thought.

"Personally, I think certain formations, like the Wildcat, are going to run their course. I think the Pistol is going to stick around, because it is so effective at creating space, and it changes the angles.

"The Wildcat formation is chiefly designed to snap the ball to a runner lined up at quarterback eliminating the hand-off or slightly modifying the angle which a back reaches the line of scrimmage. I would expect that defenses should be able to adjust to that sort of tweak fairly easily, unless offenses try to do more out of it.

"The Pistol formation is more complicated because it requires defensive coordinators to make more difficult choices. The Pistol provides the running back and the quarterback time to read the hole and react to what the defense does. The Pistol uses the defense's inertia and momentum against it. Also, the quarterback in that system can throw the ball more effectively out of it.

"Whether running or passing, offenses that develop creative ways to utilize space and are simple to execute are the models that will underpin future offensive innovations."

—————————

One of the aims of this opening chapter is to help illuminate some the more interesting aspects of Mike's coaching philosophy. Most writers and fans tend to overlook these insights, and focus instead on Mike the myth, Mike the hero, Mike the villain.

Many writers and fans have come to embrace a certain mythology about Mike Leach. The Michael Lewis piece in the *New York Times*, the *60 Minutes* interview, the so-called pirate persona, the prodigious offensive statistics, his coaching exploits. There are many ingredients from which to fashion those myths.

When reading the volumes of Leach articles, one gets the sense that Leach is college football's version of a Rorschach test. He somehow becomes whatever the writer or reader wants him to be: genius, malcontent, icon-oclast.

Some suggest that if coaches were selected by popular vote, Leach could be the head coach of virtually any major college program in America. There is a degree of truth to that observation. You see it when you walk the streets with Mike in Key West. Tourists from across the country virtu-ally mob him, shake his hand, and take his picture. They wish him well and tell him how much they wish he was coaching at their university.

Behind the myth, of course, there is substance. Mike is not shy about talking about his coaching philosophy. He speaks at dozens of coaching conferences, advises other head coaches, and frequently allows visiting coaches to shadow his coaching staff. Mike is respected by his peers, adored by his fans, but the nuts and bolts of what he does become second-ary. The mythology overwhelms the substance.

The substance comes from his technical knowledge of the game and the philosophies he chooses to embrace. These philosophies are built upon a deep foundation of learning, which goes back to his rugby days, observing LaVell Edwards at BYU, and working with coaches like Hal Mumme at Ken-tucky and Bob Stoops at Oklahoma, to name a few.

While some might be able to infer a few things about a coach based on his body of work and the arc of his career, it is probably fair to say that such an assessment, no matter how detailed, is still an incomplete ren-dering. Most fans tend to focus on the win-loss records. Former NFL coach Bill Parcells once famously declared, "You are what your record says you are." Fans and journalists for the most part have heeded that line of thinking.

If the coach has any amount of charisma, he might be fortunate (or un-fortunate, as the case might be) to have a persona bestowed upon him, fur-ther clouding the complex web of experiences that form the basis of his coaching success. What gets lost in these notional "truths" is the real truth. The philosophies, personal attributes, and ideas that helped propel a coach to the peak of his profession are ignored in favor of the better, usually sim-pler, story.

Perhaps no other college coach since the beginning of this century has been able to capture the popular imagination in the same manner as Mike Leach. It does not hurt that his teams win. It does not hurt that his offenses are among the most prolific in college football history. It does not hurt that he is considered unconventional or unapologetic about his approach to the game.

During his tenure at Texas Tech, Mike's teams recorded an 84-43 overall win-loss record (66.1 percent winning percentage), making him the school's all-time winning coach, over which time his teams recorded the nineteenth-highest winning percentage in the country (third-highest in the Big 12 after Texas and Oklahoma).* Leach succeeded at a university whose football program's annual budget ranked forty-third among 120 Division I-FBS teams (the football budgets at Texas and Oklahoma were ranked sixth and fifteenth respectively).[†,‡] This was no even playing field, yet Leach's teams were able to succeed despite such disadvantages.

That Mike's winning credentials are well established is not in dispute. His success is masked or enhanced, depending on how one might look at it, by the pirate façade (due to his curiosity in pirates, which he occasionally integrates into his coaching), his interest in poetry, literature, history, and the rest.

Mike's football credentials are atypical in some ways, but not necessarily in others. Mike was one of a handful of coaches who had never played college football. Prior to becoming the head football coach at Texas Tech, his only previous head-coaching job was in Finland where he coached the semi-professional Pori Bears for five months. "It was a lot of fun and different from what I was used to," Leach said. "Finns will drink starting at

---

* From 2005 to 2009, Leach's teams recorded a 71.9 percent winning percentage. In his final three seasons, his teams registered a 74.4 percent winning percentage.

† US Department of Education. The Equity in Athletics Data Analysis Tool. 2009 Data. Texas Tech's annual football budget was $14.7 million.

‡ US Department of Education. The Equity in Athletics Data Analysis Tool. 2009 Data. University of Texas' annual football budget was $25.1 million. The University of Oklahoma's annual football budget was $20.2 million. Ohio State's football budget was $31.8 million—the largest budget among 120 Division I-FBS programs in 2009.

nine in the morning and go all day. At halftime, there would be cigarette breaks. It was almost like the NFL back in the fifties."[1]

Few college coaches, if any, can match that kind of resume. While these sorts of stories are part of Mike's legend, they overshadow his stints as offensive coordinator where he helped transform the offenses of major college football programs like Kentucky and Oklahoma. It is easy to understand why. People want to talk about Pori, Finland and not so much about Valdosta, Georgia, but it was Mike's success in places like Norman and Lexington that foretold of his future in Lubbock.

When Mike started coaching at Texas Tech, only a handful of programs had started adopting the spread offense. After observing Texas Tech's offensive success, many schools began implementing the spread offense and experimenting with its variations. Today, virtually every top offense in college football utilizes the spread offense as a key component of their attack. High schools across Texas and even the rest of the country have embraced the spread offense. High school quarterbacks who throw for three thousand yards in a season have now become more commonplace as a result. Mike's influence has been felt far beyond the playing fields of Lubbock.

From 2000 to 2009, Texas Tech competed in not just one of the most difficult conferences in college football, but arguably *the* most difficult subdivision, the Big 12 South. During Mike's tenure, the division's heavyweights, Oklahoma and Texas, possessed two of the top three highest winning percentages in all of college football. The Longhorns and the Sooners generated a combined 83.6 percent winning percentage, recorded nine Big 12 championships, played in six national championship games, and won two BCS championship titles. The third best team in the conference over that decade was not a traditional power like Nebraska, Texas A&M, or Colorado, but Mike Leach's Texas Tech team.*

Because his teams happened to play in the brutal Big 12 South Division, his teams did not play for the Big 12 title, the winner of which appeared in the BCS championship game six times in ten years. From 2000 to 2009, winning the Big 12 South subdivision became tantamount to a birth in the national championship game or at worst an automatic BCS bid.

* During Leach's tenure from 2000-2009, Texas Tech recorded a 47-33 Big 12 Conference record (58.8 percent winning percentage).

In 2008, Texas Tech, Oklahoma, and Texas tied for the subdivision title—each team finishing with 7-1 records (Texas Tech beat Texas, Texas beat Oklahoma, Oklahoma beat Texas Tech). That season an arbitrary set of tie-breaking rules kept Texas Tech out of the Big 12 championship game.

Even though Texas Tech was ranked number seven in the BCS standings with an 11-1 record after the final week of the NCAA regular season, it was passed over by another set of arbitrary rules. In this case, the BCS did not allow three teams from the same conference to appear in one of its five contests no matter what its own rankings system said. The BCS invited two lesser teams to play in BCS bowl games instead: Virginia Tech (9-4, ACC champions, ranked 19 in the BCS standings) and Cincinnati (11-2, Big East champions, ranked 12 in the BCS standings). Five other one-loss teams from major conferences competed in a BCS game. Texas Tech was the only one-loss team from a major BCS conference that was not invited.

No matter. Mike's detractors note that he might have been able to win a lot of games, but was never able to win a conference title—evidence of his inability to win the Big One. His legend, they argue is inflated, undeserved.

Other teams might play one top-five team in a season. Texas Tech's task was usually to defeat two, one on the road, every year. The degree of difficulty is harder; the end analysis is the same. Teams that go 11-1 in other conferences are considered a lock for a BCS bowl bid. Teams that go 11-1 in the Big 12 South can be shown the door. One cannot help but wonder if Leach's fate would have been different had he coached in the ACC, Big East, the Pac-10 or even the Big 12 North subdivision over the same period. Mike shrugs off the criticism. It does not really matter to him. He had always embraced the challenge.

———————

Is he a winner or isn't he? It depends on what set of facts you choose to believe, how you interpret the inkblot.

Of course, that was 2008. For most fans, the memories of that season are already long gone.

At the end of the 2009 season, Texas Tech dismissed Mike as head coach for allegedly mistreating a player diagnosed with a mild concussion and for allegedly not cooperating with school officials during a subsequent internal investigation.

The player accused Leach of locking him in a closet. Overnight, Mike Leach somehow transformed from a congenial Shakespeare-reading pirate into the ringleader of a renegade band of prison guards. Those were the headlines. Those were the types of things ESPN said repeatedly in the run-up to and during Texas Tech's Alamo Bowl broadcast. ESPN, for its part, based its story on the details provided by an "insider," who happened to be the father of the accusing player and an employee at ESPN.

The facts of the matter, unsurprisingly, were different from what Texas Tech officials and the player's father claimed, and which ESPN's announcers later parroted.

Unfortunately, those facts would not come to light until months after the dismissal, well after the damage had been done. Facts, nevertheless, have a tendency of being stubborn things, regardless of when they are revealed.

The player whom Leach was alleged to have mistreated retracted the accusations in his sworn deposition.* The player admitted that Leach had never put him in a closet as was widely reported. The player acknowledged that his trainers, not Leach, directly administered his treatment. The trainers responsible for the player's treatment acknowledged that they had selected the facilities. In the first instance, the team's trainers placed the player in a structure (a shed) adjacent to the practice field that was as large as a one-car garage—a facility in which the team's offensive linemen would often rest to escape the heat. On a second occasion, the trainers placed the player in the team's media room where reporters were normally assembled to interview the coaches of the opposing teams. The facilities in which the player was placed were never locked. Team trainers monitored the player at all times. The player could come and go as he pleased. He had access to water and ice. The only time the player might have been in physical danger was when the player entered an electric closet, located within the media room, on his own accord, which he had earlier been instructed not to enter. Once in the closet, the player filmed himself with a mobile phone that he was not allowed to have at practice.

---

* Mike Leach vs. Texas Tech: Adam James Deposition taken March 13, 2010. Accessed April 22, 2011. http://documents.nytimes.com/mike-leach-vs-texas-tech-adam-james-deposition

A public relations firm, hired by the player's father ten days prior to the alleged incident, disseminated the video recording made by the player— alleged proof of Mike's alleged wrongdoing. What college athlete hires a public relations firm? That question would go unanswered.

When asked why he would pull such a stunt, the player claimed that he thought his entire situation was "funny."* The player would also claim the experience made him feel "like a slave."† In the fog of misstatements and misplaced allegations, that lone statement was the one which certain officials construed as their smoking gun. In his sworn affidavit, the team's physician acknowledged that the player was never in danger.

ESPN, the network that sensationalized the initial allegations against Leach, was nowhere to be found once the player's deposition was made public.

No matter. The story overwhelmed the facts. A new legend, a more sinister one, had already been spawned. The truth had become a casualty to the better story.

The supposed hot button of the day was the issue of concussions, and the public's relatively recent appreciation of the long-term health consequences of multiple concussions. Texas Tech invited famed concussion specialist, Dr. Robert Cantu,‡ to opine on the case. Cantu had no direct relationship with the case, but condemned the manner in which the player's treatment was handled based on his interpretation of the affidavits in which he presumed Leach had instructed a trainer to place the player in the shed and in the media room.§

Cantu's opinion, however, was based on a flawed assumption. Leach had never instructed the trainers to administer any medical treatment or select the facilities in which the player's care was administered. The trainers,

* Mike Leach vs. Texas Tech: Adam James Deposition.
† Mike Leach vs. Texas Tech: Adam James Deposition.
‡ Dr. Robert Cantu is a clinical professor, Department of Neurosurgery; co-director, Center for the Study of Traumatic Encephalopathy, Boston University School of Medicine, Boston, MA; chief of neurosurgery service; chairman, Department of Surgery; director of Sports Medicine, Emerson Hospital, Concord, MA; and co-director, Neurologic Sports Injury Center, Brigham and Women's Hospital, Boston, MA.
§ Mike Leach vs. Texas Tech: Affidavit of Robert C. Cantu, M.A., M.D., F.A.C.S., F.A.S.M.

who are licensed professionals, were responsible for such decisions. The trainers operated under a chain of command, which is put in place to override any coach who would have challenged their treatment instructions. The junior trainers reported to a senior trainer. There were multiple people involved in the player's treatment. The two incidences in which the trainers treated the player took place over several days, enough time for the team doctor or other trainers to intervene had anyone deemed such treatment detrimental to the player's welfare or condition. No one did. Several months later, after providing the university with their sworn affidavits, the trainers were quietly reassigned to lesser posts.

To understand Texas Tech's claims against Mike Leach, one has to understand the context behind Mike's dismissal.

In January 2008, prior to Texas Tech's historical season, the university's president offered to renegotiate Mike's contract, and the two agreed in principle to the contract's key terms that would have made Mike the third highest paid coach in the Big 12. In an unusual reversal, Texas Tech's chancellor subsequently intervened to annul the verbal agreement and delay negotiations until an undisclosed future date. This breach of protocol was even more puzzling considering university bylaws did not allow the president to renegotiate a head coach's employment contract without first obtaining the approval of the chancellor and the board of regents. Something had changed. The chancellor would thereafter assume responsibility for direct negotiations with Leach, permanently subverting the president's role and breaching the university's protocol in the process.

In spite of Mike's winning credentials and his contributions to the football program's improving revenues, he was long underpaid relative to his peers. Prior to his contract renegotiation, despite having the third-best winning percentage among Big 12 coaches, Leach received the ninth-highest salary in the Big 12. What should have been a routine renegotiation spiralled into an ugly contract battle. It wasn't about the money, but then again it was. It wasn't that Mike wasn't worth the money. He was.

Mike's manner of achieving success offended the traditional sensibilities of certain university officials and donors from the beginning. He achieved success in that most dangerous of ways—unconventionally. He passed when should have run. He went for it when he should have punt-ed. He eschewed certain boosters hungering for a slice of the limelight for a broader approach that embraced all fans. For the vast majority of supporters the formula worked. However, a certain minority felt that Leach's approach brought disgrace to their more traditional ideal of what a coach "should" be. Leach's coaching philosophy turned such convention on its head.

Despite his more contentious relationships with certain officials, Leach enjoyed broad support from the school's administration, faculty, students and fans. Over the years, most Texas Tech officials grew to appreciate Mike's innovative approach to the game and the positive attention he brought to the school. Leach's success on the field and his players' success in the classroom had won over all but the most obstinate of Texas Tech officials. During Leach's contract negotiations, those supporters implored the chancellor to reign in the worst instincts of certain board members.

Fans were coming to the games in droves. *60 Minutes* came to Lubbock to interview him. The school added luxury boxes and expanded the football stadium by eight-thousand seats. The team was playing on national television more times than it had ever done in the past.

Certain officials wanted to be a part of the success. Leach kept some of them at arm's length while embracing others. A revolving door of chancellors and presidents over a ten-year period limited Leach's ability to build relationships as they came and went. While Leach was head coach, the average tenure of a university president at Texas Tech was three years (the average tenure of a university president nationally is 8.5 years).[2] Previous contract negotiations had also made Leach wary about the intentions of certain officials. Leach was clawing for marginal salary increases, as less successful Big 12 coaches were being awarded more lavish contracts.

Leach would be branded as a troublemaker in certain corners for daring to test his value on the market by speaking with other potential employers. Texas Tech officials somehow expected Leach to accept a compensation package that was inferior to those of other Big 12 coaches whom Leach was defeating regularly, while at the same time construing his efforts to test his market value as an act of betrayal.

The more successful Leach was on the field, the more frustrated certain officials became. After Texas Tech's historic 2008 season, they realized that they were in an untenable position. If school officials refused to negotiate with Leach based on the merits of the football team's best performance in the program's history, they would have faced a mutiny from Texas Tech's fan base. They knew it, and they caved. Leach would get the contract he finally felt he deserved—one based on the market and not an incremental improvement anchored to his previous agreements.

Emails between university officials revealed that during and after the contract negotiations, certain officials were already discussing how they could rid themselves of Leach. Some would later construe the emails and memos as nothing more than evidence of school officials performing their custodial duties to protect the university—mere contingency planning, but such rationalizations strain credulity. Honorable parties accept the outcome of a hard fought negotiation. Honorable parties don't go looking for loopholes.

On Saturday, December 19, 2009, the player's father contacted Texas Tech's chairman of the board of regents to inform him of the alleged mistreatment of his son. The player's father threatened university officials that he would use his position at ESPN to publicly shame the university, and that he was considering legal action. He subsequently demanded in written correspondence that the university terminate Leach. In response to the complaint, Texas Tech conducted a cursory investigation, which occurred over two days on Sunday, December 20, 2009 and Monday December 21, 2009. University officials met with Leach, the player, the player's father, and the trainers responsible for the player's treatment. Leach and his attorneys were never allowed the opportunity to review the allegations or dispute the claims of the other parties. On Tuesday, December 22, based on the outcome of these preliminary inquiries, the university's chancellor relayed an ultimatum to Leach from the regents. Mike could either admit wrongdoing, pay a six-figure fine and sign a letter prepared by university officials, or lose his job.

So much for due process.

Leach rejected the ultimatum and later refused to sign a letter that university officials presented on Saturday, December 26, 2009. The letter itself was self-incriminating. Mike pointed out that he already had a contract that governed his conduct, which superseded any letter. University attorneys conceded Mike's point, and agreed to place the letter in Mike's personnel file unsigned. Leach offered to cooperate, but as he was on the eve of preparing his team for its bowl game, his cooperation would have to wait until after he returned from the game. University officials did not provide Leach with any indication that he was facing immediate disciplinary measures at that point. The investigation, presumably, was still proceeding. On Monday, December 28, 2009, Mike was scheduled to be in San Antonio, Texas to begin preparing his team for its Alamo Bowl appearance. As he was checking into his hotel room, he received a call from his lawyer. Leach's lawyer informed him that Texas Tech officials were suspending Leach based on the player's allegations and Leach's refusal to sign the drafted letter, which school officials now construed as an act of insubordination. The suspension meant Leach would not be able to coach in the Alamo Bowl.

Leach was two days away from receiving an $800,000 completion bonus from the university. His suspension placed his receipt of his bonus in jeopardy, not to mention the remainder of his $12 million contract. Mike's lawyers moved to file a temporary restraining order to overturn the suspension, which would have allowed him to coach in the bowl game, and receive his completion bonus plus the remaining 85 percent of his 2009 compensation (which to date has still not been paid). Texas Tech officials threatened that if Mike filed the temporary restraining order, they would terminate him. As Leach's lawyers headed to court, the university's attorney handed them a notice of Leach's dismissal that had been drafted the previous day. Just like that, on the pretense of an absurd allegation and a capricious investigation, Leach's ten-year career at Texas Tech was finished.

Leach's enemies could never have expected a gift like the player's concussion story to fall in their laps, and yet it did. A prudent institution would have taken it's time to collect facts, question the participants, perhaps even set up a panel to review the incident. Such a panel would have easily revealed that the player's claims were suspect; that the player's father had exaggerated the player's charges; that the player's father had threatened to extort the university by leveraging his position at ESPN; and that the trainers may or may not have excercised questionable judgment in their treatment of the player's injury. Any proper review, as later revealed in the various depositions, would have determined that there was not sufficient evidence to warrant a coach's suspension or termination. So why the rush to judgment in this case? One answer is motive—the other is money. Texas Tech's officials were not looking for the truth. They were looking for a reason.

When certain officials found their rationale, they acted swiftly. Texas Tech officials released documents such as affidavits from the trainers and the team physician purportedly justifying Leach's suspension, but these documents contradicted the officials' public accusations. Even the public relations company retained by the player's father, which was now inexplicably coordinating the player's public responses with those of Texas Tech officials, realized that the statements were conclusive of little and advised school officials to encourage the trainers and doctors to revise their statements. Summoning their authority as university trustees, the regents made solemn pronouncements littered with assertions, but no facts. The chancellor, who publicly proclaimed himself to be "Mike's biggest fan," claimed that Leach had been given every opportunity to re-solve the situation. Only later in court documents did the public learn that such "opportunities" required Leach to admit to a falsehood that would destroy his reputation. The only way to justify terminating a coach as popular as Leach would be to concoct a story that would at once provoke outrage while justifying the dismissal and placing the university beyond reproach, which is precisely what certain officials set out to do.

Texas Tech officials terminated Leach "for cause." By claiming that Leach was fired for cause, the university would not be liable for any further finan-cial obligations defined in Leach's contract.* The causes cited in this case included the player's allegations and unspecified claims of insubordination. The insubordination cited in this case remains unclear. Texas Tech officials would later testify that Leach's refusal to sign a pre-drafted letter did not constitute insubordination. Early on, the chancellor claimed that Leach re-acted profanely when confronted with the ultimatum from the regents. That charge remains unsubstantiated, and in any event could only be known to Leach and the chancellor. They were the only two people in the room when the alleged incident occurred. Leach, for his part, denied the chancellor's assertions. Texas Tech's final charge of insubordination appears to be based

---

* Mike Leach Employment Contract dated February 19, 2009. Article V: Termina-tion, Section A: "In the event of the University terminates this Agreement for Cause, the University's sole obligation to Coach shall be to pay his Base Salary until the ef-fective date of termination (and any Supplemental Compensation that has been earned pursuant to Article III.C.4. above). In no case shall the University be liable to Coach for the loss of any collateral business opportunities or any other benefits, perquisites, income, Supplemental Compensation, or any form of consequential damages resulting from or associated with Coach's employment."

on the circular logic that by seeking a temporary restraining order (i.e. "suing Texas Tech" as eloquently described by the chancellor) to overturn his suspension, Leach somehow fired himself. If Leach's suspension was unwarranted in the first place, and there was no reasonable evidence of a fair process, how could Leach be at fault for seeking legal remedy? These were the "causes" cited or alleged by various university officials. None of these allegations could be reasonably interpreted as "for cause," and yet these were among the justifications offered by university officials.

What gets lost in these discussions is that according to Leach's contract, Texas Tech could have legally terminated Leach at any for time— for any reason—"without cause."* Had Texas Tech exercised its option to terminate Leach without cause, Leach would have been entitled to a minimum compensation of at least $4,175,000.†

Firing Leach "for cause" was as much inspired by motive as it was by money. Leach's antagonists must have gambled that whatever blowback the university might receive from terminating Leach would be justified by saving over $4 million and installing someone they felt would be a more suitable replacement.

---

* Mike Leach Employment Contract dated February 19, 2009. Article V: Termination, Section D: "In addition to the provision set forth above, there is also reserved to the University the right to terminate this Agreement without cause at any time and for any reason. The parties agree that in the event this right to terminate is exercised, the University will pay to Coach liquidated damages in an amount equal to $400,000 (Four Hundred Thousand Dollars) for each year remaining in the Term, prorated as of the date of termination. It is agreed that the University shall pay such liquidated damages in a lump sum within thirty (30) days after the effective date of termination. University shall also pay any Supplemental Compensation set forth in Article III.C.4. above earned prior to such termination. In such event, the University shall not be liable to Coach for any other University benefits, perquisites or any collateral business opportunities, outside income revenues or guarantees or other benefits associated with Coach's position as Head Football Coach."

† According to Leach's contract, had he been terminated without cause, he would have been owed: 1) $1.6 million ($400,000 per year for the remaining four years of his contract); 2) $800,00 completion bonus; 3) $1.6 million in "Outside Athletics Related Personal Income" for the 2009 season; 4) $25,000 for achieving a graduation success rate of 65% or more; 5) $25,000 for advancing to a bowl game; 6) $25,000 for a Top 25 finish; 7) $100,000 for 8 regular season wins.

The 2009 Alamo Bowl, a contest that was only slightly less meaningless than most bowl games, featured an 8-4 Texas Tech team and 6-6 Michigan State. Over 7.8 million viewers tuned in to watch. At the time, the game was the highest rated non-BCS bowl broadcast in ESPN's history.*

During the Alamo Bowl broadcast and in subsequent interviews with the press, Texas Tech's chancellor claimed that school officials fired Mike for suing the university. Of course, the chancellor, an experienced politician and skilled lawyer himself, must have known that a temporary restraining order was considered a lawsuit by only the most technical of definitions. Temporary restraining orders are just that—temporary—lasting only until both parties can hold a hearing. No damages, penalties, or points of contention are argued when a temporary restraining order is requested.

Later, certain university officials would claim that Leach should have pursued his grievance through internal channels, ignoring that those channels were overseen by the very same individuals who were maneuvering to fire him. Leach could either take his chances with Texas Tech's kangaroo courts or a real one. Leach's contract and Texas Tech's employee manual stipulated that he could pursue either avenue. He chose the latter.

These details, however, were nothing but speed bumps to be ignored on the way to Leach's public execution. ESPN's broadcasters and producers did not bother themselves with examining such distinctions because once the public stoning starts, it's hard to stop. That's just the way it works, especially when you are the party doing the instigating.

In the weeks immediately following the aftermath of Leach's termination, Leach sued the university, claiming it defamed him, and fired him without cause. Texas Tech responded to the lawsuit by claiming that it

---

* ESPN's telecast of the Valero Alamo Bowl was the network's most-viewed Bowl game and fifth-highest-rated ever. Over 5,554,000 households tuned in for the game (7,829,000 viewers); generating a 5.6 rating. ESPN averaged 4.3 million viewers for its 22 Bowl broadcasts during the 2009–10 season (about 45 percent fewer viewers than those who watched the Alamo Bowl broadcast). "Bowl Game Audiences Grow on ABC, ESPN, and ESPN2." *Sports Media News.* January 12, 2010, accessed May 15, 2011, http://sportsmedianews.com/01/bowl-game-audiences-grow-on-abc-espn-and-espn2/.

was not guilty of any wrongdoing, and furthermore argued that the university was protected by sovereign immunity—a legal principle that means the university, as an arm of the state of Texas, is immune from civil suit or criminal prosecution.

The presiding judge of the Ninety-Ninth District Court ruled in June 2010 that Texas Tech had waived its right to sovereign immunity because of what he described as Texas Tech's egregious conduct. The district court judge allowed that Leach could pursue his breach of contract claims against the university. Texas Tech appealed the district court ruling, arguing that sovereign immunity was not a conditional protection, but a statutory one, which was applicable in all circumstances, including any contracts to which it was a signatory.

In December 2010, the Court of Appeals for the Seventh District overturned the district court ruling that would have allowed Mike to sue Texas Tech for damages. The appeals court did not allow Leach to sue Texas Tech for monetary damages because of the protections afforded to the university as a sovereign entity. Mike could not enforce his contract, a document, which, according on the appeals court's ruling, was not worth the paper on which it was written.

Some Texas Tech representatives crowed afterward that the Appeals Court ruling meant Leach had lost his case. The truth of the matter was that the actual case was never allowed to be heard.

Texas' state sovereign immunity laws, which require claimants to first petition the state legislature for the right to sue the state, are virtual relics in modern US jurisprudence. As early as 1855, the US Congress established the Court of Claims to hear monetary claims against the federal government which at the time was being overwhelmed by claims from veterans of the Mexican-American War.* Before the court was established, mone-

---

* In 1948 the Court of Claims was renamed "The United States Court of Claims." The US Congress abolished the court in 1982, and transferred its jurisdiction to the United States Claims Court (now known as the United States Court of Federal Claims) and its appellate jurisdiction to the United States Court of Appeals for the Federal Circuit.

tary claims against the federal government could only be granted through petitions to the US Congress.

In Abraham Lincoln's December 3, 1861 State of the Union address, he recognized that sovereign immunity, a right bestowed to the US federal government and separately to all individual states, should be invoked judiciously, particularly as it applied to contracts in which the federal government is a party. Lincoln noted in his speech that, "it is as much the duty of Government to render prompt justice against itself in favor of citizens as it is to administer the same between private individuals."* Since Lincoln's speech, the federal government has restricted its power to exercise sovereign immunity in areas in which it acts as a commercial party on numerous occasions. The Tucker Act of 1887, the US Board of General Appraisers (1890), the US Custom Courts (1926), US Court of Customs and Patent Appeals (1924), Board of Tax Appeals (1924) and the Federal Tort Claims Acts of 1946 are instances where the federal government sought to curb its sovereign powers vis-à-vis its own citizenry.

In similar fashion to the US federal government, state legislatures in forty-nine states have also restricted sovereign immunity powers when their state enters into valid contracts.† In   thirty-nine of these states, the legislature and the courts have held that laws governing contracts between private individuals also apply to state governments' rights and responsibilities in public contracts.‡ In ten of the forty-nine states, claimants are at the very least offered a dispute resolution channel similar to that of the US Court of Federal Claims, or are required to exhaust various administrative remedies prior to seeking resolution in the courts.⁵

Texas remains the only state in the United States that still requires a claimant to first obtain permission from the legislature to sue the state for a breach of contract claim. This particular view of sovereign immunity is shared by the likes of North Korea, Somalia, Western Sahara

---

* "State of the Union Address." President Abraham Lincoln. December 3, 1861. Lincoln was seeking to strengthen the Court of Claims' powers to include delivering judgments.
† Figures summarized from "Contractual Limitations of Liability, Warranties and Remedies." Pillsbury, Winthrop, Shaw Pittman LLP by Lawrence Schultis, Mildred Domenech, Brook Fritz, Melissa Starry and Emily Winton. November 2006.
‡ "Contractual Limitations."
⁵ "Contractual Limitations."

and Turkmenistan—states which also invoke sovereign immunity with impunity.*

_____

When do too many facts become too difficult to bother with?

Following the end of the 2010 season, the usual time when teams go shopping for new head coaches, Mike's name was brought up in nearly every major coaching vacancy. He was not a finalist in any of those searches. Fans certainly wanted to know why their schools did not consider Leach. The administrators and athletic directors of some of these programs hid behind the fig leaf that Mike Leach was off limits until his lawsuit was resolved.

To which lawsuit might these athletic directors have been referring?

Were the administrators referring to the lawsuit that related to a player's by-then discredited allegations, or were the administrators referring to the case about sovereign immunity?

Were the administrators saying that *all* Leach had to do was overturn an antediluvian state law, after which he could, of course, be considered a candidate?

The administrators' responses sounded solemn, prudent, even responsible, but the administrators did not base them on facts.

Lacking real facts, they would have to make do with imaginary ones instead.

Various administrators implied that Mike was an unsuitable candidate because he was perceived to have too much "baggage," a phrase denoting some sort of unspecified malignant history—a euphemism encouraged by

_____

* These countries are among the 37 nations that are neither observers nor members of the World Trade Organization (WTO), and like the state of Texas, observe contractual obligations indiscriminately. In contrast, WTO member countries are obliged to accept as binding international arbitration of contractual disputes to which they or their government-sponsored entities are a party, and agree not to override those outcomes by invoking sovereign immunity. If Texas was a country, its sovereign immunity stance would preclude it from membership into the WTO. Understanding the WTO: Settling Disputes. Accessed July 21, 2011. http://www.wto.org/english/thewto_e/whatis_e/tif_e/disp1 _e.htm. (Author's note: As a proud Texan, this is a difficult comparison to make, but one that is unfortunately true all the same.)

various Texas Tech officials who dismissed Leach in the first place and by others who were vested in the story line.

In the world of investments, an undervalued asset is one that most investors—the herd—overlook. The herd mentality is a powerful force. The decision of one member is echoed by the beliefs of the other members. It is a self-reinforcing phenomenon. In contrast, the opportunistic investor sees value that others ignore; he or she is willing to make a decision that others dare not based on an examination of facts ignored or misunderstood by others.

In 2010, there would be no opportunists—only the herd.

The 2010 hiring season saw twenty-two coaching vacancies filled by various coaches, none of whom came close to approaching Leach's track record and accomplishments. Only one of those programs interviewed him for a vacancy.

———————————

Mike, for his part, has adopted a sort of determined acceptance about the entire affair. On the one hand, there is no going back. On the other hand, there are wrongs to be righted. The Texas Appeals Court allowed him to clear his name in court, but disallowed him from seeking monetary damages. The Texas Supreme Court recently agreed to review his case. Leach's other alternative is to request a waiver from the Texas State Legislature— a path he is currently exploring.

Mike's bill has focused attention on a contractual matter that applies not just to him, but to any other corporation or entity that has dealings with the State of Texas. As Mike's lobbying efforts intensify, other interests are starting to pay attention. The case has touched a nerve of a different kind. In a state like Texas, where the political culture values individual rights and is influenced by a strong libertarian streak, the notion that the state's out-dated sovereign immunity laws means it cannot be held accountable for its actions does not sit well with a lot of people.

In the meantime, he waits. Not just to coach, but to coach in the right situation, at the right institution, with the right values.

When you ask Mike if he regrets what happened, he answers matter-of-factly: "You can always look back and ask yourself 'what if.' That's part of life. There are a few things I probably would have done differently, but when it comes to the key points, I think my response to the matter was justified. The facts show that I did not mistreat the player, that I did not have a role in his treatment. I was not going to sign a self-incriminating letter. I was prepared to cooperate in any reasonable way, but before I was given the opportunity, the rug was pulled out from under me. The whole incident came as a shock to me, a shock to my family. I was as stunned as anyone. Those just aren't the sorts of things you can plan for. The courts seemed like the proper avenue to pursue my case.

"My regrets have to do with the kids, the program. We were on the path to building the next Virginia Tech—a perennial top ten to fifteen team with a shot of competing for the national championship every few years. That's what you regret the most—the missed opportunity for you, for the kids, for the fans.

"We teach our players to handle adversity with dignity, with renewed focus. The same lessons apply here too. I still love the game. I still love coaching. I still love the kids. There are a lot of things on the drawing board that I want to experiment with on the field. You read about entrepreneurs who start companies, sell them, get bored, and then go off to start a new company again. That's kind of where I am at the moment. I'm looking forward to the next opportunity."

---

Mike's teams win. His players graduate and don't get in trouble. His exciting brand of football brings fans to the stadium on Saturday and gets the school's games on network television. There are no academic scandals, no recruiting violations, no one is paid under the table; there are no cover-ups, no previous run-ins with the law, no history of player mistreatment or negligence.

Those are the facts. Mike has always been willing to talk about them.

Who's ready to listen?

# THE MISSING INGREDIENT

## BY MICHAEL NEMETH

The author is a senior executive for a global information technology firm. During his thirty-five year career, Mr. Nemeth has inspired and guided the construction of some of the most complex and successful computer application systems used in the insurance, banking, and commercial real estate industries. As a result, he is a recognized expert in the analysis of complex systems and the design of improved methods and processes. Numerous business journals and press interviews have documented his innovative approaches to computer automation.

At heart, Mr. Nemeth is an unabashed college football junkie. Using forensic statistical analysis, Mr. Nemeth applied his analytical and conceptual design skills to the subject of college football and devised a fool proof approach to determine a college football national champion. In 2009, Mr. Nemeth published his proposal in a book called *Cinderella's Slipper*, a fan's plan to unveil the fairest team in all the land.

Mr. Nemeth and his wife, Vicki, live in Chattanooga, Tennessee, surrounded by their three Yorkies, three children, and four grandchildren.

———————

*"Ignorance is preferable to error, and he is less remote from the truth who believes nothing than he who believes what is wrong."*

—THOMAS JEFFERSON

At the conclusion of each college football season, the top team in the land is crowned "BCS National Champion," but not "NCAA Champion" as is the case in all other NCAA-sanctioned sports.*

Unlike all the other sports the NCAA oversees, football is the only major collegiate sport in which the NCAA does not conduct a championship competition and crown an "NCAA Champion."† The NCAA is not embroiled in controversy over any of the other championship competitions it oversees; it is not summoned before Congressional committees, it is not subject to requests from the Justice Department, and it is not exposed to vitriolic rhetoric in the media. In other sports, the NCAA does a credible job of conducting championship contests that seem fair and produce champions that seem worthy. March Madness, College World Series, and the Frozen Four all seem to satisy their fans as well as coaches, alumni, and the media. College football is the exception.

To be fair, the BCS never promised a full-blown playoff system. Instead, it undertook two half measures, which were to: (1) create a BCS Bowl Championship game from the array of existing bowl games and (2) annually identify the two most deserving teams to play in the BCS Bowl Championship game. In one sense, the BCS has done a remarkable job navigating politically polluted waters to stage a championship game without disrupting the hugely profitable bowl structure that bowl organizers,

———————

* BCS stands for Bowl Championship Series.
† The only other NCAA sport that lacks a championship competition is women's rowing.

athletic directors, commissioners of certain automatic qualifying conferences (AQ conferences), and a dwindling number of fans still revere.* The de facto national champion is now crowned on the field of play and that advancement over the voting system is no small achievement. However, a BCS championship game is meaningful only if the two best teams in the country compete and, only then, if fans and coaches agree that the competitors are, indeed, the two best teams in the land.

Like a gridiron version of *Groundhog Day*, the BCS annually chooses two teams to play for the BCS Bowl Championship and is then roundly criticized for its choices. When two—and only two—BCS conference teams finish the season undefeated, most of the ridicule is muted, but as can be observed in Table 2.1, controversy generally rules the day. Twelve chaotic finishes have required that the BCS discriminate among teams with similar records and offer a defensible explanation for the selections. This obligation to select the championship contestants leaves the BCS system reeling and gasping for breath.

Certainly, championship game combatants are the most important choices made each year by the BCS, but championship contenders aren't the only teams impacted by BCS rankings. The BCS has numerous rules governing invitations to other lucrative BCS bowl games and those rules also depend largely upon positions in the BCS standings. For example, the Rose Bowl is normally a contest between the conference champions from the Big Ten and Pac-10 conferences, unless one of those conference representatives happens to be playing in the BCS national championship game. In that circumstance, a variety of "what-if " scenarios must be exhausted before determining the Bowl's participants. One such scenario stipulates that if the Pac-10 champion plays in the BCS Championship game, the Rose Bowl committee must then consider the highest ranked champion of the five mid-major conferences contracted with the BCS. If

---

*AQ conferences include the Atlantic Coast Conference (ACC), Big 12 Conference (Big 12), Big East Conference (Big East), Big Ten Conference (Big Ten), Pacific-10 Conference (PAC 10), and the Southeastern Conference (SEC). Although Notre Dame is not affiliated with an AQ conference, should it meet certain criteria, it too is eligible as an automatic qualifier to the Bowl Championship Series.

TABLE 2.1    BCS BOWL CHAMPIONSHIP GAME CANDIDATES (AND WON
LOSS RECORDS PRIOR TO BCS CHAMPIONSHIP GAME)

| | BCS Winner (Won/Loss Record) | BCS Loser (Won/Loss Record) | Excluded Candidates |
|---|---|---|---|
| 1998–99 | Tennessee (11-0) | Florida State (11-1) | Ohio State (10-1) |
| 1999–2000 | Florida State (11-0) | Virginia Tech (11-0) | Nebraska (10-1) |
| 2000–01 | Oklahoma (11-0) | Florida State (10-1) | Washington (10-1); Oregon State (10-1); Miami (10-1) |
| 2001–02 | Miami (11-0) | Nebraska (11-1) | Oregon (11-1) |
| 2002–03 | Ohio State (13-0) | Miami (11-0) | Georgia (12-1) |
| 2003–04 | LSU (11-1) | Oklahoma (12-0) | USC (10-1); Boise State (11-1); TCU (11-1); Miami-Ohio (11-1) |
| 2004–05 | USC (12-0) | Oklahoma (12-0) | Auburn (12-0); Utah (11-0); Boise State (11-0) |
| 2005–06 | Texas (12-0) | USC (12-0) | |
| 2006–07 | Florida (12-1) | Ohio State (12-0) | Boise State (12-0); Michigan (11-1); Wisconsin (11-1); Louisville (11-1) |
| 2007–08 | LSU (11-2) | Ohio State (11-1) | Hawaii (12-0); Kansas (11-1); Virginia Tech (11-2); Oklahoma (11-2); Missouri (11-2); West Virginia (10-2); Georgia (10-2); USC (10-2); Arizona State (10-2); BYU (10-2); Boise State (10-2) |
| 2008–09 | Florida (12-1) | Oklahoma (12-1) | Utah (12-0); Boise State (12-0); Alabama (12-1); USC (11-1); Texas Tech (11-1); Penn State (11-1) |
| 2009–10 | Alabama (13-0) | Texas (13-0) | Cincinnati (12-0); TCU (12-0); Boise State (13-0) |
| 2010–11 | Auburn (13-0) | Oregon (12-0) | TCU (12-0) |

the mid-major team is ranked in the top twelve positions of the BCS standings, or if the mid-major is ranked in the top sixteen and is ranked ahead of a BCS conference champion, then the Rose Bowl will extend its invitation to a mid-major program.* That is how TCU landed a berth in the 2011 Rose Bowl rather than a team from the Pac-10 conference. Another rule stipulates a mandatory invitation to Notre Dame if it is ranked in the top eight positions in the final BCS standings. As the Rose Bowl example indicates, all of the rules that govern the invitations to BCS conference teams are in one form or another based upon the BCS standings. In order to manage these participation rules, the BCS must produce standings; and in order to produce standings, the BCS must employ a plausible ranking methodology. Based upon its history of controversy, it remains difficult not to conclude that the most important activity the BCS undertakes each season—the comparative ranking of teams—is indeed the system's Achilles' heel.

## TWO, FOUR, SIX, EIGHT, WHO DO WE APPRECIATE?

The fashionable solution to BCS ranking problems is a playoff system, because some believe that the odds of including the two best teams in a four-team field are better than the odds of choosing the two best teams to play in a single championship game. If the BCS cannot identify the two best teams using two guesses, perhaps it can increase its chances by making four guesses or even eight guesses. However, even by expanding the pool of championship candidates to the four highest ranked teams, there is no guarantee that the BCS standings would include the two best teams in a playoff field of any size. Many major BCS bowl contests in recent years reveal why a playoff system would be a flawed approach. In 2006, USC would not have been invited to a four-team playoff, but Michigan, the team they drubbed in the Rose Bowl, would have been in the field.† An eight-team candidate pool would also not have included West Virginia in 2007, but Oklahoma, the team they crushed in the Fiesta Bowl, would have received an invita-

---

* Mid Major or non-Automatic Qualifying conferences include Conference USA, the Mid-American Conference, the Mountain West Conference, the Sun Belt Conference and the Western Athletic Conference.

† Prior to the game, USC was ranked number 5 in the BCS Standings while Michigan was ranked number 3.

tion.* Similarly, in 2008, undefeated Utah would have gone begging in a four team playoff, but Alabama, the team they demolished in the Sugar Bowl, might have played for the National Championship.† Likewise, in 2009, Florida would have been left standing at the altar, but Cincinnati, whom the Gators dismantled in the Sugar Bowl, would have made the field.‡

These examples suggest that neither a four-team nor an eight-team field playoff would be able to address such oversights. The bottom line is that a playoff system—even a two-team, one-game playoff—is only as good as the ranking system that drives the selection of teams for the playoff field. Nonetheless, most fans, many members of the media, a plethora of experts, not a few coaches, members of Congress, and even the president, are calling for an expanded field of teams that could play their way into a title game appearance.

Proponents of a playoff seem to think that deciding a champion is like pearl diving—the more oysters you bring up from the ocean bed, the better the chance that one contains a pearl. Although the odds of discovering one pearl increase as more oysters are harvested, the odds of finding a pearl in every oyster never improve.

The expanded playoff model presumes that a larger field of football teams would surely include the best team in all the land and that the best team would ultimately assert itself in the playoff games. This approach, however, is more than a little naive. Upsets abound in a single elimination playoff and the rate of upsets increases in relation to the number of teams in the field. As a result, the best team in the field cannot be counted upon to win the playoff and the corollary is that the winner of the playoff may not be the best team in the field. Would anyone really argue that the University of Connecticut men's basketball team that finished in ninth place in the Big East conference with a .500 conference record was the best men's college basketball team in America in 2010–11? The Huskies peaked at the right time in the NCAA tournament, played in favorable matchups, and

---

* Prior to the game, West Virginia was ranked number 9 in the BCS Standings while Oklahoma was ranked 4.

† Prior to the game, Utah was ranked number 6 in the BCS Standings while Alabama was ranked number 4.

‡ Prior to the game, Florida was ranked number 5 in the BCS Standings while Cincinnati was ranked number 3.

benefited from some lucky escapes, proving that UConn was more a fortu- nate survivor than the best men's team in college basketball that season.*

Although the BCS viscerally reacts to any mention of a playoff, it stages a playoff today—a small one consisting of just two teams and one game. The problem with the current playoff system is not so much the small number of teams involved, as it is the suspicion that the *wrong* teams are involved. In order to overcome the public's skepticism about its selection methodology, the BCS must first learn how to rank college football teams in a manner that would be convincing to any reasonable person not sitting inside a BCS boardroom.

## THE ASSOCIATED PRESS, COACHES', AND HARRIS POLLS

Despite being lavishly equipped with two human polls and a raft of com- puter systems, the BCS ranking process differs little from the popularity polls of the pre-BCS era. Before the BCS was invented to turn subjectivity into objectivity, a panel of coaches and a panel of sportswriters cast sub- jective votes to name "mythical" National Champions.

One of those polls, the Associated Press (AP) Poll, supposedly reflects the consensus wisdom of currently sixty-five sportswriters and broad- casters from forty-one states. The AP voters are notionally required to monitor all 120 Division I-FBS teams, which cumulatively play around 1,350 football games per season. By taking on the solemn duty of voting on behalf of the nation's conscience, AP voters must theoretically devote themselves to watching about seventy games or so per week (equivalent to around 215 viewing hours per week), which of course would require over thirty viewing hours per day.[†] The current poll obliges these chosen sportswriters to rank teams from one to twenty-five.[‡] Teams ranked num- ber one receive twenty-five points, teams ranked number two receive

---

[*] This author should add that the 2010–11 Connecticut team had a great tourna- ment run, and was a fun team to watch in a highly memorable tournament.

[†] The AP poll excludes writers from the states of Alaska, Delaware, Maine, Montana, New Hampshire, North Dakota, Rhode Island, South Dakota, and Vermont—all states that do not have Division I-FBS football programs.

[‡] The AP poll ranked twenty teams from 1936 to 1961, ten teams from 1962 to 1967, twenty teams from 1968 to 1988, and twenty-five teams from 1989 onward.

twenty-four points, and so forth until reaching the twenty-fifth ranked team, which receives one point. One cannot help but wonder how poll system apologists would feel if such a panel of journalists determined US presidential elections in the same manner.

The Coaches' Poll (now the *USA Today* Coaches Poll)* consists of fifty-nine head coaches at Division I-FBS institutions who are also members of the American Football Coaches Association (AFCA). These individuals, in addition to coaching their teams, must also somehow find another thirty hours per day to keep pace with their AP counterparts.

Since 1954, the Coaches' and AP polls have differed in their final verdicts on eleven occasions (19.3 percent of the time). In those eleven instances, fans were presented with two National Champions, neither of which was recognized by the NCAA's banana republic as the champion of anything.[†]

## THE BIRTH OF THE BCS

In 1997, the BCS sought to improve this situation by combining the two popularity polls with a slate of computer ranking systems to form a single algorithm that would determine two title game contestants. Fans greatly appreciated the idea of a conclusive championship game, but in the very first season, the system's weakness was apparent. One-loss Florida State was allowed to play for the championship, while another one-loss team, Ohio State, was excluded.

---

* In 1991, *USA Today* and CNN co-sponsored the coaches' football poll. In 1997, ESPN took the place of CNN as co-sponsor. Following the 2005 season, ESPN withdrew its support citing its discomfort with the controversial 2004 BCS outcomes and resulting conflict of interest, which precluded it from being able to objectively cover the story, leaving *USA Today* as the sole sponsor. ("ESPN severs ties to coaches' poll," by Jack Carey. *USA Today*. June 7, 2005)

† 1954: UCLA (Coaches), Ohio State (AP); 1957: Ohio State (Coaches), Auburn (AP); 1965: Michigan State (Coaches), Alabama (AP); 1970: Texas (Coaches); Nebraska (AP); 1973: Alabama (Coaches), Notre Dame (AP); 1974: USC (Coaches), Oklahoma (AP); 1978: USC (Coaches), Alabama (AP); 1990 Georgia Tech (Coaches), Colorado (AP); 1991: Washington (Coaches), Miami (AP); 1997: Nebraska (Coaches), Michigan (AP); 2003: LSU (Coaches), USC (AP).

In 2000, only one team (Oklahoma) managed to stay undefeated while one-loss Florida State was once again allowed to play in the championship game. There is nothing wrong with appearing in the championship game as a one-loss team, unless, of course, there are multiple one-loss teams. That type of scenario does represent a problem, which is precisely what happened in 2000 when Florida State, Washington, Oregon State, and Miami failed to cooperate with the BCS by also losing just one game during the regular season. Suddenly, the BCS was right back where it started. There was little to distinguish among the four contenders and BCS officials could choose only one of the four one-loss teams. Controversy followed again in 2001 when one-loss Nebraska was destroyed 62-36 by Colorado in the final regular-season game, yet was selected to participate in the BCS championship game.* Nebraska did not even appear in the Big 12 conference championship game, much less win it. That honor went to Colorado instead. Meanwhile, one-loss Oregon, whose only defeat came midseason against a 9-2 Stanford team, was denied its opportunity for the ring (Oregon subsequently outclassed Colorado 38-16 in the Fiesta Bowl.)†

## THE AP LEAVES THE PARTY

The BCS's relationship with the AP was under strain almost from the start. When the BCS first established its polling system, it failed to obtain formal permission from the Associated Press (AP) to use its college football rankings in the BCS algorithm. The AP seemed willing to tolerate its inclusion in the BCS standings for the first few years, but things took a turn for the worse in 2004, invoking memories of the 2000–01 controversy.‡ Only this

---

* Game result, November 22, 2001. Colorado defeats Nebraska 62-36.

† Game result, January 1, 2002. Oregon defeats Colorado 38-16 in the Fiesta Bowl. Game result, October 20, 2001. Stanford defeats Oregon 49-42.

‡ "'By stating that the AP poll is one of the three components used by BCS to establish its rankings, BCS conveys the impression that AP condones or otherwise participates in the BCS system,' the letter [from the Associated Press to BCS Coordinator Kevin Weiberg] said. 'Furthermore, to the extent that the public does not fully understand the relationship between BCS and AP, any animosity toward BCS may get transferred to AP. And to the extent that the public has equated or comes to equate the AP poll with the BCS rankings, the independent reputation of the AP poll is lost.'" ("AP removes its poll from BCS ratings." SportsLine.com wire reports. December 21, 2004).

time, instead of a controversy concerning how one of the two teams had been selected for the championship game, the BCS was faced with a scenario whereby four undefeated teams were left standing: Oklahoma, USC, Auburn, and Utah, only two of which could eventually go on to play in the national championship game. The lucky participants in this case were Okla-homa and USC. The BCS deflected fan and media criticism for this particular incongruence by explaining that Auburn had initially been ranked too low in the preseason polls, and that Utah's GDP per capita did not quite meet economic forecasters' five-year expectations. The BCS's response to the controversy was to suggest that the polls delay their rankings until some real games had been played.* The AP responded to the BCS's suggestion by effectively telling BCS officials to take a flying leap off a tall bridge.

After seven seasons of relentless criticism over the BCS team selections, the AP demanded that the BCS drop its poll from the algorithm so it could duck out of the line of fire and revert to using its poll as a harmless device to sell newspapers. When the BCS lost the use of the AP poll, it gained an opportunity to tip the balance in its algorithm away from subjectivity and toward objectivity. Instead, the BCS ran around looking for a replacement opinion poll. Finding no other credible poll to act as a substitute for the Writers' Poll, the BCS decided to invent a popularity poll of its own. Prior to the start of the 2005 season, the BCS engaged Harris Interactive Corporation, a reputable marketing firm with a recognizable "name" in the polling business, to manage the new poll. The Harris Poll, unlike the AP Poll, would begin counting votes after most teams had played four games. Certainly, the Harris organization would collect and count votes efficiently, but, according to published reports, Harris merely replaced the AP's sportswriters with its own assortment of ex-coaches, ex-jocks, and perhaps even a few ex-husbands.

Table 2.2 compares the Top 10 preseason predictions and the final rankings as determined by both the Coaches' Poll and the AP Poll from 2000 to 2010. The table reveals many factors at work. First, the writers and coaches display a virtually equal inability to accurately forecast Top 10 teams (the coaches actually exhibited a marginally better performance than the writers did). Both polls were able to correctly predict a Top 10

---

* Kyle Whittingham, the head coach of the Utah Utes, responded to the controversy by assigning his team its only first place vote in the final Coaches' poll.

team about 50 to 55 percent of the time—a predictive capability slightly higher than a coin toss. Second, the two polls reflect a depressingly common consensus between writers and the coaches. Remarkably, writers and coaches, based on virtually no evidence, managed to project the same preseason number one team every single year between 2000 and 2010, and reached an agreement on the championship claim of the BCS championship victor on ten of eleven occasions—the lone exception coming in 2003.

For those who might wonder, coaches and writers seem to have pet teams they like to include in the Top 10 each year, no matter how undeserving the teams might actually be. Over an eleven-year period, the teams that were predicted to be Top 10 teams and failed to end the season in the Top 10 the most times were: Florida (five times), Michigan (four times), Texas (four times), Florida State (three times), Oklahoma (three times), and Virginia Tech (three times). If you are someone who suspects that the preseason polls are biased toward the "big names," it appears that you have an argument (Notre Dame was, of course, excluded in this analysis).

## THE MONSTERS HIDING UNDER THE BED

When the BCS began operation in 1998, the basic premise was that computerized ranking systems would be used to balance the subjectivity of the popularity polls. Unable to distinguish one ranking model from the next (or at least unwilling to engage in a conversation over the matter), the BCS sought consensus instead by including a range of analytics-based ranking systems in its ranking model.

In 1999, the BCS algorithm included rankings from eight system suppliers, three of which were sponsored by major news organizations—the *New York Times,* the *Seattle Times,* and the Scripps Howard news organization. Also in the fold were systems from Dave Rothman, the acknowledged pioneer in the field of computerized rankings, Jeff Sagarin (possibly the only person who makes a living out of the computerized ranking of sports teams), and a system developed by the Dunkel Index, which has been collecting sports statistics since your grandpa was a toddler.

After the debacle in 2004, the BCS changed its algorithm in two significant ways. First, the BCS handed one-third of the ranking power to the

Harris Poll and another one-third to the Coaches' Poll, which for all practical purposes—based on the two polls' astonishing ability to rank the same teams with the same degree of inaccuracy—was really one poll, but with two different names. The other one-third of the ranking power remained with the BCS computer systems.* Because the BCS could not explain to fans and coaches how any of the systems worked and why the systems produced rankings different from the popularity polls, the BCS chose to avoid criticism by "dumbing down" the computer systems to something more digestible by the masses.

The second major change was to reduce the number of analytical services from nine participants to six participants. Dave Rothman, who has since passed away, the Dunkel Index, Scripps Howard, and the *New York Times* left the fold. Anderson and Hester, the reporters who were the inspiration behind the *Seattle Times* system, struck out on their own but stayed in the pack. Jeff Sagarin also remained in the fold, but with a watered-down system that complied with BCS rules. He now publishes two sets of rankings on his Web site, the ones from his Sagarin system and the ones from the system he supplies to the BCS. The BCS made four roster changes to its collection of computer systems in its first seven years of operation and finally settled on six compliant computer systems that have been in continuous use since 2004. The BCS algorithm now includes just two popularity polls and six computer systems with the voting power split two-thirds for the polls and one-third for the computers.†

While the BCS system purports to include six systems, every week the BCS system drops the highest and lowest computer rankings for each

---

* This chapter borrows the shorthand term of "computers" to denote the various analytics-based models used to determine BCS rankings, as in "those new-fangled computers sure seem complicated." We may use a variety of technologies and software and even call those tools by their proper names in our daily lives, but in the world of the BCS, any tool that seeks to objectively measure the relative capability of college football teams is simply referred to as a "computer."

† Since 2004, the BCS has included ranking methodologies developed by Peter Wolfe (http://prwolfe.bol.ucla.edu/cfootball/descrip.htm), Wes Colley (http://www .coll-eyrankings.com/), Jeff Sagarin (http://www.usatoday .com/ sports/ sagarin/ fbt06 .htm), Richard Billingsley (http://www.cfrc.com/), Kenneth Massey (http:// www .massey ratings.com/theory/massey.htm), and Anderson and Hester (http:// www .anderson sports.com/football/ACF_frnk.html).

TABLE 2.2   COMPARING PRE-SEASON POLLS WITH FINAL POLLS (COACHES' POLL AND AP POLL, 2000–2010)

| Year | Number of Incorrect Top 10 Pre-Season Predictions Coaches' Poll | Number of Incorrect Top 10 Pre-Season Predictions AP Poll | Pre-Season Prediction No. 1 Team (Coaches, AP) | Final ranking of No. 1 Pre-Season Team (Coaches, AP) | Final No. 1 Team | Pre-Season Ranking of Final No. 1 Team (Coaches, AP) |
|---|---|---|---|---|---|---|
| 2000-01 | 5 | 5 | Nebraska | 7, 8 | Oklahoma | 21, 19 |
| 2001-02 | 3 | 3 | Florida | 3, 3 | Miami | 2, 2 |
| 2002-03 | 6 | 6 | Miami | 2, 2 | Ohio State | 12, 13 |
| 2003-04 | 4 | 5 | Oklahoma | 3, 8 | LSU, USC | 15, 8 |
| 2004-05 | 6 | 6 | USC | 1, 1 | USC | 1, 1 |
| 2005-06 | 5 | 5 | USC | 2, 2 | Texas | 2, 2 |
| 2006-07 | 5 | 4 | Ohio State | 2, 2 | Florida | 8, 7 |
| 2007-08 | 3 | 4 | USC | 2, 3 | LSU | 2, 2 |
| 2008-09 | 5 | 6 | Georgia | 10, 13 | Florida | 5, 5 |
| 2009-10 | 4 | 4 | Florida | 3, 3 | Alabama | 5, 5 |
| 2010-11 | 5 | 6 | Alabama | 11, 10 | Auburn | 23, 22 |
| | 46.4% | 49.1% | | | | |

further diminishing the power of the computers. Since the BCS cannot possibly know which of the six rankings is the most or least accurate, the practice produces results of unknown quality. It also leads to the curious situation whereby different combinations of computer systems may rank teams in one weekly rendition of the standings, and another combination may rank them the following week.

This concern leads naturally to a question about how these systems are tested and certified. Some of the current suppliers note on their Web sites that their ranking results are compared to the popularity polls to ensure they are producing consistent and reasonable results. That analytical models are supposed to produce not just different but *better* results than the popularity polls now seems almost beside the point even to the analytics suppliers themselves.

It is puzzling as well that the six computer systems can produce strikingly different results since they all ingest a very short list of data to process. As best as can be determined from public information, the input data used to produce rankings are limited to a handful of variables:

- Game result (win or loss)
- Game location (home, away, neutral site)
- Game date
- Game score
- Team records/winning percentages
- Opponent rating
- Opponent ranking

Missing from this list is the toxic element known as margin of victory. Margin of victory is the shorthand used by fans and voters to form an initial opinion about the relative strength of two competitors following a head-to-head encounter. The margin is easily deduced from the game score, but its use in ranking algorithms was outlawed by the BCS prior to the 2002 season in a misguided attempt to foster good sportsmanship. In 2010, the BCS may or may not have noticed that Wisconsin wore the leather off the football against Indiana (83-20) and then posted seventy points against Northwestern two weeks later in spite of the rule change.*

---

* Game result, November 13, 2010; Wisconsin defeated Indiana 83-20. Game result, November 27, 2010; Wisconsin defeated Northwestern 70-23.

One can only wonder how the BCS interpreted those results next to other contests that were determined by less than a field goal. None of the systems appears to make any attempt to evaluate actual team performance.

Voters in the polls have access to much more information than that which the analytical systems are allowed to analyze. Voters can watch games and can be influenced by the color commentary. Voters can watch game tape and talk to coaches; read press clippings; analyze box scores and a plethora of other statistics. Yet the consistent characteristic of the computer systems is that the inputs are few and focus exclusively on game results.

## GARBAGE IN, GARBAGE OUT

To compensate for the skinny list of input variables, and to appear to have applied high-tech approaches to the job, the BCS computer gurus use very sophisticated mathematical tools to slice and dice the numbers. Unless you are a math wizard, you might be impressed by the fact that the BCS computer systems employ seemingly impenetrable techniques like Elo Chess, Bayesian correction, standard deviation, the Bradley-Terry-Luce model, Laplace's Method, and simultaneous equations. In reality, using sophisticated mathematical tools to rank football teams is a bit like using a newspaper printing press to write your grocery list. Not only are the tools overkill for the job at hand, they are also the wrong tools for the job.

One of the BCS computer systems is based upon Elo Chess, a ranking methodology developed by a Hungarian physics professor who wanted to produce world rankings for chess masters. In the world of chess, players make tiny incremental improvements in play over a period of many years, a context rather different from a twelve-game college football season. Over the course of decades, Elo Chess fine tunes the list of master chess players through minute adjustments based on a robust history of matches. The method awards more rating points for defeating an opponent of greater skill than for beating an opponent of lesser skill, and deducts more rating points for an expected loss to a lower-rated opponent than for an expected loss to a higher-rated opponent. The problem with using Elo Chess to rank college football teams is that there is no accurate rating for any college football team at the beginning of a season, there is no long history to evaluate, and the composition (i.e. rosters) of the teams change every year. Rather than assessing ratings based on a rich archive of performance data, Elo Chess is used primarily to calculate the consensus rating abilities of journalists and coaches.

Two of the BCS computer systems are based upon versions of the Bradley-Terry-Luce Model (B-T-L Model). In this approach, a model of real-world events is constructed by connecting college football teams through head-to-head clashes and mutual opponents to create something like a family tree. The main problem with the B-T-L model with respect to its application to college football polls is that it presumes a measure of order that in reality does not exist. B-T-L is normally applied to paired comparisons, such as Chevy or Ford, Yankees or Red Sox, sparkling water or still. For college football, the model presumes that the better team wins the vast majority of all games and when upsets occur, the number of mutual opponent connections is sufficient to absorb the disorder, albeit lowering the probability that the model is correct.

In fact, we know with absolute certainty that ranking college football teams is not a decisive process like choosing between a Mercedes and a BMW. Individual game results are not conclusive proof that the winner is the better team, or will continue to be the better team, or will improve as the season progresses. We know that there are good wins and ugly wins, good losses and bad losses, and these nuances are lost in a binary outcome of a single game.

One of the computer models attempts to improve the B-T-L model by adding a strength-of-vote adjustment based upon the score of the game. The strength-of-vote adjustment is essentially a probability that the same team would win a rematch. This model presumes that winning by a score of 45-27 is better evidence of an ability to repeat the victory than would be winning by a score of 35-27. This adjustment would have had some difficulty predicting Auburn's 56-17 thrashing of South Carolina in the SEC Championship game based upon the weak evidence of outright superiority provided by Auburn's come-from-behind 35-27 victory over the Gamecocks during the regular season.\* Most fans recognize that game scores are circumstantial evidence of team quality at best, and are not the football equivalent of DNA evidence, but this model somehow manages to reach a "conclusive" verdict anyway.

Two other systems in use by the BCS are a bit less sophisticated than the four above. One is an undisguised replica of the discredited RPI technique, and the other is a Rube Goldberg-esque collection of assorted factors packaged in a black box. The public has no way of determining on what factors the sixth system is actually based since the system does not publicly reveal its methodology.[†]

## YOU ARE NOT NECESSARILY WHAT YOUR RECORD SAYS YOU ARE

The root cause of all ranking problems is the assumption that a team is precisely as good as its record. America's obsession with winning ranks near the top of a list that includes sex, celebrities, scandals, automobiles, and money. In the public perception, winning is good, losing is bad, and there isn't anything very complicated about the matter. Winning is the only object of the games we play and thus it seems logical to gauge the quality of a team by the size of the number in its win column.

As unassailable as this line of thinking seems to be, it is also the very logic that sparks the controversy surrounding the BCS and fuels debate over the polls. "Win" and "lose" are like pass or fail grades on a test in school; they are binary summaries of complex events and much information is lost in the summation. Take, for example, a situation in which four students take a math test on which they score marks of 99, 71, 69, and 29. If the test is graded on a pass/fail basis with a score of 70 being the minimum requirement to pass, two students fail the test and two students pass. As a result, the passing scores of 99 and 71 represent equivalent mastery and the scores of 69 and 29 represent equivalent failure. A pass/fail divide of 70, however, suggests that the results of 71 and the 69 are as far apart as

---

[*] Game result, December 4, 2010; Auburn defeated South Carolina 56-17. Game result, September 25, 2010; Auburn defeated South Carolina 35-27.

[†] See Ranking methodologies footnote, page 49.

the Grand Canyon when the reality is that both scores represent a near equal performance. Clearly these four students exhibit widely divergent degrees of mathematical competence (a qualitative measure), but that is not apparent if all that is visible are two "Passes" and two "Fails" (binary measures). "W" and "L" expose the same amount of information as "Pass" and "Fail," and they conceal the same amount of information. If we want to know how well these four students know math (a qualitative measure), we would not limit our investigation to whether they passed or failed the test. We would examine the actual test scores to obtain an accurate assessment. The same is true when comparing wins and losses for football teams.

A remarkable fact about college football is that a team can play poorly and still win, or play well and still lose. We have all witnessed games in which a team won "ugly," or games in which neither team could "get anything going." As binary statistics, won/lost records treat all wins equally, thus the team that wins "ugly" receives the same credit as the team that dazzles us with its scintillating performance. Auburn received no less credit for squeaking past mediocre Clemson and inept Kentucky than it did for blasting a strong South Carolina team in the 2010 SEC title game.* Conversely, the losers of crowd-pleasing games, like the Oregon- Stanford contest in 2010, receive no more credit in a won/lost record than do the losers of blowouts, like Michigan State's 37-6 shellacking at the hands of Iowa this past season.† The embarrassing outcome was represented by just one "L" in the Spartans' loss column.

In every contest, one team plays *relatively* better than the other does. Winning does not automatically mean that a team is "good"; it simply means that the winning team played *relatively* better than the losing team, on game day, under a certain set of circumstances. Therefore, winning and losing are relative measures and not always definitive or decisive events. If the circumstances were changed or if the teams played a second time, the outcome could well be different.

Won/lost records are merely the sum of pass/fail results for some number of tests without any qualifying information about the difficulty of the

---

* Game result, September 18, 2010; Auburn defeated Clemson 27-24. Game result, October 9, 2010; Auburn defeated Kentucky 37-34.

† Game result, October 30, 2010; Iowa defeated Michigan State 37-6.

tests or the grades achieved on the tests. A student is not well educated simply because he or she passes tests; a student is well educated because he or she understands the subject matter. Similarly, a team is not good because it wins; a team wins because it is good. In order to turn a won/lost record into a qualitative measure, the quality of the playing performances and the quality of the opponents must be measured and added to the equation. The key factor that is missing from the BCS ranking algorithm is *the measurement of performance.* After adding this *missing ingredient* to the ranking stew, it becomes possible to differentiate one unbeaten record from another or differentiate an unbeaten record from a one-loss record. And then it becomes possible to comparatively rank college football teams.

## EPIPHANY

There are but four ways to judge college football teams, and the most natural of these is to watch the games and form subjective opinions. In the media, this method is often referred to as the "eyeball test." Thanks to cable and satellite television, most fans have access to more football games than they have time to watch. When watching some games, the difference in quality between Oregon and UCLA in 2010 can be obvious (the Ducks defeated the Bruins 60-13), but the difference between Ohio State and Stanford is much harder to discern.* Neither the Buckeyes or The Cardinal played each other and neither team shared any common opponents during the 2010 season. For the average viewer, offense pleases the eye more than defense; therefore, an overwhelming high scoring victory might seem more impressive than a lower scoring outcome achieved by a similarly dominating defensive performance. A conquest of an SEC opponent might carry more weight than a win over a team from Conference USA. Personal favorites tend to receive more credit than they deserve and the exploits of hated rivals are trivialized. The heralded "eyeball test" is a simple thought process that is inevitably biased, and thereby unreliable. While some fans might readily acknowledge their own biases, the so-called experts, and the voters, are somehow expected to be objective and see traits that the average fan misses.

---

* Game Result, October 21, 2010. Oregon defeated UCLA 60-13.

The second option we have for judging football teams is to listen to the experts and accept their opinions. However, it is difficult these days to find unadulterated information about sports. Virtually all broadcast sports content is a mixture of showmanship, opinion, slanted salesmanship, and a few selected facts. When we hear expert opinions, we have to remember that the first job of a broadcast expert is to entertain viewers, the second job is to sell advertising time, the third job is to pump up future viewing events, and way down at number four is the job of sharing their expertise.

The third option to judge college football teams, the option taken by most computer systems, is to intuit cosmic meaning from wins and losses. We trust that the winning team deserves our respect because it has performed relatively better in some way than the losing team. The computer systems, however, are unable to explain what the winner did or how it was able to emerge victorious.

## THE MEANINGLESSNESS OF STATISTICS

The fourth option for judging football teams is to analyze statistical information in order to determine how one team won and the other team lost. We assume that the voters in the polls examine the statistics and find the factors that determine the games' outcomes. The obvious place to look for statistics is in the traditional box score.

The typical football box score contains only a few basic bits of data that represent action on the field: first downs, yards gained, penalty yardage, turnovers, and time of possession. Each of these statistical categories is subdivided to expose a bit more detail—yards gained is subdivided into rushing yards and passing yards, turnovers are subdivided into fumbles and interceptions—but basically, these five statistics are entrusted with the task of telling the story of a football game. It would be logical to assume that playing performance, as measured by these five statistical categories, should determine the outcome of football games and the teams that performed better in these categories should win most games. Why else would these few statistics be the primary ones discussed by color analysts and widely reported in the press?

The author conducted an analysis of box score statistics for games played by twenty-four sample teams ( "Sample 24 teams"), representing the best teams during the 2010 season, to find a correlation between eye-popping stat sheets and winning.* The analysis, which simply tracked the frequency with which the teams won without a statistical advantage or lost in spite of having an advantage, revealed that *none* of the five traditional statistics had a causal relationship with the outcome of the games. An unambiguous cause-and-effect relationship could be established if winning teams virtually always led in these statistical categories while losing teams virtually always trailed in these categories, but such is not the case. These traditional statistics served more as descriptors, like your height, weight, and hair color describe your physical attributes, and failed to explain the game outcomes in the same way that your physical attributes fail to define you as a person. The Sample 24 teams evidenced a remarkable ability to win football games without an advantage in the traditional statistical categories and suffered a stunning number of losses when they enjoyed a statistical advantage, which means that good teams have capabilities not measured by traditional statistics. Table 2.3 presents the results of the analysis and compares the relative impact of each statistical category on game outcomes.

Not only was it impossible to discern a correlation between winning and the traditional statistics, it was nearly impossible to formulate a consistent interpretation of the traditional statistics. For example, a team that enjoyed more time of possession may have forced its opponent into repeated three-and-out possessions, garnering all the clock time for its own offense. Just as probably, the team with the dominant clock time might have plodded down the field three yards at a time only to be denied somewhere along the way to the end zone, or it may have been sliced up by an opponent that scored quickly. Certainly, Oregon's quick-strike offense suffered little in 2010 despite trailing in time of possession in eight of its twelve victories.

---

* Sample 24 teams include the six BCS conference champions, all ten teams invited to BCS Bowl games and all teams ranked in the top ten in either the Coaches' poll or the BCS standings. The analysis encompasses 272 games played by Sample 24 teams.

TABLE 2.3    BOX SCORE STATISTICAL CORRELATIONS FOR SAMPLE
24 TEAMS

|  | *Time of Possession* | *First Downs* | *Total Yards* | *Penalty Yards* | *Turnovers* |
|---|---|---|---|---|---|
| *Percentage of games lost with an advantage* | 35.4% | 35.4% | 29.2% | 52.3% | 13.8% |
| *Percentage of games won without an advantage* | 69.6% | 57.6% | 45.9% | 81.6% | 66.3% |

First downs were weakly correlated with winning, but this fact defied consistent interpretation as well.* Teams that enjoyed excellent field position naturally required fewer first downs to score than did teams hamstrung by poor field position. Teams that scored on long offensive plays weren't credited with a first down for the long play while other teams may have racked up six or seven first downs covering the same ground. Teams that scored with special teams or defensive plays sacrificed offensive possessions and the associated first downs, but used the bonus points to outscore their opponents. Alabama was the poster child for the first-down statistic, recording more first downs than all thirteen opponents in 2010, including against the three opponents that sent the Tide to defeat.

As with first downs, total yardage is more a by-product of field position than of quality play—good field position produces more points but depresses total yardage while poor field position provides the necessary landscape to roll up big yardage. If total yardage was a causal factor in winning, all teams would win a high percentage of the games in which they produce more yards, but they don't. As a result, it can be said that yardage is often a by-product of winning, but it cannot be said that yardage is a causal factor of winning and losing football games.

Penalty yardage is usually considered a negative statistic, but its impact is situational. An untimely penalty can have a devastating impact on the

---

* See Table 2.3.

outcome of a football game, but no distinction is made in the box score between penalties that changed the course of a game and those that were merely irritants. In fact, Sample 24 teams won more frequently without an advantage in penalty yardage (81.6 percent) than they did with an advantage (77.2 percent), suggesting that aggression is a necessary attribute of winners, even though the aggressive attitude prompts the occasional slap on the wrist.

The most common event leading to good field position is the turnover. Of the five traditional statistics, only turnovers had a correlation with winning strong enough to interpret as an influential element in the outcome of football games. Sample 24 teams won 94 percent of the games in which they committed fewer turnovers, but just 13.8 percent of the games in which they had more giveaways than takeaways. The weaker opponents of Sample teams won a mere 33.7 percent of the games in which they enjoyed an advantage, suggesting that turnovers are like a scalpel in the hands of a surgeon but a dull knife in the hands of a butcher.*

However, highly ranked teams enjoyed a takeaway-giveaway advantage in less than half of their games (47.6 percent). Since turnovers don't necessarily produce victories for ordinary teams, and since even the best teams produce a takeaway advantage in less than half of their contests, turnovers can't be said to have a conclusive cause-and-effect impact on winning any more than the other traditional statistics.

Games that can't be explained by box score statistics are commonplace in college football. The statistics that seem to explain one set of outcomes fail to produce the similar outcomes in other games. Teams strive to earn first downs, pile up yardage, dominate the clock, and avoid mistakes and yet the rewards for these achievements are inconsistent and unpredictable. North Carolina had more time of possession, more first downs, more total yards, fewer penalty yards, and one less turnover than LSU but still lost its season opener.† Nevada had no statistical advantages in its game against Fresno State yet managed a one point victory.‡ Ohio State gained more yards, surrendered fewer penalty yards, ate more clock time, and commit-

---

* The analysis of traditional statistics tracked the number of times the winning team had an advantage in turnovers.

† Game played September 4, 2010; LSU defeated North Carolina 30-24.

‡ Game played November 13, 2010; Nevada defeated Fresno State 35-34.

ted the same number of turnovers as Wisconsin and yet was knocked out of the No. 1 ranking by the Badgers in a 31-18 rout.* While there is always the possibility that football is a silly game that can be won without the systematic application of any specific skills, a safer bet is that box score statistics were meant to explain the outcome of football games, but simply do a poor job of it.

## THE KISS PRINCIPLE

The inescapable conclusion drawn from the analysis of box scores is that traditional statistics are not *deterministic*; that is, they do not represent the factors that determine game results. In order to measure playing performance, statistics must be deterministic, must offer an explanation for the game result, and must work in favor of teams of all quality levels. When a weak team produces advantages in deterministic statistics, the advantages should translate into victories just as surely as they produce victories for stronger teams.

This is not rocket science. Playing well can be defined succinctly as doing the things that produce victories and being good can be defined as repeatedly doing a better job than opponents at the things that produce victories. When these "things that produce victories" are identified and measured, a grade for team playing performance can be calculated and used to place a value on its won/lost record. It follows that if each team is assigned a performance rating, the strength of a team's schedule can be calculated by combining the performance ratings of its opponents. In this manner, won/lost records can have a value beyond pass or fail and teams can be ranked comparatively.

Many fans and friends were consulted for advice about how to find the factors that determine football game outcomes, but a conversation with a friend I'll call "Bob" crystallized the approach. When asked to describe how one team defeats another in a college football game, Bob didn't hesitate to compose a lengthy, philosophical response. He didn't talk about establishing a running game to open up the passing game. He didn't say that winning teams are built on the foundation of a strong defense. He didn't spout clichés like, "Games are won in the trenches." He simply said, "They score

---

* Game played October 16, 2010. Wisconsin defeated Ohio State 31-18.

more points, stupid!" His statement wasn't intended as an insult. Bob is an information technology guru and in that world, the maxim is, "Keep it simple, stupid," which is known as the KISS principle. "They score more points, stupid" is the application of the KISS principle to the world of college football.

In another day and age, Bob might have said, "Oh, this is elementary, my dear Watson," for the idea that winners score more points than losers is surely as elementary as any football theory can get. Good offenses score points and good defenses prevent points. Good teams combine an ability to score with an ability to prevent scores in order to consistently outscore the opposition. It's that elementary. No matter how well a team stuffs the box score with gaudy statistics, if the yards and first downs don't produce points, the team loses. Logically then, the "things that produce victories" can be paraphrased as, the "things that produce or prevent points."

## METHODOLOGY

In order to identify the things that produce or prevent points, the author analyzed the best teams from the 2007, 2008, 2009, and 2010 college football seasons.* In each year, all six BCS conference champions, all ten teams invited to BCS bowl games, and every team that reached the Top 10 in either the Coaches' Poll or the BCS standings were included in the sample. Over the four-year period, these ninety-six teams ("Sample 96 teams") played 1,422 games against teams of all skill levels; and the resulting statistics represented both the ways in which good teams won and the ways in which lesser teams lost.

The first principle applied to the analysis was that all points have equal value, irrespective of the manner in which they were scored. A team can score on offense or on defense or on special teams; it is all the same to the scorekeeper. The people who invented the game gave equal weight to

---

* The author read all 1,422 play-by-play accounts and recorded occurrences of the statistics described in this article. The records were maintained in spread sheets. To the extent that the play-by-play accounts were an accurate recounting of the game, and to the extent that the author's record keeping was accurate, the resulting statistical base is valid for the purpose of drawing the conclusions presented herein.

CHART 2.1   HOW SAMPLE 96 TEAMS ARE MOST LIKELY TO SCORE
            (2007-2010)

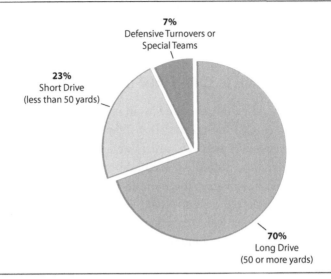

**7%**
Defensive Turnovers or
Special Teams

**23%**
Short Drive
(less than 50 yards)

**70%**
Long Drive
(50 or more yards)

touchdowns scored on runs from scrimmage, passes from scrimmage, interceptions, fumbles, punt returns, and kickoff returns. We have to respect their wisdom and treat these scores as equally reflective of quality playing performance.

In order to facilitate the analysis, scoring was subdivided into three categories to separate the circumstances surrounding the scores and better identify the things that produce points:

1. Scoring the hard way (scoring drives of more than fifty yards in length)
2. Opportunistic scoring (offensive scoring on possessions starting from inside the opponent's fifty-yard line)
3. Non-offensive scoring (scoring by the defense or by special teams)

## HOW DO GOOD TEAMS SCORE?

The first revelation of this analysis is that the best college football teams in America scored a significant proportion of their points on long offensive drives (see Chart 2.1). Just like their professional counterparts, good college football teams score most of their points the old-fashioned way—by sustaining long scoring drives. Sample 96 teams scored just 23 percent of their total points after getting the ball on the enemy side of the fifty-yard line and fewer than 7 percent of their points on defense or by special teams.

## THE NEW METRICS: LONG FIELD AND SHORT FIELD OPS

As noted earlier, total yards generated by an offense is perhaps one of the most misleading of all football statistics. Teams that generate the most yards do not necessarily win. To understand this relationship, or lack thereof, is to understand a simple principle about football: the shorter the distance that must be covered, the more likely the drive will result in a touchdown; the longer the distance that must be covered, the more likely the drive will fizzle like a wet firecracker on the Fourth of July. To gain a better understanding of how good team score, long and short field opportunities should somehow be recorded and ranked, which they are not. This simple fact of football life is a prime example of why traditional statistics are not useful in the measurement of playing performance and why new statistical measures must be developed.

Instead of trying to solve this puzzle with conventional statistics, allow me to formally introduce the Long Field and Short Field Opportunities Statistic, or "Long Field Ops" and "Short Field Ops," which respectively describe possessions starting greater or less than fifty yards from the end zone.

## DOING HARD TIME

The ability to sustain a long scoring drive was the most critical success factor for Sample 96 teams. The bulk of all points were produced on scoring drives of more than fifty yards in length (see Chart 2.1).

The vast majority of possessions took place in the form of long drives. As seen in Table 2.4, Sample 96 teams started 84 percent of their offensive possessions in their own territory.

Table 2.5 shows, as expected, that Sample 96 teams were much more likely to score on long drives than were their lesser opponents, but in the

TABLE 2.4    LONG FIELD AND SHORT FIELD OPS: SAMPLE 96 TEAMS
AND OPPONENTS (2007-2010)*

| | Short Field Ops | Long Field Ops | Percentage of Short Field Ops | Percentage of Long Field Ops |
|---|---|---|---|---|
| *Sample 96 Teams* | 2.1 | 10.9 | 16.0% | 84.0% |
| *Opponents* | 1.3 | 11.7 | 9.9% | 90.1% |

TABLE 2.5    LONG FIELD SCORING PROFICIENCY

| | Long Field Ops | Scoring Frequency | Points per Long Field Op | Long Field Points per Game |
|---|---|---|---|---|
| *Sample 96 Teams* | 10.9 | 38.0% | 2.28 | 24.9 |
| *Opponents* | 11.7 | 21.8% | 1.28 | 15.0 |

case of long field possessions, the difference was more pronounced than it was on short field possessions. Sample 96 teams scored on 38.0 percent of their long possessions, while their opponents scored on just 21.8 percent of their long field scoring attempts. As a result, Sample 96 teams were also more proficient than their weaker counterparts, scoring an average of 2.28 points per long field possession while holding their opponents to an average of 1.28 points per possession. Sample 96 teams scored an average of 24.9 points per game on long field possession, while lesser teams were only able to muster 15 points per game in similar circumstances.

## ANALYZING SHORT FIELD OPS

Sample 96 teams were also better at generating Short Field Ops than their opponents, and consequently found themselves in fewer long field situations.

Table 2.6 demonstrates that Sample 96 teams and their weaker opponents benefited from the principle of good field position to a somewhat

---

* Analysis presumes an average team has thirteen offensive possessions per game.

TABLE 2.6    SHORT FIELD SCORING PROFICIENCY

|  | Short Field Ops | Scoring Frequency | Points per Short Field Op | Opportunistic Points per Game |
|---|---|---|---|---|
| *Sample 96 Teams* | 2.1 | 67.4% | 3.95 | 8.3 |
| *Opponents* | 1.3 | 57.0% | 3.14 | 4.1 |

similar degree. Sample 96 teams scored on 67.4 percent of their short field possessions while their opponents scored on 57 percent of their short field possessions. Sample 96 teams were more proficient at converting short field opportunities, outscoring their opponents 3.95 points/possession to 3.14 points/possession. The disparity in scores was influenced by the quality of the opposing team. Sample 96 teams were by definition superior to most of their opponents, hence were better at scoring points in short field opportunities. Sample 96 teams scored an average of 8.3 opportunistic points per game.* Their lesser opponents averaged just 4.1 points per game.† Based on these calculations, we can observe that, short field possessions contributed, on average, 4.2 points to the winning margin for the best teams in the land.‡ Overall, Sample 96 teams won 87.1 percent of the games in which they had more short field opportunities.

More interesting, perhaps, is an examination of the causes of short field possessions as summarized in Chart 2.2. Fully half of all short field possessions are the result of turnovers. This is one major reason why turnovers seem to impact game outcomes, but the turnover is not so much the deterministic factor as is the resulting short field opportunity that facilitates an easy score. After all, not every turnover produces a short field opportunity, but most short field opportunities produce a score. Punt returns and kick-off returns produce another 30 percent of short field opportunities and yet another 8 percent occur when, late in games gone bad, des-

---

* The figure 8.3 points per game is determined by multiplying 3.95 points per Short Field Op with 2.1 Short Field Ops per game.

† The figure 4.1 points per game is determined by multiplying 3.14 points per Short Field Op with 1.3 Short Field Ops per game.

‡ The average point differential of 4.2 points per game is determined by subtracting 4.1 points per game from 8.3 points per game as calculated in the two previous footnotes.

CHART 2.2   HOW SAMPLE 96 TEAMS GENERATE SHORT FIELD OPS

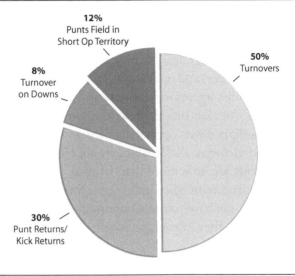

perate teams turn the ball over on downs in their own territory. That leaves just 12 percent of short field opportunities that result from punts fielded in enemy territory, and most of those are blown-up punt attempts or shanks that fly out of bounds after traveling far less than the average punting distance.

## DEFENSIVE AND SPECIAL TEAMS' SCORES DON'T WIN MANY GAMES (BUT THEY ARE FUN TO WATCH)

As exciting as it is to see a punt returner weave his way to a score, or to watch a kick-off returner find a seam and pick up a wall of blockers on the way to the end zone, neither play happens very often in college football. As demoralizing as it is for the offense to have a defender scoop up a fumble or pluck an errant pass from the air and then put points on the scoreboard, such points also do not happen very frequently in college football either. Over the course of four seasons, Sample 96 teams averaged just 2.1 points per game on scores by the defense or by special teams, roughly 6 percent of their average total points per game.

Non-offensive scores occur infrequently. Sample 96 teams posted more non-offensive points than their opponents in just 25.5 percent of all games.

In most games, neither team scored points while on defense or during special teams, but when Sample 96 teams or their opponents did score non-offensive points, the added points had a negligible influence on game outcomes. For example, Sample 24 teams for the 2010 season played 272 unique games (45 games were against other members of the Sample 24 for a grand total of 317 games) and only thirteen of them—4.8 percent of the contests— were decided by non-offensive scoring.* Connecticut was the primary beneficiary of non-offensive scoring during the 2010 season. Twice the Huskies slipped past opponents with non-offensive scores and without those two victories, the Huskies would have been a .500 team. Non-offensive points are little more than frosting than the cake, but do have to be taken into account when judging a team's playing performance because these scores can have tremendous emotional impact and change momentum more than they impact the scoreboard.

## PUTTING IT ALL TOGETHER

As we can see in Table 2.7, in an average football game of thirteen possessions, Sample 96 teams started eleven possessions in long field situations, scored 4.4 times, and put twenty-five points on the scoreboard. Their opponents took over possession in their own territory 11.7 times per game, scored 2.6 times and rang up just fifteen points. The ten-point scoring margin on long field possessions can be added to 4.1 points of margin derived from short field opportunities and a very small margin created by non-offensive scoring to arrive at the overall fifteen point margin of victory for Sample 96 teams.

To hammer home the significance of long field scoring, Sample 96 teams won a whopping 94.5 percent of the games in which they enjoyed that advantage, and lost only 5.5 percent of the games in which they had better long field statistics than their opponents. Weaker opponents rode the long field advantage to victories 73.5 percent of the time. It is equally amazing that Sample 96 teams won only one game in four when they were at a disadvantage in long field scoring. This analysis strongly indicates that the ability to score on long drives, while preventing opponents from

---

* A game is considered to have been decided by non-offensive scoring if the outcome would have been different had neither team scored non-offensive points.

TABLE 2.7    SCORING OUTPUT BY TYPE OF POSSESSION
(2007–2010)

|  | *Sample 96 Teams* | *Opponents* | *Point Differential* |
|---|---|---|---|
| *Points off Long Field Drives* | 24.9 | 15.0 | 9.9 |
| *Points off Short Field Drives* | 8.3 | 4.1 | 4.2 |
| *Points off Special Teams / Defense* | 2.1 | 1.2 | 0.9 |
| *Total Points* | 35.3 | 20.3 | 15.0 |

scoring on their long drives, is *the* defining characteristic of superior football teams.

Long field proficiency (points per long field possession), and to a lesser extent short field frequency (short field possessions as a percentage of all possessions) and short field proficiency (points per short field possession), are statistics that pass the three tests for good statistics. They determine the outcome of football games, explain the outcome of football games, and produce victories for good teams as well as mediocre teams.

## LONG FIELD OP FORENSICS

At the end of the day, the meat and potatoes of football success are to be found in the long field possessions. In order to assess the performance capabilities of football teams it is important to examine the mechanics of a long scoring drive and reach an understanding of why good teams sustain drives and weaker teams do not.

Two detailed analyses of long field possessions were performed, one for the twenty-four sample teams from the 2008 season and one for the twenty-four sample teams in 2010 (see Table 2.8).* These forty-eight

---

* The author maintained records of long field possession results for sample teams in 2008 and 2010. The author researched play-by-play accounts of all games played by the sample teams and recorded the long field possessions' outcomes in a separate spread sheet.

TABLE 2.8    LONG FIELD RESULTS

|  | Scores | 3 & Out | Offensive Mistakes | Defensive Stops |
|---|---|---|---|---|
| Sample Teams | 38.2% | 19.3% | 19.9% | 22.6% |
| Opponents | 22.5% | 26.7% | 27.5% | 23.3% |

sample teams ("Sample 48 teams") from those two seasons began 6,611 offensive possessions on their own end of the field. Over the course of those two seasons, Sample 48 teams scored on a 38.2 percent of their long field possessions. In 2008 Texas Tech was the most efficient at producing points in long field situations, scoring on 50.4 percent of its long field possessions, while Nevada led the pack in 2010 with a 51 percent efficiency rating.

The possessions that did not culminate in a score were divided more or less equally among three other kinds of results. Table 2.8 compares long field drive results for Sample 48 teams with the results of their opponents; the table may make it easier to follow the numbers quoted in the narrative that follows.

Sample 48 teams failed to launch a drive, otherwise known as a three-and-out, on 19.3 percent of their long field possessions. Not coincidentally, Auburn and Oregon, arguably two of the best teams in the country in 2010, suffered the fewest three-and-out possessions with just eighteen apiece over the course of the entire season.

Once the chains begin moving, inertia is overcome and the typical drive tends to maintain its own momentum unless it is derailed by a turnover, a sack, or a major penalty. Wisconsin and TCU, the teams that met in the 2011 Rose Bowl, committed the fewest drive-killing mistakes, falling on their own swords only seventeen times during the entire 2010 season. Texas A&M suffered self-inflicted failure more often than any other sample team—forty-eight of the Aggies' long field possessions ended with an interception, a quarterback buried under a mound of enemy players, or a field decorated with bright yellow hankies. In total, 19.9 percent of the Sample 48's long field possessions ended with one of these ignominious events.

Naturally, some drives ground to a halt from a simple inability to gain ten more yards. Defenses would like to take credit for all of these circumstances— 22.6 percent of all long field possessions—but this category includes missed low-probability field goals, missed high-probability field goals, time expiring when teams were trying to score, and time expiring when teams wanted to get off the field. While good teams make mistakes that kill drives, they are rarely prevented from making a first down by opposing defenses.

Opponents of the Sample 48 teams were naturally playing against better defenses and their poorer long field offensive possession statistics bear this out. For Sample 48 opponents, scoring was the least likely outcome of a long field possession, occurring on just 22.5 percent of long field possessions. The most likely outcome for weak teams was a drive-killing sack, penalty, or turnover. These unfortunate endings occurred on 27.5 percent of long field possessions. Three-and-out possessions followed close behind with a failure rate of 26.7 percent, and defensive stops accounted for the last 23.3 percent of long field possessions.

One curious conclusion to be drawn from these stats is that once Sample 48 team defenses allowed their opponents to achieve a first down, they were not any more able to stop weak opponent offenses, than the weak defenses were able to stop Sample 48 offenses. Other conclusions are that good teams launch drives with an initial first down at a better rate than weak teams (an aggression measure?), and that good teams make far fewer big mistakes (sacks, major penalties, turnovers). These conclusions lead us to believe that the two keys to success on long field possessions are: (1) pulling the cork out of the bottle with an initial first down, and (2) keeping the drive alive by avoiding catastrophic mistakes. The corollary is true for the defense: (1) stopping a drive before it starts and (2) bringing pressure on the opposing quarterback to produce sacks, fumbles, and interceptions.

## BIG PLAYS MATTER

Less obvious is one last statistical fact that must be introduced to complete the analysis of long field scoring—the impact of the "big play." The enemy of all offensive drives is the distance to the goal line, but this distance can suddenly be negated by big plays. Long field possessions morph instantly into short field possessions with the assistance of a "big play." Big plays are defined here as offensive plays covering more than twenty-five yards or a major penalty on the opponent (as in the ten- or fifteen-yard variety). Big plays are like rolling double sixes in a board game and moving your game piece halfway around the board in a single turn. A play of twenty-five yards almost always turns a long field possession into a short field possession, and we have now established that short field possessions produce points at a considerably high rate. In 2010, Oregon launched fifty-eight big plays from scrimmage in thirteen games and Auburn exploded for sixty big plays in fourteen games, proving that they were very good teams for reasons that actually contributed to their success.

As can be seen from Chart 2.3, Sample 48 teams used big offensive plays to fuel 55.3 percent of all long field scoring drives, while major opponent penalties assisted 13 percent of all long scoring drives. Only 31.7 percent of all long field scoring drives were unaided by the helping hand of a big play. To put these numbers into context, when a Sample 48 team produced a big offensive play, it was successful in scoring 82.8 percent of the time, more than double its scoring average overall.* The flip side is that without the big offensive plays and major opponent penalties, Sample 48 teams scored on only 18.3 percent of their possessions.†

Sample 48 opponents were even more reliant upon big plays. More than 70 percent of the opponents' scoring drives were propelled by a big play from scrimmage or a major defensive penalty. When Sample 48 opponents could not turn in a big play and were not blessed with a major infraction committed by the Sample 48 teams, they could only convert a score on 8.4 percent of their possessions. However, when a mediocre team was able to pull a rabbit out of the hat and make a big offensive play, it had a 72.4 percent probability of going on to score.

---

\* Of the 3,312 long field possessions initiated by the Sample 24 teams during the 2010 season, 876 included at least one offensive play covering at least 25 yards and 725 of those possessions resulted in an offensive score.

† Of the 3,312 long field possessions initiated by the Sample 24 teams during the 2010 season, 2,266 possessions did not include a big offensive play or a major defensive penalty. Sample 24 teams were able to score on only 415 of those possessions.

CHART 2.3    BIG PLAYS AS A CONTRIBUTING FACTOR TO LONG PLAY
             SCORING DRIVES FOR SAMPLE 48 TEAMS (2008, 2010)

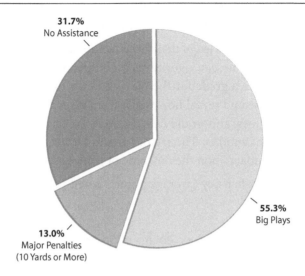

**31.7%**
No Assistance

**55.3%**
Big Plays

**13.0%**
Major Penalties
(10 Yards or More)

## DAZZLING DEDUCTIONS

College football is a game of big plays and big mistakes, and these dramatic events are the essence of winning college football. The best teams in America principally do five things better than their opponents to win football games and these things all revolve around big plays and big mistakes:

1. Achieve short field possessions through turnovers, punt returns, and kickoff returns
2. Deny their opponents short field possessions by taking care of the ball and covering punt returns and kickoff returns
3. Score on long field possessions by:
   a. making big offensive plays
   b. avoiding the dreaded three-and-out
   c. protecting the quarterback against sacks
   d. avoiding major penalties
   e. protecting the ball against turnovers
4. Prevent opponent long field scores by:
   a. preventing big offensive plays
   b. generating frequent three-and-outs
   c. avoiding major penalties

    d. pressuring the opposing quarterback into turnovers

    e. sacking the opposing quarterback

5. Exhibit superior special teams play, which directly impacts non-offensive scoring and short field opportunities

Armed with the knowledge that these factors determine the outcome of college football games, an algorithm combining the factors can be constructed to produce a grade for the playing performance of a team in a game. The grade would reveal how well a team played irrespective of the outcome (win or loss) and would help differentiate one win from another and one loss from another. The factors would be weighted according to their historical impact upon the outcome of games as follows:

1. Long field proficiency (average points scored per long field possession)
2. Big offensive plays
3. Short field frequency (percentage of possessions started in enemy territory)
4. Turnovers
5. Major penalties
6. Three-and-out possessions
7. Special teams big plays
8. Short field proficiency (average points scored per short field possession)
9. Sacks
10. Non-offensive scores

These factors would be graded both for the offense and for the defense and the two grades would be combined to produce a team grade for a game.

Winning and losing can't be ignored, of course, but as statistics, they leave much to be desired. Thus, the value of a victory (and the value of a loss) must be added to the performance grade to develop an overall team rating. A simple solution for placing a value on a victory is to award the victorious team the rating points of the vanquished opponent. The opponent's rating represents a precise measure of the strength of the opponent and the value of the victory, and, therefore, differentiates one win from another. Similarly, some losses could have a potential positive effect if the loss was against a good opponent and the playing performance was of high quality (the so-called "good" loss). A sliding scale could represent the combination of opponent strength and playing performance grade in order to calculate a value for a loss. By combining a win/loss value with a performance grade, a game rating can be produced and the accumulated game ratings for a season can represent a team's overall rating.

Subsequently, team grades can be comparatively ranked, and the BCS can stage a credible title game or a full-blown playoff with the assurance that the best teams are competing for the championship.

Naturally, computers are the best tool for this job and it follows that rather than fearing the mechanical beasts, the BCS should embrace the objective machines and should ask major computer software system developers to construct computer programs to do the job. It also follows that instead of limiting the creativity of the suppliers and the input variables available to the suppliers, the BCS should throw open the door to innovation.

The BCS is a failure today simply because its title game matchups are neither credible nor inclusive of teams from conferences other than the six BCS partner conferences. Title game selections fail to satisfy football fans because the BCS ranking method is subjective, illogical, and mathematically bizarre.

The missing ingredient in the ranking process is a measure of the intrinsic play-making ability exhibited by the teams being ranked, and, that playing performance measurement must be predicated on the factors that determine game results. As Sherlock Holmes might once have said, the best way to determine the two teams most deserving of a place in the BCS championship game is "elementary, my dear Watson, elementary."

# SLAYING DAVID

*Making a Case for FBS v. FCS*
*Matchup in College Football*

BY CAROLINE E. FAURE,
KAREN B. APPLEBY,
*and* CODY L. SPARROW

Caroline E. Faure, EdD; ATC, is an assistant professor of Sport Science and Physical Education at Idaho State University. Dr. Faure teaches undergraduate and graduate course work in sports medicine and sports law. Her dissertation, "An Examination of the General Understanding of High School Football Coaches Relative to Concussion," earned her the prestigious Kole-McGuffey Award. The study helped expose the need for better educational programs for coaches when it came to concussion identification and management. In addition to establishing quality concussion education programs, Dr. Faure enjoys doing research on her other passion, NCAA college football.

Karen M. Appleby, PhD, is an associate professor and chair of the Department of Sport Science and Physical Education at Idaho State University. Her academic training is in Sport Psychology, Sport Management, and Cultural Studies. Dr. Appleby teaches both undergraduate and graduate courses in Research and Writing, Sport Psychology, Management of Athletics, and Sport Sociology. Her research interests include gender issues in sport, injury in sport, and the master's athlete population.

Cody L. Sparrow is a graduate assistant at Idaho State University. He is currently pursuing his master's degree in Athletic Administration with an emphasis on NCAA compliance.

## INTRODUCTION

On September 1, 2007, the Appalachian State Mountaineers pulled off what many believed was one of the biggest upsets in college football history by knocking off fifth-ranked Michigan 34-32 on the Wolverines' home field.[*] It was the first time that a Football Championship Subdivision (FCS) football program had beaten a nationally ranked Football Bowl Subdivision (FBS) team since the NCAA split its Division I teams in 1978.[†,‡,§,1] Not only did the Wolverines lose the game, they paid the Mountaineers $400,000 for the privilege.[2] The week after the upset, the Associated Press announced it would make FCS schools eligible for votes and potentially a

---

[*] Michigan would finish the season with a 9-4 record, good for eighteenth place in the final 2007 BCS rankings.

[†] The NCAA referred to Football Bowl Subdivision (FBS) programs as Division I A programs from 1978 to 2005.

[‡] The NCAA referred to Football Championship Subdivision (FCS) programs as Division I AA programs from 1978 to 2005.

[§] The NCAA defines Division I as the highest level of intercollegiate athletics. In 1973, the NCAA introduced a classification system that distinguished college athletics programs based on a variety of characteristics such as attendance, number of athletic programs, and so forth. Large athletic programs were defined as Division I programs while schools with smaller athletic programs were designated Division II or Division III status. In 1978, Division I football programs were further subdivided into Division I-A (denoting larger football programs) and Division I-AA (denoting smaller football programs).

national ranking in its weekly Top 25 poll. Appalachian State received two votes that week while Michigan dropped completely out of the rankings.

Games pitting small schools against top-ranked schools are becoming increasingly common in college football, especially since a NCAA rule change in 2006 that allowed teams to play a twelfth regular season game. The NCAA also allows FBS programs to use one win over a FCS opponent to count toward the six wins required to become bowl eligible. Since 1998 (the first year of the Bowl Championship Series), there has been a near twofold increase in the number of FBS versus FCS games in college football (these contests peaked in 2009). The FCS and FBS are NCAA subdivisions only relevant to college football, and do not apply to other sports overseen by the NCAA. While both sets of schools are Division I programs, the NCAA considers football attendance numbers and scholarships as primary subdivision determinants. FBS schools, for example, must demonstrate the ability to generate and average of at least 15,000 spectator per home game over a "rolling two-year period."[3] They are also granted the right to distribute up to eighty-five athletic scholarships.[4] FCS teams are restricted to providing full scholarships to only sixty-three athletes, although full awards can be split among eighty-five players. In 2009, 91 of the 710 total games involving teams from Automatically Qualifying conferences were played against FCS opponents (12.8 percent of games played). This total included fourteen games featuring teams ranked in the final AP Top 25. In games against ranked FBS opponents, Top 25 teams outscored their FCS counterparts 761 to 168. The average margin of victory was 37.1 points.

While Appalachian State's win garnered a great deal of national media attention, the reality is that such upsets are uncommon. On the same weekend the Mountaineers beat Michigan, twenty-one other NCAA Division FCS schools played FBS schools. Twenty times, the larger schools won (Nicholls State was the only other FCS team to beat an FBS foe, knocking off unranked Rice University 16 to 14). In the FCS teams' losses, no team came closer than two touchdowns, and the average margin of loss was 32.8 points. Table 3.1 traces the historical outcomes of intersubdivision (FBS versus FCS) games.

The practice of FBS programs scheduling FCS opponents is cloaked in controversy. The media and fans tend to criticize top-ranked FBS schools for scheduling teams that appear to be "cupcakes."[5] Small schools can be

TABLE 3.1    FBS HISTORY VERSUS FCS TEAMS[6]

| Year | FBS Winning % | Record | Differential |
|------|------|------|------|
| 1996 | .851 | 40-7 | 15.1 |
| 1997 | .857 | 30-5 | 20.8 |
| 1998 | .872 | 41-6 | 21.8 |
| 1999 | .865 | 45-7 | 22.9 |
| 2000 | .709 | 39-16 | 19.7 |
| 2001 | .860 | 49-8 | 21.3 |
| 2002 | .877 | 57-8 | 24.8 |
| 2003 | .859 | 61-10 | 23.6 |
| 2004 | .893 | 50-6 | 21.5 |
| 2005 | .963 | 52-2 | 25.4 |
| 2006 | .910 | 71-7 | 26.7 |
| 2007 | .886 | 70-9 | 25.9 |
| 2008 | .977 | 85-2 | 28.9 |
| 2009 | .947 | 89-5 | 29.1 |
| 2010 | .913 | 63-6 | 27.4 |
| **TOTAL** | **.890** | **842-104** | **24.4** |

chastised for compromising their athletes' safety and spirit for the sake of big money.* In the eyes of the critics, no one wins. But in the eyes of the athletic directors who schedule the games, the benefits can be considerable.

## STUDY BACKGROUND

Between 2009 and 2011, the authors of this study (the "researchers") reviewed the scheduling history of FBS and FCS schools. The researchers contacted athletic directors at FBS and FCS schools whose teams regularly participated in inter-subdivision games. The researchers then contacted the athletic directors by e-mail and invited them to participate in a study to investigate their perspectives on the scheduling of inter-subdivision college

---

* Interview with FCS Athletic Director #4 (FCS4), September 3, 2009. To maintain confidentiality of the athletic directors surveyed, the authors refer to them as FBS 1, 2, 3, etc. (denoting different FBS athletic directors) and FCS 1, 2, 3, etc. (denoting different FCS athletic directors).

CHART 3.1    PARTICIPANT PROFILE

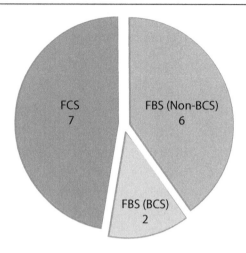

football games. On the FBS side, emphasis was placed on teams perennially ranked in the AP Top 25. Of the twenty-four athletic directors who were invited to participate in the study, fifteen accepted (63 percent). Eight of those athletic directors represented FBS schools whose teams finished the 2010 season ranked in the Top 25 and seven represented FCS schools (see Chart 3.1).*

## THE PERSPECTIVE OF FBS ATHLETIC DIRECTORS

Despite ongoing national criticism that FBS teams should not be allowed to play FCS opponents,[7] FBS athletic directors at top-ranked schools were consistent in their perspectives on scheduling FCS opponents. FBS athletic

---

* Interviews with all of the athletic directors were scheduled and conducted over the telephone. The interviews followed a semi-structured protocol and were recorded and later transcribed. To ensure the credibility of the responses, a written copy of the completed interview transcript was sent to each athletic director. Each athletic director was encouraged to make necessary edits and/or add comments. To ensure confidentiality, final transcripts were coded using processes known as open and axial coding to help with pattern analysis. Social scientists use open coding to analyze text and identify common properties and dimensions (categories and subcategories). Axial coding is a process whereby data is reassembled once the properties and dimensions have been defined by making connections between the various categories.

directors cited flexibility of scheduling, cost savings, and the opportunity for players, particularly backup players, to get valuable game experience as the primary reasons for scheduling FCS opponents. It also did not hurt that FBS teams happen to defeat FCS opponents with great regularity.* While some might believe FCS games would hurt FBS schools in national rankings, this did not appear to concern of FBS athletic directors.

## A "GUARANTEED" WIN (...THEY HOPE!)

Talk to top-ranked FBS athletic directors and few will tell you they are looking for a "guaranteed" win when scheduling FCS opponents. As one critic suggested, "You can arrange the win, you can pay for it in full, but still there are no guarantees. The game still has to be played and in the end, the players on the field get to decide what happens."[8] Three of the FBS athletic directors said that they schedule FCS teams because their football teams were *more likely* to register a win against an FCS opponent than they were against an FBS opponent. Schools in conferences that automatically receive bids to the BCS are among the most active recruiters of FCS games.[†]

The Big 12 Conference provides an interesting analysis of the significance that FCS schools can play in FBS teams' scheduling and performance. Table 3.2 summarizes records against FCS opponents from 1998 to 2010.[‡]

Since 1998, Big 12 teams have scheduled eighty-one FCS opponents, which Big 12 teams defeated on seventy-nine occasions (97.5 percent of all matchups).[§] Overall, FCS opponents made up 7.3 percent of all games (including bowl games) played by Big 12 schools.

---

* Interview with FBS Athletic Director #4 (FBS4), February 4, 2011.

† Conference champions from the ACC, Big Ten, Big 12, Big East, Pac-10, and SEC conferences are granted an automatic berth into one of the five Bowl Championship Series (BCS) games. These conferences are referred to as Automatic Qualifying (AQ) conferences. Notre Dame, which is not a member of an AQ conference, receives special status and can achieve AQ status should it meet certain requirements. Schools in the remaining conferences are regarded as members of non-AQ conference and, as the designation suggests, receive invitations to BCS contests on a subjective basis.

‡ The year 1998 coincides with the introduction of the BCS format.

§ Northern Iowa defeated Iowa State by the score of 24-13 in 2007 and Montana State defeated Colorado by the score of 19-10 in 2006.

TABLE 3.2    FCS SCHEDULING BY BIG 12 MEMBER SCHOOLS
             (1998–2010)

| | FCS Opponents (1998-2010) | FCS Losses | Total Wins (1998-2010) | FCS wins as Pct of All Wins |
|---|---|---|---|---|
| Baylor | 10 | - | 44 | 22.7% |
| Kansas | 10 | - | 69 | 14.5% |
| Iowa State | 10 | 1 | 67 | 13.4% |
| Kansas State | 11 | - | 100 | 11.0% |
| OK State | 9 | - | 88 | 10.2% |
| Missouri | 8 | - | 92 | 8.7% |
| Texas Tech | 8 | - | 106 | 7.5% |
| Texas A&M | 5 | - | 91 | 5.5% |
| Nebraska | 5 | - | 115 | 4.3% |
| Oklahoma | 2 | - | 134 | 1.5% |
| Colorado | 2 | 1 | 78 | 1.3% |
| Texas | 1 | - | 133 | 0.8% |
| TOTALS | 81 | 2 | 1117 | 7.3% |

FCS opponents have played a more significant role in the fortunes of some teams than others. The Baylor Bears, the worst performing team in the Big 12, won just forty-four games in the thirteen years measured here. During that time, victories against FCS opponents made up nearly 23 percent of the football program's total wins. FCS wins comprise over 10 percent of the overall win totals for four Big 12 teams (Kansas, Iowa State, Kansas State, and Oklahoma State) over the period. On the opposite end of the spectrum, the University of Texas played just one FCS opponent in twelve seasons.

Teams that are members of Automatic Qualifying conferences (AQ conferences) are guaranteed berths to big money bowls which leads to bigger football revenue. AQ conferences receive additional tens of millions of dollars in revenue annually from BCS bowl games alone.[9] The team that gets the invite to a BCS bowl is not the only one that makes the money; every team in its conference gets a share of bowl revenues. For the 2010 bowl season, the Big Ten and SEC both received $22.2 million to share with their member schools. Each of the other AQ conferences received $17.7 mil-

TABLE 2.3    FBS V. FCS WINNING PERCENTAGES, 1996–2010[10]

| Conference | FCS Opponents | Record Against Winning % |
|---|---|---|
| SEC* | 78-2 | .975 |
| Big 12* | 87-3 | .967 |
| WAC | 74-3 | .961 |
| Pac-10* | 37-2 | .949 |
| Mountain West | 48-3 | .941 |
| Big East* | 64-4 | .941 |
| Conference USA | 68-5 | .932 |
| ACC* | 82-7 | .921 |
| Big Ten* | 52-5 | .912 |
| Independents | 52-16 | .853 |
| MAC | 95-27 | .779 |

* denotes Automatic Qualifying Conference

lion.[11] With such big sums of money on the line, it seems rational for FBS schools to look for guaranteed wins. Bringing in FCS schools appears to be the way they get them. Collectively, AQ conference schools are 400-23 (95 percent win percentage) against FCS opponents since the FCS classification began (see Table 2.3).

## THE CUPCAKE PHENOMENON

Athletic directors from FBS and FCS programs have a broad spectrum of views regarding the level of competition that takes place. One FCS athletic director concedes the obvious mismatch:

> [FBS programs are] looking for a win. We know that. They want to get [us] in for their first game so that their starters look fabulous and their season ticket holders go, "Oh yeah, it's going to be another good year."[†]

---

† Interview with FCS4.

Another FCS athletic director concurs:

> They've got eighty-five scholarships, and we've got sixty-three.
> Their kids are going to be bigger and stronger. So, I mean we
> don't have much of a chance.*

FBS athletic directors' views about the quality of FCS competition range from respect to indifference. The games are clearly overwhelming mismatches, and that leads critics to contend that FCS opponents are mere "cupcakes,"† FBS athletic directors, however, do not typically discredit the quality of football played:

> You have situations where the [FCS] schools have some success.
> Jacksonville State beat Ole Miss [in 2010] and of course Appalachian State beat Michigan. You have so many examples of
> really high-quality football—sometimes better than [FBS]
> schools.‡

> There are some really good FCS schools across the country. Our
> fans may not recognize their names but they're really good.⁵

Another FBS athletic director noted that he schedules the FCS games three to five years in advance. He's not concerned about whether that team is good once it comes time to play:

> In all sports, there are peaks and valleys. If I schedule an [FCS]
> team five years from now and they come in here and are having a
> down year, maybe they are three and seven, and someone says to
> me. "You know what's [school] doing scheduling these people?" I
> couldn't care less about that. I just don't care about the criticism.‖

---

* Interview with FBS Athletics Director #2 (FBS2), February 2, 2011.
† Amy Daughters, "College Football," ¶ 22.
‡ Interview with FBS2.
⁵ Interview with FBS Athletic Director #6 (FBS6), February 3, 2011.
‖ Interview with FBS Athletic Director #1 (FBS1), February 3, 2011.

Amid the criticism of the inter-subdivision games, FBS athletic directors say name recognition is important in order to sell the game's credibility. However, they are also aware of the risks associated with scheduling FCS schools. Three FBS athletic directors noted these risks:

Of course, there is always that *chance* that the big school could lose. If that happens, it can be catastrophic:

> What's the biggest threat? That you get upset! When that happens, it's on *SportsCenter* for seven straight days. Ask Michigan!*

> You can't lose. You can't lose. That's what scares you. It happens every single year. When that happens you are like, "Oh my goodness, what have we done?"†

## SCHEDULE FLEXIBILITY

According to all of the FBS athletic directors interviewed for this study, the primary reason FBS athletic directors schedule FCS opponents is the small schools' flexibility in scheduling. With 120 FBS schools to choose from, top-ranked teams could play other FBS schools from other conferences, but other FBS programs are rarely as flexible with their availability, especially from the middle to latter part of the regular season. Some conferences, like the SEC, establish their schedules as early as four to five years in advance.‡ That means those FBS athletic directors know what their open dates are and they can begin the courtship of a FCS opponent early.

While some media and fans would like to paint the games as examples of Goliaths picking among a bevy of helpless Davids,⁵ some FBS athletic directors say it simply is not so:

---

* Interview with FBS Athletic Director #3 (FBS3), February 1, 2011.
† Interview with FBS6.
‡ Interview with FBS1.
⁵ Amy Daughters, "College Football."

I have never had a problem scheduling [an] FCS school. We get a significant amount of interest. FCS [schools] will reach out to us as opposed to us reaching out to them. I think that a chance to play in our facility against our team is attractive and it appeals to the competitiveness of those schools.*

Further, other FBS athletic directors were quick to point out the potential value playing an FBS school may have for the FCS athletes.

It gives [the student-athletes] the chance to play on the big stage. Instead of playing in front of two or three thousand fans, it gives them the chance to play in front of ninety thousand fans.†

Interestingly, one FCS athletic director suggested that he had significant impact in the negotiations in relation to money and tickets when it comes to scheduling FBS opponents:

[The FBS school representative] actually called me the first time in July of 2008 and said, "Are you interested in a game with us?" and I said, "Oh maybe if all the circumstances—money, tickets, everything—were right," and they said to give them a ballpark number. I gave them an amount and they said, "No thanks." They called back in August and asked if I was still interested and I told them the same numbers and they said, "No." Then they called me again in September and asked if I was still interested and I said, "Yeah...same numbers" and they said "No" again. But then in October they called me for a fourth time and said, "Are you still interested?" and when I said "Yep. Same numbers" they said, "OK, we'll do it."‡

This commentary seems to negate the idea that FBS schools are the ones who hold the most power when scheduling and playing smaller FCS schools. Other FCS athletic directors concurred that it takes two to make it work:

---

* Interview with FBS1.
† Interview with FBS2.
‡ Interview with FCS4.

Scheduling is like anything. It's like dating. It takes two schools
that need games to make it happen. I needed a game; they needed
a game, and it just ended up happening. There wasn't any magic
formula to it. They were desperate for a game in October and I
had an open date that matched up.*

Once FBS schools decide to *play down*, the focus turns to finding the
right team to play. FBS athletic directors say they look first to nearby FCS
schools. Sometimes, however, they suggested the need to look beyond their
immediate geographic region in order to fill a particular date. Typically,
athletic directors from FBS programs will place personal telephone calls
to schools that have a history of scheduling games against other FBS programs. Other FBS programs will simply use a mass e-mail addressed to
athletic directors at FCS schools:

[Name of FBS school] is looking for a FCS opponent to come to
[City] on Sept. 10, 2011 (preferably) or Sept. 24, 2011 (possibly).
[School] is offering an attractive guarantee. Please call [name] at
[number] if you are interested.†

## FINANCIAL IMPACT ON FBS SCHOOLS

Despite the big money payouts, the FBS athletic directors interviewed in
this study said playing FCS teams actually *saves* them money. FBS teams
are granted twelve games to play during the regular football season. For
the largest conferences, nine of those matchups are typically dedicated to
their conference schedule. That leaves teams with three open dates to fill.
Considering home games generate substantial revenue, especially at top
FBS schools, FBS teams prefer scheduling as many home games as possible.‡ Bringing in an FBS school is risky. Top-ranked schools, especially
those in strong conferences, like the SEC, need wins. A loss, which at least
statistically is more likely to occur playing an FBS opponent than an FCS

---

* Interview with FCS Athletic Director #2 (FCS2), September 9, 2009.
† Electronic Mail transmission to FCS4, January 31, 2011.
‡ Although in some instances, neutral site games can generate similar or more profit
than homes games are able to produce.

CHART 3.2    PAYOUT PER TEAM BY BOWL GAME (BASED ON
             2010–11 TOTALS)

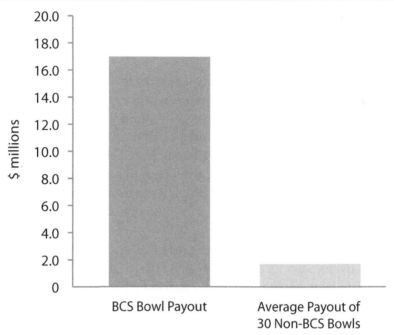

opponent, can be devastating. The BCS Championship game, and the other
four BCS games each pay out $17.0 million per team. Lesser bowl games
pay significantly less (between $325,000 to 4.25 million). A single loss to
a non-conference opponent could have significant implications for a top
tier team (see chart 3.2).

In 2011, the BCS distributed more than $174 million from its five bowl
games (see Table 3.4). Of that total, $145.2 million (83.4 percent of total
BCS revenues) went to AQ conferences. The Big Ten, Pac-10, and SEC were
each able to generate $27.2 million because two representatives from each
conference participated in BCS games. The pay-outs received by AQ conferences were six times higher than those received by non-AQ conferences.
As the distributions indicate, the BCS format offers a winner-takes-all opportunity for its participants.

The incentive to produce a strong season and reduce the risk of losing
can have significant financial implications for a team. Boise State, a member

TABLE 3.4    BCS REVENUES GENERATED BY CONFERENCE 2010–11[12]

|  | Payout | Pct of Payout |
|---|---|---|
| *AQ Conferences* | *$145.2 million* | *83.42%* |
| Big Ten, Pac-10, SEC | $27.2 million (per conference) | 46.88% |
| ACC, Big 12, Big East | $21.2 million (per conference) | 36.54% |
| *Non-AQ Conferences* | *$24.72 million* | *14.20%* |
| Mountain West | $12.75 million | 7.32% |
| WAC | $4.05 million | 2.33% |
| Conference USA | $3.34 million | 1.92% |
| Mid-American | $2.64 million | 1.52% |
| Sun Belt | $1.94 million | 1.11% |
| *Other* | *$4.15 million* | *2.38%* |
| FCS Conferences | $2.25 million | 1.29% |
| Notre Dame | $1.7 million | 0.98% |
| Army | $0.1 million | 0.06% |
| Navy | $0.1 million | 0.06% |
| **TOTAL** | **$174.07 million** | |

of the non-AQ conference was ranked number four heading into the eleventh week of the season with an unblemished 10-0 record. The Broncos' BCS hopes ended in 2011 when they were upset by Nevada (a fellow WAC member). The loss dropped Boise State out of BCS contention. Instead of participating in a BCS game in which it would have earned $17 million, the Broncos settled for the Humanitarian Bowl where it earned $750,000. Boise State's loss to Nevada was without a doubt the most "expensive" loss of the season. It is no wonder that top-tier teams aim to reduce the risk of scheduling overly competitive non-conference opponents given the money at stake.

Not only is the risk of losing to an FBS opponent higher, getting another ranked, non-conference FBS team to accept the challenge with the same conditions as FCS schools is highly unlikely. FCS schools will agree to single away game contracts. Lower-tiered FBS schools rarely agree to the same specifications. Instead, they often negotiate *home and home* contracts— meaning each team is guaranteed a home game against the other. Such deals guarantee that both teams have an equal chance to generate considerable revenue. Playing a mid-major or lower-tiered FBS team is an option, but again it does not always make sense to top-ranked FBS programs:

> The net is still more than what we'd make going on the road but we try to manage that expense category the best we can. It's tough though because FBS [schools] that are willing to go on the road and play single, one-time road games know that they can demand a big guarantee. Most of them want a return game or a two-for-one or three-for-one. Those FBS [teams] willing to come play a one-time game on the road want big numbers.*

Another FBS athletic director suggested a tremendous difference in overall cost:

> If we were to go out there and get [an] FBS school from another conference and if they agreed to just play us one time at our place, the cost would be substantially more than what we pay for [an] FCS school. We'd have to pay them maybe twice as much to come in to our place. Plus, they'd demand a lot more tickets for their fans. You're talking at least a half million to three-quarters of a million dollar difference there. That adds up.†

Examples of the ambitious FBS-to-FBS pay-outs are abundant. The Georgia Bulldogs paid $875,000 to host Louisiana-Lafayette from the Sun Belt Conference in 2010.[13] They will also pay $925,000 to New Mexico State from the Western Athletic Conference for a game in 2011, $1 million to host Florida Atlantic from the Sun Belt Conference in 2012, and $975,000 to host North Texas also from the Sun Belt Conference in 2013.[14] Arkansas State, another Sun Belt Conference member, received $1 million to play Auburn in 2010 and they have another $1 million payday in 2011,

---

* Interview with FBS3.
† Interview with FBS Athletic Director #7 (FBS7), February 9, 2011.

courtesy of Virginia Tech.[15] Nebraska courted Boise State from the WAC for a game in Lincoln in 2011, but Boise State's price tag, a reported $1 million, was allegedly too steep for the Huskers to stay interested.[16] Boise State's payday to play Virginia Tech in 2010 was a reported $1.25 million. Thanks to outside sponsorship of the game (Washington Redskins owner Daniel Snyder was behind the scheduling and hosted the game at the Redskins' FedEx Field), Virginia Tech also received a game guarantee of $2.35 million, a figure that likely exceeded what Virginia Tech would have generated had the game been played in its home stadium.[17]

The simple fact is that higher-echelon teams are most likely to sell out their stadiums regardless of the opponent. They are also likely to continue signing lucrative media contracts, securing corporate sponsorships, raising funds from supporters, and selling merchandise. That is why a single home game against an FCS opponent makes sense. FCS schools *cannot* command anything but a single away game contract. They also *settle* for sums between $450,000 and $750,000.* However, as mentioned before, negotiating still takes place. One FBS athletic director discussed this negotiation in the following comment:

> We negotiate. We will negotiate. It's just the nature of the beast. We try to stay below the market because we know that even though we've been sold out for seventy-four straight games, we only have fifty-five thousand seats, so that impacts our resource base. It's tough for us to try to compete in a market with those that have one hundred thousand seats. They can pay a lot more. I will tell you we have a couple of future games that have significant guarantees.†

Playing a team within the region is not only more attractive to the nationally ranked school, it is also a selling point for the small school. While game guarantees typically provide for game tickets and sometimes even hotel rooms and meals, transportation to the host site is not usually a negotiable item. A trip across the country means the FCS school will have to charter a plane and that cost will come out of what that school pockets from the game's guarantee. A plane ride can cost upward of $70,000 to

---

* Interview with FBS2.
† Interview with FBS3.

$100,000. Buses to transport the team a state or two away are a fraction of that cost ($3,000–$5,000).* As one FCS athletic director suggested, if FBS schools are forced to find an FCS team that must travel a significant distance in order to play the game, they will certainly be asked to give a greater guarantee:

> Trying to play poker, if you will, is not always a great thing to do. We want [FBS] games that are within our geographic region. If an opportunity does arise, we'd prefer not to travel three time zones away.[†]

FCS teams typically do not travel with a huge fan base. That means the allotment of seven thousand to ten thousand tickets the top team usually doles out to visiting FBS teams is reduced to one thousand to two thousand. This gives the big school even more tickets to sell to their own fans.

> [Playing an FCS team] opens up more tickets that you can sell to the general public than perhaps our season tickets. Usually you'll hold five thousand to seven thousand tickets for the visiting teams. Let's say the visiting team takes one thousand tickets. Now you have five thousand to six thousand people who have maybe never been to a game before that can come. And it's usually a game that starts at noontime or one o'clock because it's not nationally televised. So with it not being a night game, it's a situation where there are a lot of people that can come and enjoy a game at our stadium. That may be the only time that they're ever able to come.[‡]

## GAME EXPERIENCE

FBS athletic directors in this study also mentioned the gap that exists between the talent levels of the two teams as another reason why they favor FCS opponents. Top-ranked FBS athletic directors admit they expect to win these games. They expect that playing FCS teams will often give the

---

* Interview with FCS4.
† Interview with FCS1.
‡ Interview with FBS2.

FBS teams' coaches an opportunity to put second and third teamers on the field.

> The percentages are heavily weighted toward the [FBS] schools winning. And sometimes that's by a large margin. If the games aren't too close, it allows schools the opportunity to play individuals that would never get to play against a conference opponent. The benefit there for our program is that you get guys that have worked just as hard as the starters and just as hard as those second teamers, and they have a chance to play. I think for someone to get that chance—it's kind of like the *Rudy* movie. You get in the game there and he's able to say, "I was able to play against [FCS1] or [FCS2]" or against another [FCS] school. It means a lot to the walk-ons who would perhaps never have the chance to get on the field.*

## EFFECT ON FINAL RANKINGS

Playing FCS teams has little effect on the final rankings for top-ranked FBS teams in BCS-qualifying conferences. As stated previously, FBS teams are allowed to count one FCS game toward the six wins required to be bowl-eligible. Even with that FCS game, athletic directors whose teams play in the SEC, Big Ten, Big 12, and Pac-10 say the strength of their conference schedule is enough to justify a high ranking at the end of the season. Of the twenty-five teams in the final BCS rankings, only Ohio State (sixth), Oklahoma (seventh), Boise State (tenth), and Oklahoma State (fourteenth) did not have FCS games on their 2010 schedule.

Virginia Tech finished the 2010 season ranked sixteenth despite a 21-16 loss to FCS opponent James Madison (a loss that perhaps was even more surprising than Michigan's 2007 loss to Appalachian State). The Hokies also appeared in a BCS game as the champion and automatic qualifying representative of the ACC.† Virginia Tech's other losses came to nationally

---

* Interview with FBS2.

† Virginia Tech was ranked tenth in preseason Associated Press polls, and went 8-0 in ACC conference play. Unlike Appalachian State, which went on to win the 2007 FCS national championship, James Madison finished the 2010 season with a 6-5 record losing to fellow Colonial Athletic Association members Delaware, New Hampshire, Villanova, Massachusetts, and Richmond—good for eighth place in the ten-member conference.

ranked opponents Boise State (the week before playing James Madison) and Stanford (in the BCS Orange Bowl). Historically, FCS games have not proven to be a factor in the final strength of BCS schedule calculations. Thirty-one percent (eight out of twenty-six) of the teams that have played in the BCS national championship game and 35 percent (40 out of 114) of teams that have played in other BCS Bowl games (Sugar, Fiesta, Rose, and Orange) have played FCS teams during the regular season. For top-tier teams from the AQ conference, scheduling FCS teams does not negatively impact their overall bid for a BCS bowl and, therefore, is non-threatening:

> I don't want this to come across as arrogant but it is just the fact of the matter that when you play the teams that we play in our league, our strength of schedule will take care of itself. [Playing FCS schools] does not impact us at all and I am just never concerned about that.*

Table 3.5 shows the increasing trend of playing FCS teams and the lack of impact it has had on BCS Bowl teams.

## THE NON-AQ PERSPECTIVE

Scheduling FCS opponents seems to have minimal impact on the ability of teams from AQ conferences to obtain a BCS Bowl berth. Teams which are not members of AQ conference are much more sensitive about the possibility of losing a BCS berth because of pollsters' perceptions about their suspect strength of schedule. One athletic director from a non-AQ conference school said he has "a high degree of concern" about how playing FCS opponents could have an adverse impact on his school's BCS bowl selection prospects.† He said that for teams like his, strength of schedule has become an increasingly important factor. His conference is not considered strong, so the three outside games his team plays must be stacked with high-quality FBS opponents in order to gain national credibility. Because of these concerns, he tries to avoid scheduling FCS teams. Another athletic director from a non-AQ conference school concurred:

---

* Interview with FBS1.
† Interview with FBS Athletic Director #5 (FBS5), February 9, 2011.

TABLE 3.5    BCS BOWL GAME PARTICIPANTS AND THEIR HISTORY
             WITH THE FCS*

| | Bowl Game | Teams that Played FCS Opponents |
|---|---|---|
| 1999 | Orange | Florida |
| 2000 | Rose<br>Sugar** | Wisconsin<br>Virginia Tech |
| 2001 | Fiesta** | Oregon State |
| 2002 | | |
| 2003 | Fiesta** | Miami (FL) |
| 2004 | | |
| 2005 | Sugar<br>Fiesta | Auburn, Virginia Tech<br>Pittsburgh |
| 2006 | Sugar<br>Orange | West Virginia<br>Florida State |
| 2007 | Orange<br>Fiesta<br>National Championship** | Wake Forest<br>Boise State<br>Florida |
| 2008 | Rose<br>Sugar<br>Orange<br>National Championship** | Illinois<br>Georgia, Hawaii<br>Kansas, Virginia Tech<br>Ohio State |
| 2009 | Rose<br>Sugar<br>Orange<br>Fiesta<br>National Championship** | Penn State<br>Utah<br>Virginia Tech, Cincinnati<br>Texas, Ohio State<br>Florida |
| 2010 | Sugar<br>Orange<br>Fiesta<br>National Championship** | Florida, Cincinnati<br>Iowa, Georgia Tech<br>TCU<br>Alabama |
| 2011 | Rose<br>Sugar<br>Orange<br>Fiesta<br>National Championship** | TCU<br>Arkansas<br>Stanford, Virginia Tech<br>Connecticut<br>Auburn, Oregon |

Note: Prior to 2007, the BCS National Championship game was played as the
Rose, Sugar, Orange, or Fiesta Bowl. Starting in 2007, the National Championship
game was separated from those Bowl games.

** denotes BCS National Championship Game.

---

* Authors' calculations using each team's schedule and cross-referenced with opponents' NCAA football classification.

If you have a weaker schedule in your conference and you have
an FCS school on your schedule, it could hurt you in the ratings
in the end.*

## THE FCS PERSPECTIVE

Playing against FBS schools can also have a significant effect on FCS teams
hoping to make their subdivision's postseason field. FCS athletic directors
in the study pointed out that losses affect computer rankings and hurt
their chances of qualifying for postseason play.[†] The FCS takes only their
top sixteen teams to the postseason tournament. A loss, no matter who it
is to, counts:

> At the end of the day, you're going to probably lose those [FBS]
> games when you play them and that loss could hurt your chances
> to get in the playoffs at the end of the season, especially when there
> are other teams in your conference that didn't play [FBS] teams.
> If there are other teams in your conference that don't play these
> games, they may not have that loss and so their record might be
> better and that will help them get into the playoffs. When you play
> two [FBS] teams in a season, that means you really have to win a
> lot more during your conference schedule to get in the playoffs.[‡]

Some FCS athletic directors whose teams are not usually playoff contenders are especially proactive about pursuing top-ranked teams. These

---

* Interview with FBS6.

[†] The FCS football champion is determined by a sixteen-team playoff format. Automatic bids are awarded to the champions of eight FCS conferences. Members of
these conferences that do not automatically qualify are eligible for the remaining eight
slots. FCS playoff eligibility also extends to members of the Metro Atlantic Athletic
Conference, Pioneer Conference, and Northeast Conference—although none of these
schools has ever participated in the FCS playoffs, (schools in these conferences do not
offer football scholarships). The remaining eight-playoff slots are determined by a
committee, comprised of FCS athletic directors, which primarily relies on an unpub-
lished internal ranking system.

[‡] Interview with FCS Athletic Director #1 (FCS1), September 14, 2009.

programs experience even less of a downside from scheduling FBS opponents than their more competitive FCS peers.

Without question, the guarantee of securing a large financial payout is the single biggest reason FCS athletic directors schedule FBS opponents. With six-digit sums as the single game guarantees, the decision is obvious for many FCS schools—especially those that struggle generating football revenue due to low ticket sales.

Every FCS athletic director who participated in this study described the widespread effect the FBS game guarantee money had on their athletic department. One FCS athletic director said the money his school received ($375,000) helped to take the "pressure" off his institution.* If he did not agree to the FBS game, his university would been required to generate significantly more money to fund his athletic department. He said smaller, non-BCS conferences could not offer those types of payouts, but if he was fortunate enough to continue to land a Pac-10, Big 12, or Big Ten school, he could make anywhere from $250,000 to $600,000 for a single game. Another FCS athletic director's school was paid $350,000 to play a Top 25 program in 2009 while two other FCS athletic directors said their schools landed payouts ranging from $200,000 to $500,000 for their games against BCS opponents in 2009. One FCS athletic director, who suggested his athletic budget was "probably the smallest in the [conference]," said the money produced by scheduling FBS opponents helped him break even. He said the sum brought in from their single game against a Top 25 FBS opponent ($375,000) accounted for 6 percent of his department's total revenue.

The financial impact FBS games have on FCS schools is tremendous. One FCS participant said his team went 1-11 in 2008 and accepted two invitations to play Top 25 teams in 2009. One game paid out $450,000 and the other paid out $510,000. Though his football coach "was not excited" about having to play the games, this athletic director said the games were necessary in order for his school's athletic department to survive state-appropriated funding cutbacks:

> Our holdback was roughly $630,000 from the state appropriated funds and one of those game guarantees was $510,000. [If we didn't play the game] I was going to lose $510,000 from our budget

---

* Interview with FCS1.

and I just didn't know how we were going to do it. We could have easily picked up another school for $350,000 or $400,000 that was a lesser [FBS] school and we would have competed a little bit better, but still would have had to make up that other number. Five hundred thousand dollars is the budget of a small sport at our school and we couldn't afford to drop another sport. We're at our minimums for NCAA sports for Division I already. If we dropped another sport, we'd have to drop to Division II. Playing the game was one of our only options.*

In addition to the two games in 2009, this athletic director accepted invitations to play two more FBS opponents in 2010. Those games yielded an additional $775,000. Faced with a significant need to generate revenue, he conceded his immediate focus was on making money with his football team rather than winning games. He said his school desperately needed to upgrade athletic facilities and progress toward Title IX compliance, neither of which were possible without significant sums of money. The money generated from playing FBS opponents has helped offset the purchase of a new basketball court, construct the school's new softball stadium, and add new field turf to the football stadium. Two existing women's sports locker rooms were upgraded and two more were constructed. This athletic director also pointed out that once his athletic department was stable and facilities upgraded, he had no doubt that his football team would resurrect itself in the win column. A majority of the FCS athletic directors surveyed also said they were able to make significant upgrades to their school's athletic facilities because of the FBS game guarantee money. They all plan to continue the practice.

## THE OPPORTUNITY OF A LIFETIME

According to the athletic directors interviewed for this study, FBS matchups offer FCS athletes the opportunity of a lifetime. FCS athletic directors indicated that scheduling top-ranked teams gives their players a chance to experience a big-time college football atmosphere and play against some of the best players in the game:

---

* Interview with FCS4.

This is maybe [our players'] only chance to play in a stadium that seats ninety thousand while getting the national exposure. Some people view it as a payday, but it's totally different for these kids.*

We played two games against [FBS] opponents in 2008. That was a great experience for our kids. They don't get those kinds of experiences very often. They got to play in front of one hundred thousand fans in those two games. They got to run out of the tunnel and take the field in front of all those people, in huge stadiums, and play against established programs with top-caliber athletes. That is something they don't get to do very often and it's going to be something they remember for the rest of their lives. They cherish things like that.†

Making sure the experience is a good one is also a priority for the FBS schools. Two FBS athletic directors said they understand how positive the games can be for FCS schools:

We treat them first class and they respond. They write us nice letters and are so happy to have been here. I will tell you more often than not it is a very positive thing for the FCS school. They get a good payday, they get a big-time experience and good exposure for their program, and their kids get a great [opportunity] to play in our stadium.‡

We played [an FCS] school and their athletic director said, "You have no idea how much our student-athletes love playing a game like this." Our key thing here is to make sure everybody has a great experience. At the end of the day, that's the most important thing— to make sure everybody has an experience that they can carry with them forever.⁵

---

* Interview with FCS Athletic Director #3 (FCS3), September 8, 2009.
† Interview with FCS1.
‡ Interview with FBS1.
⁵ Interview with FBS2.

Victories like Appalachian State's resonate at FCS schools. Stories like these are used regularly to motivate players and convince them that a modern day David can, indeed, beat Goliath. One FCS athletic director mentioned:

> We want them to be able to stick with [the FBS team] and to know it's just a mind game. We can play with these guys. They played high school ball just like us. They maybe even played across the line of scrimmage from some of our guys. And then, when we get into conference, we can say, "Hey, we've seen worse than this, we'll be just fine." That's what I expect—a good growing experience.*

When questioned about scheduling an FBS opponent, one FCS athletic director reminded people this was a one-time opportunity for his athletes:

> What you have to remember is that on any given Saturday, you can play with someone. When people ask me about why we did it, I have to remind them that we didn't play [the FBS team] in a best of seven series. We played them for one game.†

## NATIONAL EXPOSURE

Many top-ranked teams have regional or even national television contracts. Even if some FBS programs cannot offer FCS schools that type of exposure, it is safe to assume that the game's highlights will be streamed across every sports channel on cable. In the unlikely event the small school pulls off an upset, the publicity generated can fuel unprecedented amounts of exposure nationwide. As one FCS athletic director pointed out, "Appalachian State won four national titles and I'm sure if you asked someone there, they'd say the value of beating Michigan did more for that school and their recruiting and image than any of those I-AA national titles."‡

Any added degree of regional and national exposure can help, especially when it comes to recruiting. Several FCS athletic directors said the national

---

* Interview with FCS4.
† Interview with FCS1.
‡ Interview with FCS1.

media coverage helped to put their schools *on the map* and that their coaches used the FBS games as a recruiting tool. They also said football fundraising improved:

> Our fundraising for the [FBS] game was fabulous. It was ten times better than I thought it would be. We took some good people with us, we treated them really well, and we had a great dinner the night before the game. We even had a nice suite up in the press box during the game. Because of that game and those experiences, our fundraising was outstanding. It built some relationships and our entire university is getting a lot more money because of it.*

## INSULT AND INJURY

FCS athletic directors know the odds of an upset are slim. What they are more afraid of is the likelihood of insult and injury to the players. There is belief among many that the emotional toll of a well-publicized and lopsided loss can lead to the diminution of team morale. Coping with competitive stress and anxiety is part of the experience in competitive sports. However, repeated experiences of losing are especially detrimental from a long-term perspective. Often, some fear that these experiences can lead to the devaluation of players' self-esteem, a fear of failure, and a loss of interest.[18] An unlikely win, however, could be invaluable. Winning creates confidence that facilitates both performance and intrinsic motivation.[19] Fueled by their win over Michigan, Appalachian State went on to win the national FCS championship in 2007. The possibility of being demoralized by a lopsided loss, however, might make some players question their own ability to perform in subsequent games. While most FCS fans, coaches, and players support the games, there are still those who disapprove of the scheduling. Just like FBS schools, they would rather play a *cupcake*, too, such as a Division II school:

> You know, there are a few here and there that say what a great opportunity it is to go and play a big-time team in their big stadium,

---

* Interview with FCS4.

but I've heard a few people say, "Why are you [selling out] the foot-ball team?" They just don't understand how an athletic department works.*

Demoralizing the other team is not something FBS schools want either. As one FBS athletic director stated, "Our coaches get it. They're not sitting here trying to score 110 points on these [FCS] teams."†

Added to the emotional risk of a huge loss is always the risk of injury. This risk also concerned every athletic director in this study. For example, one FCS athletic director said the thought of his players getting injured crossed his mind every single day after he agreed to play the top-ranked opponent until after that game was over. He said he felt fortunate that none of his players were significantly hurt while playing the games and that he would have had to "go into hiding" if they had been. It is not just the FCS athletic directors who are concerned about the risk of injury. One FBS athletic director shared the concern as well:

> I don't want anyone to get hurt…I want to win the ball game, but I want the other school to come in here and have a positive experi-ence. I want them to have a good payday, but I don't want anybody to get hurt. My biggest fear is somebody getting hurt…The only thing I worry about with these games is somebody getting hurt.‡

## CONCLUSION

While upsets like Appalachian State's 2007 victory over Michigan can res-onate for years, FCS wins over top-ranked FBS opponents are relatively rare. Responding to the critics, John Jentz, the associate athletic director at the University of Wisconsin, told his local newspaper, "The reality in college football is there's the group of schools that wants to have the home games no matter what, and there's the group of schools that will travel for a check at any cost."[20] The findings of this study suggest that there are

---

* Interview with FCS4.
† Interview with FCS1.
‡ Interview with FBS1.

positive and negative aspects of scheduling these competitions for both FBS and FCS schools.

Whatever the drawbacks may be, the upcoming 2011–12 schedule offers further evidence that the practice of scheduling FCS opponents is unlikely to slow down anytime soon. As of the date of this writing, among the sixty-six member schools from AQ Conferences, fifty-five of those programs (83 percent of teams) have scheduled games against fifty-six FCS opponents.*

It is also clear from these findings that, in light of financial rewards, potential media exposure, and the opportunities the games afford student-athletes, the scheduling of these types of games is likely to continue.

### BIBLIOGRAPHY

"2009–10 Revenue Distribution Data," *Bowl Championship Series* (2010), http://www .bcsfootball.org/news/story?id=4856975.

Aschoff, Edward, "Scheduling Games Part of Business," *Gatorsports.com,* ac cessed January 28, 2011, http://www.gatorsports.com/article/ 20090910/ ARTICLES/909109920?p=2&tc=pg.

Associated Press, "Blocked Field Goal Secures Appalachian State's Upset of Michigan," *ESPN.com,* September 1, 2007, http://scores.espn.go.com/ ncf /recap?gameId=272440130.

Bouchet, Adrian, and Matthew Scott, "Do BCS Schools Have an Advantage Over Non-BCS Schools in APR Rankings? An Early Examination," *The Sport Journal,* 13:2 (2010), http://www.thesportjournal.org/article/do-bcs-schools-have-advantage-over-non-bcs-schools-apr-rankings-early-examination.

Carey, Jack, "For Small Schools, There's a Big Payoff to Road Trips," *USA Today,* September 3, 2009, http://www.usatoday.com/sports/college/football/ 2009-09-02-smallschool_payoffs_N.htm.

Congressional Budget Office, *Tax Preferences for Collegiate Sports,* Washington, DC: US Government Printing Office, 2009.

Cripe, Chad, "National Title Is Not on Boise State Football Team's Goal List; Redskins Expect 86,000 Fans for Boise State-Virginia Tech." *Idaho Statesman,* September 3, 2010, http://voices.idahostatesman .com/2010/09/03 / ccripe/national _title_not _boise_state_football_teams_goal_list_redskins.

---

* North Carolina State is scheduled to play two FCS opponents (Liberty and South Alabama). Mississippi, Oklahoma, Oklahoma State, Texas, Texas A&M, Boston College, Ohio State, Stanford, Colorado, USC, and UCLA have not scheduled FCS opponents for the 2011 season.

Daughters, Amy, "College Football: Should FBS vs. FCS Games Be Banned Permanently?" *Bleacher Report,* September 28, 2010, http://bleacherreport .com/articles/475339-college-football-should-fbs-vs-fcs-games-be-banned-permanently.

Everson, Darren, "Goliath Hasn't Gone Anywhere," *Wall Street Journal,* September 21, 2010. http://online.wsj.com/article/SB10001424052748703556 604575501740109812272.html.

Hanin, Yuri, "Fear Of Failure in the Context of Competitive Sport: A Commentary," *International Journal of Sports Science & Coaching* 3:2 (June 2008): 185-189.

Jacobi, Adam, "Boise State Wanted $1 Million to Play Nebraska?" *CBS Sports.com,* September 9, 2010. http://college-football.blogs.cbssports.com /mcc/blogs/entry/24156338/24447857.

Polzin, Jim, "UW Officials Insist FCS Opponents Are Here to Stay," *Madison.com,* September 15, 2009, http://host.madison.com/sports/college /football/article_a1f81f9a-a274-11de-b121-001cc4c002e0.html.

Reeve, Johnmarshall, Bradley Olson, and Steven Cole, "Motivation And Performance: Two Consequences Of Winning And Losing In Competition," *Motivation and Emotion* 9 (1985): 291-297.

Strauss, Anselm and Juliet Corbin. Basics of Qualitative Research. Thousand Oaks: Sage, 1998.

Tucker, Tim, "Georgia Adds Florida Atlantic to 2012 Football Schedule – At Cost of $1 Million," *Atlanta Journal Constitution,* November 30, 2010, http: //blogs.ajc.com/uga-sports-blog/2010/11/30/georgia-will-pay-1-million -for-2012-football-game-vs-florida-atlantic/

"What's the Difference between Divisions I, II and III?" Last modified February 7, 2007, *National Collegiate Athletic Association,* http://www.ncaa.org /wps/portal/ncaahome?WCM_GLOBAL_CONTEXT=/ncaa/NCAA /About+The+NCAA/Membership/div_criteria.html.

# THE RISE OF AN AMERICAN SPORT IN KING ARTHUR'S COURT

NEIL REYNOLDS

The author has covered the NFL as a journalist and broadcaster since 1991. He currently serves as co-presenter of BBC Radio's weekly NFL show, providing studio analysis and live game commentaries from the United States.

Based in London, England, Reynolds writes a weekly NFL blog for the BBC Sport Web site and serves as a roving reporter and occasional studio guest for Sky Sports' NFL show. During his time covering the NFL, Reynolds has interviewed some of the biggest names in the sport, including legends such as Joe Montana, Jerry Rice, Dan Marino, John Elway, Dick Butkus, and Y.A. Tittle.

Reynolds co-hosted the NFL Fan Rally in front of 38,000 fans in London's Trafalgar Square in October 2010 and hosted Super Bash—the official NFL Super

Bowl party for three thousand fans at London's O2 Arena in February 2011. He hosts all video content and weekly podcasts on nfluk.com and serves as a columnist and feature writer for the official NFL Web site for fans in the UK.

Reynolds is author of *Pain Gang: Pro Football's Toughest Players*. He has also written for *NFL.com*, the *Atlanta Journal-Constitution*, the *Green Bay Press Gazette*, the *Dallas Morning News*, and the *Pittsburgh Post-Press Gazette*. He has served as editorial consultant to the NFL for the five International Series game day magazines produced and sold at Wembley Stadium, writing many articles in each published edition. Readers can follow Neil on Twitter at *@neilreynoldsnfl*.

––––––––––––

Less than a month before Auburn quarterback Cam Newton became an instant multimillionaire and the number one pick of the Carolina Panthers in the 2011 NFL Draft, a college football season of a very different kind was being played to its own thrilling conclusion.

More than four thousand miles away from the bright lights and flashing cameras of New York's Radio City Music Hall, the Birmingham Lions and Portsmouth Destroyers were giving their all in pursuit of national championship glory in Leeds, England.

By the normal college football standards applied by fans in the United States, the 2011 British Universities American Football League (BUAFL) Championship Game was a modest affair. The best description of John Charles Stadium would be "cozy" or "intimate." The stadium itself is attached to a leisure center located in an industrial estate in the north of England where most visitors head straight for the public swimming pool. On this unseasonably warm early April day, the stadium was packed to the rafters with one thousand ardent gridiron fans who were treated to an afternoon of high drama.

The championship showdown was not Auburn-Alabama or Florida State-Miami. Not even close. But it was hugely meaningful to the players and coaches involved.

The teams served up a thriller that was packed with the kind of twists, turns, and excitement fit for the sport's very highest level. With less than a minute on the clock, the defending champion Birmingham Lions were closing in on a third successive national title. They trailed the upstart Portsmouth Destroyers by a score of 20-19 and had certainly been given a bloody nose by the upstart club from England's south coast.

For much of the hard-hitting contest, the Destroyers had dominated the proceedings. Trailing 20-6 in the fourth quarter, the Lions were reeling. Faced with the prospect of losing their crown, Birmingham launched a furious comeback, scoring twice in the final period to move to within a single point of the Destroyers.

The second of those fourth-quarter touchdowns left Lions head coach Wayne Hill with a tough decision, kick the extra point and play for overtime or go for two and win the championship game there and then.

Hill opted for the latter.

The crowd held its collective breath as the Lions broke from the huddle and lined up for the play that would determine their season.

Birmingham's Sope Dirisu, the Lions' backup quarterback, took the snap and rolled to his right. Dirisu, who led the frantic comeback attempt after entering the game in the final period, displayed perfect timing by delivering the option pitch to star running back Dan Conroy.

For a split second it was very much advantage Birmingham Lions. Just five yards of open field stood between Conroy, the end zone, and the chance to write his name in his university's sporting history books.

Conroy secured the football, lowered his shoulder, and prepared to dive into the end zone. The Lions had put the game on the shoulders of their most productive offensive player and BUAFL Championship glory beckoned. But out of nowhere, Destroyers safety D.J. Demuren came flying across the field, delivering a textbook blow to knock the Birmingham runner out of bounds at the half-yard line. The breath-taking defensive play, which also featured a timely assist from cornerback Itai N'Danga, secured Portsmouth's first national championship.

The fans were stunned, as were the players—but only for a moment. The Portsmouth players knew instantly what Demuren's tackle represented—the school's first National Championship title.

Portsmouth's victory capped a memorable season both on and off the field for the BUAFL.

While Portsmouth's players and coaches celebrated finishing top of the pile, league officials were patting themselves on the back for a job well done. The 2010–2011 season was among the most competitive in British college football history, evidenced by the Destroyers knocking Birmingham from their championship perch for the first time in three years. The playoffs were filled with nerve-racking, back-and-forth showdowns between evenly matched teams. The next season will kick off with as many as half a dozen schools harboring genuine title ambitions.

Off the field, the BUAFL remains one of the fastest growing university sports in the United Kingdom,* and that growth shows no signs of slowing in the immediate future.

For now, the league's aim is to drive participation. The BUAFL is not about to discover the next Cam Newton or Andrew Luck, but league officials are fine with that; this is a league very comfortable in its own skin and one that is happy to accept that the playing standard is not on a par with the mega-rich schools in the United States.

British American Football Association (BAFA) director for Student Football Development Andy Fuller admits, "Our aim is to grow the game and to get universities playing. The standard may not be particularly high, but there is a bug at the moment so it is a case of enabling that bug to bite. Once it bites, it's easier to start working on development issues—after a team has been established, it can start to progress from there.

"The premise of the BUAFL over the past four years has been to give people a greater opportunity to play, to establish teams while there is this interest, and to place the emphasis on participation. With increased participation comes credibility and with credibility comes increased opportunity."

---

* The term "United Kingdom" officially refers to the United Kingdom of Great Britain and Northern Ireland, and is used interchangeably with the terms "UK," "Britain," or "Great Britain."

As Fuller suggests, there is a growing passion for the sport of football in the United Kingdom and the sudden upturn in interest can be attributed to the National Football League's decision, starting in 2007, to begin playing regular season games in London's Wembley Stadium.

---

Since January 1983, when Channel 4 (in the UK) aired its first live broadcast of Super Bowl XVII between the Washington Redskins and Miami Dolphins, the NFL has been able to maintain a foothold in the British public consciousness.

Most of Britain's first generation of NFL fans began their love affair with the sport after that Super Bowl game twenty-eight years ago, when over four and a half million people tuned in to watch (about 8 percent of Great Britain's population).

To understand the significance of that Super Bowl is to understand the significance of the television network that hosted the game's first live broadcast in Great Britain.

In 1982, Channel 4 became the newest entrant into a highly regulated television market, which at the time included just three other networks: BBC1, BBC2, and ITV. There was no cable television, Internet, or anything of that sort at the time. Channel 4's mission was to provide more programming alternatives for the British viewing public. A typical Channel 4 lineup would include shows about the contemporary arts, historical documentaries, and classical music programs. Part of the channel's programming was designed to cater to the interests of various ethnic minorities. It was here in this bastion of politically correct drudgery that American football would be introduced to the British public—a sort of American-style "National Geographic," which offered a glimpse of the American psyche through the cultural window of an NFL highlights program.

Back then, television viewing options on Sundays at 6:00 p.m. were limited. Viewers had the choice of watching an antiques show on one channel or religious programs on the other two channels. It was during this time slot that Channel 4 broadcast the NFL highlight show. Whether by genuine interest, default, or some display of religious apathy, the six o'clock time slot offered an opportunity for many British fans to develop a passion for the sport.

That particular program showed highlights of the previous week's NFL matchups, and served as the only way for NFL fans to keep up with game results and storylines.

At the time, American football offered British audiences a fresh sport. American football was exciting and different. In the early to mid-1980s, US pop culture was thriving in Great Britain. Watching the NFL was part of a larger trend of entertainment and products coming from the United States, which included Michael Jackson, BMX bikes, and Rubik's Cubes. Channel 4's NFL highlight program and those live Super Bowl broadcasts left an indelible memory on many people in Great Britain.

One way to get a sense of the cultural legacy of those programs is to employ the "Taxi Driver Test." London cabbies are not generally the most passionate fans of NFL football or other kinds of pop culture, but they can provide a useful indication of a fad's enduring cultural relevance. American football is one of those phenomena that pass the Taxi Driver Test. When prompted, a London cab driver will tell you, "Oh yeah, I remember American Football. The Fridge. Dan Marino. Joe Montana," and that's where it usually ends. The most successful NFL teams from the eighties—Miami, San Francisco, Chicago, Washington, Dallas—were the teams that British fans watched week in and week out, and they are still well supported in Britain today.

The NFL broadcasts evolved from showing highlights show, to televising tape-delayed games from the previous week, to providing a mixed-version that showed highlights in the first half and transitioned to a live game in the second half. As interest in the sport grew, Channel 4 began showing additional highlight programs on Monday nights and a magazine program on Saturday afternoon.

———————

The NFL has endured many highs and some notable lows during the course of its history in the United Kingdom.

From 1986 to 1993, the NFL sponsored one live preseason football game a year at Wembley Stadium. The games were part of the "American Bowl" series, which the NFL launched to promote the league outside of the United States. Different versions of the American Bowl were held in cities like Tokyo, Sidney, Toronto, Osaka, Berlin, Monterrey, Mexico City, Barcelona, Dublin, and Vancouver.

These games were exciting at first. Live American football was a unique event in a city like London, which is home to thousands of different entertainment alternatives. While the initial games were well attended, over time interest began to wane. British fans realized that the teams' best players might play for a series or two before being replaced by backups and other hopefuls. Once viewers began watching live regular season games on television, interest in the lesser preseason matchups declined even further.

The World League of American Football represented the next stage in the evolution of the NFL's presence in Europe. The World League, founded in 1990, was initially made up of ten teams from five countries.* The World League primarily served as a player development league for the NFL, similar to the minor leagues in baseball. The teams were made up almost entirely of American players. At least one non-US player was required to participate in every other series of downs. In the United Kingdom, the World League was represented by the London Monarchs. The Monarchs won the World League's inaugural championship game, beating the Barcelona Dragons 21–0. That season, the Monarchs averaged crowds of forty thousand fans per contest over five games.

Despite what seemed to be a promising start, the World League was unable to turn a profit in its first season. Its financial fortunes failed to improve over the following season, prompting league organizers to suspend operations after the 1992 season.

In 1995, the World League resumed operations as a strictly European competition, adding new teams from Amsterdam, Düsseldorf, and Edinburgh. The London Monarchs moved their "home" stadium to the much smaller White Hart Lane as a cost-saving measure.† With the exception of a few diehards, fan interest continued to sag. In 1998, the London Monarchs

---

* 1990 World League Teams by Country: UK: London Monarchs; Spain: Barcelona Dragons; Germany: Frankfurt Galaxy; Canada: Montreal Machine; United States: New York/New Jersey Knights, Orlando Thunder, Raleigh-Durham Skyhawks, Birmingham Fire, San Antonio Riders, Sacramento Surge.

† White Hart Lane is also the home stadium to the Tottenham Hotspurs football (soccer) club of the British Premier League.

were renamed the England Monarchs and instead of playing contests at home, the team travelled across the country in the hopes of exposing the sport to more fans. Changing stadiums, rebranding, and other efforts proved to be no match for fans' apathy toward what they perceived as a weak imitation of the real thing. Following the conclusion of the 1998 season, just three years after resuming operations, the World League surrendered to the inevitable and suspended the Monarchs' operations.

In 1996, Great Britain's "northern" team, the Scottish Claymores,[*] was established to build upon nascent fan interest in that part of the country. The Claymores obliged their fans early on, securing a World Bowl championship in the team's second season by defeating the defending champions Frankfurt Galaxy 7-3 in 1997.

After the Monarchs were disbanded, the Scottish Claymores would remain Great Britain's lone representative in NFL Europe, until 2004 when its operations were also suspended due to limited fan interest.[†,‡]

In spite of Britain's lackluster fan support for NFL Europe, NFL decision makers remained convinced that a sizable fan base existed. What was needed was the right product to awaken their interest. The NFL had tried pre-season teams and development leagues. What it had not yet delivered was the product fans craved most: real teams, real players, real competition.

In 2007, the NFL announced that it would hold its first ever regular season competition held outside of the United States at London's revamped Wembley Stadium. The initial NFL International Series Game between the Miami Dolphins and New York Giants sparked a massive scramble for tickets. The NFL received over half a million applications for eighty thousand available tickets in just seventy-two hours, causing the NFL Web site to crash repeatedly over those first few days.

---

[*] A "claymore" is a distinct type of two-handed Scottish sword, which was used in late Medieval and early modern periods by the Highlanders of Scotland. The average sword was about fifty-five inches in length, and weighed between five and six pounds.

[†] In 1997, the World League rebranded itself yet again, this time as the NFL Europe League (or NFL Europe).

[‡] NFL Europe would rebrand itself on more time as NFL Europa in 2006. The league folded following the 2007 season.

While there was always considerable fan support for the NFL, those regular season games have elevated interest in the sport to new levels. Each contest since 2007 has been a sell-out.* Viewing figures for those watching NFL games on stations such as Sky Sports, BBC 1, Channel 4, Channel 5, and ESPN have grown by 60 percent since 2006. Registrations on the offi-cial NFL Web site in the UK—nfluk.com—have soared from 37,000 in 2006 to more than 260,000 in 2011.

Ahead of the 2010 International Series Game between the 49ers and Broncos, more than 38,000 Brits packed into London's famous Trafalgar Square for a fan rally. Former 49ers Hall of Fame wide receiver Jerry Rice and the all-time leading points scorer in NFL history, Danish kicker Morten Andersen, made special appearances.

The momentum created during the International Series weekend in October—which also saw Wembley Stadium break single-day merchandise sales records—continued through the playoffs and up to Super Bowl XLV.

More than 4.3 million viewers tuned in to watch the Green Bay Packers defeat the Pittsburgh Steelers on BBC 1 and Sky Sports, which is no mean feat given that the game kicks off around 11:30 p.m. on a Sunday night. Add in those who listened live on BBC Radio, and the number of British fans following the NFL title showdown soared to 8.4 million.

---

One of the clear beneficiaries of the increased fan numbers associated with the NFL activity in the UK is the BUAFL.

Prior to the first NFL regular season game in London in 2007, there were 2,490 players and coaches associated with the BUAFL representing forty-two teams spread across the UK. As of the date of this publication, seventy-five teams now play, and participation numbers have increased by 45 percent. The BUAFL boasts that more than 3,500 members are involved with the league as players or coaches, representing forty-six nationalities.

---

* Subsequent matchups have included the New Orleans Saints and San Diego Chargers in 2008, the Tampa Bay Buccaneers and New England Patriots in 2009, the San Francisco 49ers and Denver Broncos in 2010, and the Buccaneers again scheduled to play the Chicago Bears in 2011.

"The NFL is the driver," Fuller admits. "Whenever we talk about things that spark interest, the NFL is the common response and the thing that sparks people's interests. That leads to people looking to start a team or to join a team already in existence on a campus.

"It's no great surprise that there is a correlation between the NFL regular season games being played in the UK and that growth in our student sport."

NFL representative Matt Joyce, who is responsible for fostering relationships between the NFL and the grassroots level of the game in the UK, notes that, "The development of the BUAFL over the last four years has made it the largest, fastest-growing UK university sport.

"There are more university teams and more people playing throughout the UK than ever before. It is fair to say this popularity has occurred in line with the increase in NFL regular season games.

"It is a great [advertisement] for the NFL to have more young people playing and enjoying the sport at all levels. The growth of the NFL hinges on connecting young fans to the sport, of which universities are a key factor."

While the NFL has driven participation in the BUAFL, the BUAFL has helped to generate new fans for the NFL. As Joyce points out, the relationship works both ways.

The man who lifted the national championship trophy in Leeds—Destroyers offensive lineman Ben Peddie—is a perfect example of how the BUAFL and NFL reinforce each other.

While training to be a science teacher at Portsmouth University, Peddie was looking for an engaging team sport to take part in to fill his spare time. He chose American football, played for the Destroyers from 2006 until 2011, and is now a passionate fan of all forms of the game, particularly the NFL.

"I had watched the Super Bowl on TV and would stay up for that as a kid, but I didn't really have a clue about the sport," Peddie explains. "I didn't know the rules, I didn't know the players, and I didn't really know much about the teams.

"Until I got involved with the Destroyers, I didn't really know much about the sport. Playing in the BUAFL helped me become an NFL fan. Before I came to university, I played quite a lot of rugby, but I injured my back and that put me out of the sport for two years. By the time I came to university, I thought I would try a different sport, and having seen the Super Bowl on TV and the hype that surrounded that, I felt like giving American football a go and that's how I got into the sport.

"The NFL has definitely had a knock-on effect when it comes to BUAFL participation numbers. We definitely see more people coming to try-outs who have been to a London game, who have been watching it more on TV, and who want to get involved. There are more people becoming fans and, through that, we are getting more people playing the game. It definitely has increased participation."

Adam Lillis who played quarterback, wide receiver, and kick returner for the University of Kent Falcons from 2003 to 2007 offers a similar story.

"I was aware of the NFL prior to playing at the University of Kent, but I didn't have a strong interest in the sport," Lillis explains. "I had played some *Madden* games and watched a Super Bowl but that was about it.

"When I started university, I played soccer, rugby, and cricket, but I wanted to try a different sport. Once I tried American football, I was hooked. It was definitely the teamwork aspect that appealed to me.

"I have always been involved in soccer, rugby, and cricket, and preferred these to individual sports such as golf, snooker, and tennis. And with American football, there is a stronger aspect of teamwork and camaraderie than any other sport I have experienced.

"Unlike other sports, an American football squad requires a group of individuals that have a huge variety of different skills. You could be strong but slow, fast but weak, lack hand-eye coordination, but have an abundance of aggression—whatever mental or physical frame you fit, there is a place for you on an American football team.

"Outside of teamwork, it was definitely the contact that appealed to me. When playing rugby, I craved the contact side of the sport but always felt like I wanted to do more, which is why American football appealed to me so much. I loved the idea of twenty-two players engaging in contact every play, regardless of who had the ball!

"The NFL was only ever a passing interest for me before I played for the Falcons, so it is very likely I wouldn't have invested any time or money into the sport if I hadn't played the game myself. But because I played, I naturally gained an interest in the NFL and soon became a fan of the Miami Dolphins."

The relationship between the NFL and the BUAFL extends into the social side of playing football. With most BUAFL games being played in the fall on Sunday afternoons, the NFL offers the perfect post-match viewing opportunity later in the day.

Fuller explains, "There is a culture in British university sports that most teams play on a Wednesday and, after they have played, Wednesday night becomes student sports party night.

"Because we don't play on a Wednesday, we are slightly disenfranchised from that. But what has emerged is a unique culture where the teams will play during the day, travel back to their respective universities and then get together and take in the NFL games on a Sunday night."

"There are things that bind you on the field and there are things that bind you off it. Playing for the Kent Falcons was a huge part of my university life," adds Lillis.

"As well as the playing side of the sport, the Falcons had a busy social calendar. It was not difficult to make lifelong friends through the team due to the nature of the sport. Many of my teammates from eight years ago are close friends to this day.

"Since playing college football, I have become involved in various coaching roles and play locally for the (British American Football Association Community League) East Kent Mavericks. I am currently coaching the Falcons and have done so for the past four years. I have done this for three reasons: to stay involved with my college team, to improve my knowledge of the game, and purely because I enjoy it too much."

The national championship-winning Portsmouth Destroyers take their BUAFL commitment to excellence extremely seriously, but they always make time in their busy football schedule to watch the NFL.

"The NFL is a huge benefit to our league—it is what our kids watch," explains head coach Russ Hewitt. "Everything we do in the university is structured around the NFL. We get back mid-September so the NFL season has started and all our sponsor and hospitality activity is centered around bars and clubs showing the NFL.

"We watch the games together on Sunday evenings, we have our own Thanksgiving Day party, we have a Super Bowl party, and we even had a draft party. Our kids are now so into football because of the NFL, and their interest in it is huge, and I encourage that.

"When we watch the NFL games, it is an opportunity for the kids who are new to the sport to ask questions. And all these kids support teams that have been successful in recent years, so you can see there are new people coming into the sport. You can tell how long a kid has been into the sport by the team he supports. There is a big link between the NFL and the BUAFL."

The students might enjoy a post-match beer or two together, but they take just as much delight in reeling in a touchdown pass or dropping the opposing team's quarterback for a sack.

"All the players and coaches take it very seriously. They want to win," Fuller insists.

Portsmouth offensive lineman and team captain Peddie adds, "Whether it's winning a championship or getting a first win for a team, no matter what the situation, everyone wants to feel like their effort has been rewarded.

"When we got our very first victory in February 2007, we had travelled to play Reading University. At the time, we were 0-5. We ended up winning in overtime and you could see what it meant to the whole team. Everybody was on the field, piling on top of each other.

It was the exact same scene when we won the final. To win that final was incredible, especially for someone like me who had been there five years.

"I remember our very first league game; we had to go on a five-hour bus ride to play Plymouth and we got absolutely spanked. To go from that to beating the two-time national champions in the final was just incredible."

---

It is no coincidence that the two teams that butted heads in the 2011 BUAFL Championship Game—the Birmingham Lions and Portsmouth Destroyers—take a very serious approach to the sport, and are striving to build football dynasties that can dominate the gridiron landscape.

"A number of the teams and programs in our league are incredibly well run," Fuller explains. "They are teams that have a very good standard of coaching and have, as a consequence, put together really strong performances on the field. These teams are comparable to any other British university sport to a point, with the exception that you don't have the athlete pathways from a young age. So your raw material is slightly more raw than someone coming into cricket or rugby.

"The standard is very high with some of our teams and that provides great opportunity for some of our players who have aspirations to play at schools in the United States. It gives those players a tremendous opportunity to take that extra step.

"Many coaches who are seeking to increase American football performance standards in Britain have reached out to their counterparts at colleges and high schools in the US. These relationships and the learning opportunities created by those interactions have allowed British coaches to adopt best practices and apply them in the UK.

"The best examples are represented by our two finalists this year. Portsmouth head coach Russ Hewitt spends time with the Miami Hurricanes and has learned an awful lot from them. The Birmingham Lions were led for many years by Tony Athersmith, and he is very well connected in the US—having built strong relationships with coaches like Mike Leach while he was at Texas Tech University, current Seattle Seahawks head coach Pete Carroll, and several of their other coaches."

Athersmith guided the Lions to back-to-back national championships in 2009 and 2010 before bowing out midway through the school's run to the 2011 title showdown. He provides a unique insight into the challenges of trying to run a football program to NCAA standards within a British university where sports such as rugby, cricket, and soccer will likely always be of paramount importance.

"Overall as a squad, I would say that the Birmingham Lions would be considered a very good American high school team. If we put an all-star team of university players together in the UK, we would be the equivalent of a Division III team in the US." In the past, the Lions played against two Division III squads, Lakeland College and Carthage College in Wisconsin. "We didn't win those games, but the games were competitive.

"The athleticism is there, but the infrastructure is not," Athersmith continues. "That's somewhat understandable when it comes to American football because it is still considered an emerging sport.

"A handful of British players are playing at various divisions at the college level in the United States. The starting quarterback at Birmingham, Tristan Varney, received a number of Division I scholarship offers in the US, and our running back, Dan Conroy, has the physical ability to play at the Division II level."

The process of developing a good football team in the BUAFL has slightly different challenges than what most NCAA coaches have probably experienced.

"We literally start from scratch," Athersmith admits. "We show them how to put their pants on, their shoulder pads; 'here's how to get into your stance.' You start with the absolute basics, get them lined up, and try to keep them safe.

"You have to understand that roughly nine out of ten kids who try out for the team have probably never played American football before they come to university, but they have seen it on TV.

"Those who are interested in American football see it as another option instead of playing rugby or soccer. They've probably watched the game on television, played *John Madden* on *PlayStation*, and just want to find out what the sport is all about.

"At Birmingham, we would have about three hundred fifty kids try out in the first week. Over a series of days, you tend to end up with sixty or seventy players who are willing and able to commit. Once you put the pads on and start the contact drills, the number of players who really want to play reduces significantly.

"We start practice the first week of October, which serves as an induction week. We move to pads by the second or third week of October and tend to play our first game in the first week of November. Most of these kids have about eight practices to learn football from a standing start—putting on pads, getting used to contact, and playing in their first game. It is a challenge. Our aim is to teach players about the fundamentals of contact rather than scaring them off, but there is not much time to get them up to full speed."

When Athersmith was in charge of the Lions, he would devote considerable amounts of time to improving his team and getting them ready for each season and each weekend within the campaign.

The thirty-six-year-old was not only holding down a full-time job with the West Midlands Ambulance Service, he was also plotting a championship course for the Lions and doing so as the only paid head coach in the BUAFL.

Here is how a typical week would unfold for Athersmith…

*Saturday or Sunday*…Game day

*Monday*…Break down game film and begin scouting film for the following week. Produce the game plan on Monday and send the draft plan to the coaching staff for comments and changes.

*Tuesday*…Introduce the game plan to the players during meetings, film study, and conditioning practice from 7:00 to 10:00 p.m.

*Wednesday*…Review the game plan again for minor changes. Work on the practice schedule for Thursday.

*Thursday*…Install the game plan during a two-hour, on-field practice.

*Friday*…Day off.

Athersmith estimates he dedicated thirty to thirty-five hours per week of his own time to the Lions, but it was a price he was willing to pay, having been well and truly bitten by the coaching bug.

"I played youth football and moved into club football where I became fascinated by the idea of coaching," Athersmith reveals. "I had a passion for the chess match. By the time I was eighteen, I knew I wanted to become a coach.

"I have had the opportunity to be around a lot of coaches from the United States. I was introduced to Mike Leach when he was head coach at Texas Tech and he was very generous to me. He invited me to Lubbock to spend time with his team. I spent ten days with the team during 2002 spring training. Mike gave me full access to every meeting and told me I could conduct myself as if I was a member of the coaching staff. I could watch all of their film, spend time with the coaches, and stand on the field during practices. It was an intense experience.

"On the first day I was overwhelmed by the quality of the facilities. It was an 'Oh my God' moment. Coaches have their own offices and teams have their own film rooms, weight rooms, and physiotherapy facilities! You are in awe of the whole setup of Division I college football, but once you get to the practice field, it's just football.

"Mike and I stayed in touch, developed a friendship. He kept tabs on how my teams were doing and how I was developing as a coach.

"Mike met up with me in the UK while he on holiday in 2003. He wanted to visit London, see the castles, and learn more about the history of England. One evening, after we were hanging out and pretty tired after a couple of days on the road looking at the different historical sites, I admitted to Mike that after spending all that time watching his practices, I still didn't really understand the spread offense. I asked him if he wouldn't mind going through the offensive system with me step by step.

"Mike took a piece of paper and a pen and spent the next couple of hours explaining the entire concept to me. From that discussion, I was able to develop a clear idea of how the system works. He taught me how he teaches the system to his players and how he teaches it to his quarterbacks.

"From there, I just ran with it and we installed the spread offense as soon as I joined Birmingham's coaching staff. Virtually everything we ran on offense was based on what I learned from that evening session with Mike at my house.

"I also had the opportunity to develop a relationship with Pete Carroll while he was at USC. In the summer of 2010, some of Birmingham's coaches got to spend a few days with the Seahawks, Coach Carroll and his staff. Pete still keeps track of our team's progress and likes to know how we're developing."

Throughout the course of a typical season, Athersmith had to call on every ounce of his coaching knowledge as he battled to get his fresh-faced novices up to speed. More often than not, he succeeded and turned the Lions into one of British college football's true powerhouses.

"As the season goes on, you can build up the game plan gradually," he explains. "Of course, the level of experience contrasts with US college teams where players have a full year of off-season, two full weeks of summer camp and have been playing since they are six years old. They already know the system at a high level. They know how to hold a ball, how to line up, how to catch a ball. Here we start at point zero."

Once his players get hooked, Athersmith and other coaches in similar situations, face a rather unique problem. After going from never having donned a helmet and shoulder pads before, the players can suddenly be exposed to playing too much football and face the threat of wearing down their young bodies.

"The off-season could often be difficult for us," Athersmith stresses. "Some of the kids participate in the senior, nationwide club league (British American Football Association Community League), which allows anyone over the age of eighteen to play.

"That league starts right after the university season finishes in April and runs through the end of the summer with the championship game being played in late September. Lots of our kids basically end up playing six seasons in three years. Instead of being in peak physical condition, some of the kids are worn down and beaten up because of the punishment they have taken. We don't really have the ability to prevent them from playing in other leagues, although we try to encourage them not to participate in those club leagues."

During his time at Birmingham, Athersmith enjoyed very good support from the university, although nationwide the programs are run on even smaller budgets.

"Different universities have different budgets," Athersmith says. "At Birmingham, the program's annual budget is about £20,000 (approximately $32,000), which represents the largest football budget in the UK. That budget enables us to buy equipment and replace it every few years. Most universities have nothing like that sort of funding. Their players are required to pay for all their own equipment."

With good university support, exposure to quality coaching and a history of winning, it is easy to see why Birmingham's players are dedicated and driven to lift trophies each and every season.

But Athersmith insists such passion and commitment is not restricted to his former team, stating, "All players want to win. They want to improve, they want to compete, and they don't want to lose.

"This is their NFL. This is their Super Bowl. They are passionate, enthusiastic, and committed—and that message has to be communicated to them from the head coaches down."

———————

Another man who shares Athersmith's commitment and passion to build an American football dynasty is Russ Hewitt, who has just replaced his former rival as the reigning national champion. Hewitt has spent considerable time picking the brains of the Miami Hurricanes' coaching staff, and his aim is to develop a production line of quality players that can be relied upon every season.

"For us at Portsmouth, it is 100 percent about creating a quality football program," Hewitt explains. "I think you need to aim high and we do that with our football and we do that with our ideas. I want us to be the best team in the country. Participation can be quite frustrating but we do need kids playing football and we do need the numbers.

"My philosophy is based on the NCAA model where teams recruit about twenty-five freshmen every season. Every three years, NCAA Division I teams have seventy-five players go through their program so that they are not in a position where they are rebuilding a team every year. My aim is to develop a program that will continually allow us to challenge the best teams."

The Destroyers have come a long way in a relatively short time. They endured some growing pains in their first three seasons, but have gone 18-2 over the past two winters, including a perfect 11-0 mark in the 2010-2011 campaign.

Like Athersmith, during his time at the Lions, Hewitt will take newcomers to the sport. But they have to earn their stripes by going through a testing process based on the NFL Combine model. And if they make the team, they are coached up—hard and fast.

"We have a Freshers Fair like everyone else," Hewitt explains. "We will take NFL fans because each university starts with the same caliber of kids. We hold a combine and we have one hundred fifty to a hundred sixty kids involved in that and from there we select thirty-five based on their athletic ability. We test them similarly to the way college athletes are tested at the NFL Combine to see if they have any athletic ability.

"Our aim is to build a sixty-man squad. I usually have about thirty-five veterans on the team, which leaves room for twenty-five rookies. We select those players from the thirty-five candidates we identify during the combine. We never close the door on anyone, but because my number is twenty-five rookies every year, some players might not make the team.

"We have fourteen coaches and pull in qualified coaches as consultants during our combine so we have one positional coach and one assistant at every spot. One of the keys to our success has been the ability to develop a cohesive group of coaches who have a strong understanding of the game.

"A lot of teams who just want to participate in the sport will give themselves five weeks to prepare for the season, and then install six offensive plays, one defense and two coverages. Once you start playing them, you can pull them from pillar to post because they have only been taught a certain amount and they have a ceiling that they cannot go past.

"We push our guys to master five or six coverages, four or five defenses, two blocking schemes, four protections, and we can take all of that into the game. Rookies do struggle and they have to show some glimpses of ability and understanding to get on the field. But we have always had rookies starting for us at all positions over the years."

Hewitt is brash, confident in his team's ability, and unapologetic. He offers firm views on the future of British college football and insists there must come a time when league officials place more emphasis on creating a quality product than participation numbers.

"I think the game should be more competition-based rather than focusing on participation because then you have more chance of pulling people in to watch it.

"We're definitely good enough to compete against very good US high school programs. But I think you need to have aspirations to be a Division III school or to develop a European version of the NCAA. You need to put everything in place to achieve that and then need to get funding in place for things like gym access. Whether you follow the booster route or you work the government funding route, it has to come with results."

Those results could be more positive than anyone in the UK might first have dared to dream. With NFL Commissioner Roger Goodell openly talking about exploring the option of a British franchise within the next decade, the future of the sport in Great Britain suddenly has seemingly endless possibilities.

And that should reflect healthily on the college game.

"The NFL regular season games played in London have increased awareness of the sport," Kent Falcons coach Lillis concludes. "I am optimistic about the future of American football and the NFL in the UK. The continuation of those games will help the sport grow and become even more popular."

And if that is the case, the BUAFL should continue to go from strength to strength and will be in a position to act more aggressively on matters of playing standards and participation.

"It is a fact that we are a sport driven by membership subscriptions," Fuller says. "People pay to play the sport and a percentage of that fee goes into the running and administration of student football. The more people who play, the more money we have to invest in a variety of different projects, whether that be in growing the game or in talent development.

"The NFL will remain the touch point for 99 percent of new people who come into our sport. We will become increasingly influenced by the NCAA, but the NFL is the primary tool for driving participation.

"It will be NFL-driven for the foreseeable future because those guys are the superstars. Whatever the value of college football, there is still always that element of which players will make the NFL Draft. The NFL drives the interest, the NCAA becomes a frame of reference, but then it cycles back to the NFL and you want to see how the players on your favorite college team fare in the NFL.

"From a UK point of view, as we increase participation, the British American Football Association will look at starting a girls' league and flag football programs. The overall aim is to extend the reach of the game to the point where it is no longer a niche interest.

"I don't think we're going to be a soccer, rugby, or tennis but I think we're ploughing our own furrow because of the unique heritage that comes from the United States."

While the likes of Fuller, Athersmith, and Hewitt advance the sport's grassroots growth in the UK, the NFL—and the owners of the thirty-two teams—is passionate about growing its game internationally and making the game so popular in the United Kingdom that the clamor for a franchise will become too difficult to ignore.

In order for that to happen, a younger fan base needs to be introduced to the game. The NFL knows it cannot rely on those who first saw American football when the Redskins took on the Dolphins in Super Bowl XVII back in 1983.

The regular season games at Wembley Stadium undoubtedly play a major role in creating those new and passionate followers. The BUAFL, for its part, is also helping to turn casual fans into avid consumers of the NFL brand. And that seems like a fair deal, given that the BUAFL is benefiting from the NFL in terms of player numbers. It is a partnership that suits both sides and both have certainly adopted the "long may it continue" approach.

"We have close links with the BUAFL and continue to work, support, and guide the development of the league," the NFL's Joyce concludes. "There is definitely a strong link between participation and fandom for the NFL.

"The greater the growth of the game in the UK, the stronger the base we'll have to develop future fans of the sport."

# GOING FOR IT ON FOURTH DOWN

## Understanding "Game-Winning Chance"

BY FRANK FRIGO

*with* CHARLES BOWER, PhD

Frank Frigo is a decision theory expert, and a former winner of the World Backgammon Championship in Monte Carlo. He has held the number one international ranking in both live tournament and online play. Frank has an active career in commodity markets specializing in structuring wholesale energy transactions. He has more than twenty years of experience in the power and natural gas industries.

Frank received a bachelor of science degree in geology from Western Illinois University and attended the master's program for applied geophysics at the University of Houston. He resides in Louisville, Kentucky, with his wife and two children.

Charles Bower, PhD, has an extensive background in both computer modelling and statistical interpretation of data. He received a bachelor of science degree with a major in mathematics from Purdue University and spent five years in the Bell System as a programmer analyst before returning to academic life. Chuck holds a master of science degree in Physics and a PhD in Astrophysics from Indiana University. He was employed by NASA as an X-Ray astrophysicist and he worked on the Chandra X-Ray Satellite at the Marshall Space Flight Center in Huntsville, Alabama. Most recently, Chuck served as a senior scientist in experimental particle astrophysics at Indiana University. He has written over forty articles that have been published in various physics journals. His hobbies include playing and writing about backgammon, in which he specializes in the statistical interpretation of computer modelling results of this ancient game. Chuck is married and resides in Bloomington, Indiana.

Collaborative History: Chuck and Frank co-developed a decision-making computer model for the NFL called ZEUS™. Over the past several years, they have consulted with several NFL head coaches, general managers, and directors of player personnel. They have provided expert commentary on decision theory in football for a number of major media outlets including: *ESPN, Fox Sports, Wired Magazine, Le Monde, Technology Review, Business Week,* the *Wall Street Journal,* the *Christian Science Monitor,* as well as being regular contributors to the *New York Times.* They were honored as *Esquire Magazine's* "Best and Brightest" of 2006 and were the subject of a feature story on Showtime's "Inside the NFL."

In 2010, they formed ViMass Group, LLC (www.vimassgroup.com), where they provide analytical and predictive consulting services for corporate clients and sports organizations.

---

Sports fans love to second-guess coaching decisions. When we disagree with their choice, and it fails, we "know" we are correct. "How could that high-salaried buffoon be so clueless?" we like to say to our friends over a cup of coffee on Monday morning. In hindsight, the "correct" decision always seems so obvious to the casual observer. When a coach makes a difficult decision, the court of public opinion is, almost by definition, split down the middle. As a result, approximately one-half of the observers will believe they had a better choice than the play-caller, a choice that would have resulted in a more favorable outcome than the one they witnessed.

Nowhere is this type of thinking more evident than among the faithful fans of American football. The most dramatic and critical calls generally fall into one of the following categories: onside kicks, two point conversions and fourth-down attempts. In particular, the fourth-and-short situations provide the greatest fodder for passionate Monday-morning quarterbacks. Seemingly equal doses of "I can't believe they went for it" and "I can't believe they kicked it" can be heard during the course of a long college or NFL season. Not surprisingly, the fortunes (and misfortunes) of many teams are attributed to this class of decisions.

While fourth-down decisions have been sources of controversy for as long as the modern game has been in existence, it has only been during the last decade that this class of problems has caught the attention of scientists and mathematicians. A groundswell of analysis has been published in recent years arguing the merits of more aggressive actions on fourth down. David Romer, a professor of economics at the University of California-Berkeley, produced a compelling argument for the cost (in expected points) of punting on fourth down in many common situations. Other academics followed suit. The consensus was mounting and the evidence was in. Teams in both college and the NFL were punting too much and the cost was great. But how great?

When Chuck Bower and I developed the ZEUS™ computer play-calling model, we set out to answer this very question. We didn't want to know just how much a poor decision cost an average team in expected points, but more importantly what it cost a specific team in expected wins for a game or an entire season. We focused on the metric of Game-Winning Chance or "GWC."

## UNDERSTANDING GWC

GWC evaluates a play based on the highest probability of winning a game. If a running play has a 2 percent greater GWC than punting, it means if

CHART 5.1    EQUITY PROGRESSION CHART—EXPLAINING GWC

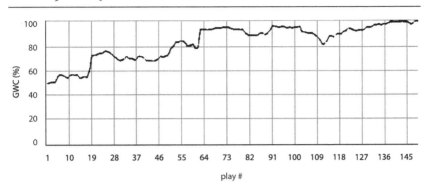

the situation occurred one hundred times, choosing the run would, on average, produce two more victories than punting.

Chart 5.1 helps to explain how GWCs are measured during a normal game, which in this example consists of 154 total plays. Assuming two equal and average teams, the GWC begins at 50 percent and progresses as a tug of war. At the beginning of the game, both teams have an identical GWC and by the conclusion of the game, one team will reach 100 percent and the other will end up at 0 percent. The model calculates the GWC for each of the 154 plays or "increments". To be more precise, each of those increments has a range of values based upon the difference between the optimal play choice from scrimmage and the lesser alternatives. The model can assess this range at any juncture (play from scrimmage) and assign a cost to suboptimal choices and a benefit for optimal play calls in a given scenario. The GWC percentages plotted on the graph for each play increment represent a mean value of that range. While we have identified the respective GWC values at the beginning of each of the 154 plays, we pay particular attention to fourth downs, which represent more directional (or binary) types of choices.

By simulating outcomes beginning with any critical decision and accounting for the unique characteristics of the opposing teams, the ZEUS model was able to produce a cost of suboptimal decisions in GWC units over the course of single game, and subsequently over an entire season. The findings were remarkable. Just two errors per game (each with a 3 percent magnitude) would cause an average NFL team to squander nearly one game per season in expected wins on fourth-down decisions alone.

We could only imagine how much a typical NFL franchise would value this information. The difference between a 9-7 record and a 10-6 record is often the difference between the postseason and an early vacation.

During the next couple of years, we set out to make our case to a large number of NFL organizations. While the average NFL team was leaving about 0.9 wins per season on the table, the range of 0.6 to 1.3 games revealed surprising uniformity amongst teams. They were all making similar misguided decisions with regularity. The early adopter, we reasoned, would garner the most benefit. While the findings seemed like a slam-dunk and the teams were extremely interested in the analysis, no one was jumping at the solution. After more than fifteen meetings with general managers, head coaches, and other key staff across the NFL, a couple of common themes began to emerge: risk aversion and conformity. It may be all about winning in the NFL, but only as long as you look like your peers while you are doing it.

Going for it on a fourth down and two from a team's own twenty-eight-yard line may offer a coach the highest expectation of winning the game, but the prospect of being stuffed is typically too much to bear. Punting and losing is simply remembered as a loss. Throw an incomplete pass on fourth down and it is a controversial loss.

Amazingly, little has changed in the NFL in recent years. According to our research on critical calls, the cost of conservative decisions on fourth downs has remained relatively stable over the past decade. Aside from the infrequent courageous efforts of a few head coaches, on average, the 2011 season is likely to look very similar to the 2002 season. We had to ask ourselves, "Wasn't anyone listening?" As it turns out, someone was.

## FIRST DOWN OR BUST

Kevin Kelley is the head football coach at Pulaski Academy High school, a private prep school located in Little Rock, Arkansas. He has compiled an impressive 81-15-1 record over the years (83.5 percent winning percentage) with a rather unconventional strategy. His team NEVER punts on fourth down and they onside kick approximately 75 percent of the time. This is an excerpt from Steven Levitt's *Freakonomics Blog*:

Kelley says that when he began to shun the punt, people thought he was crazy: "It's like brainwashing; people believe you are required to punt." Players and the home crowd needed to get acclimated to it. "When we first started going on every fourth down," he says, "our home crowd would boo and the players would be distressed. You need to become accustomed to the philosophy and buy into the idea. Now our crowd and our players expect us to go for it, and get excited when no punting team comes onto the field. When my ten-year-old son sees NFL teams punting on short yardage on television, he gets upset because he's grown up with the idea that punting is usually bad."

Several years ago, Kelley began to research the work of David Romer and became a student of the ZEUS model. Because of his findings, he enthusiastically decided to shun punting altogether regardless of the situation. While we must commend him for having the courage to implement his convictions, we do wonder if he may have taken a good idea too far. It is hard to argue with success especially when it is attributed to a revolutionary strategy. However, as much as we often condone aggressive actions, all fourth downs are not created equal—even for the mighty Pulaski Bruins.

## THE FOURTH-DOWN CONUNDRUM: CRACKING THE CODE

Fourth downs offer a delicate class of problems. The choice between punting, kicking a field goal, and going for the first down with a run or a pass is a very complicated problem of risk and reward. The many important factors to consider include the score difference, timeouts, ball position, yards to first down, and the relative strengths and weaknesses of the opposing teams. While it is certainly true that coaches most often err on the conservative side of the equation, a single brushstroke of aggression will not solve the problem.

Any fourth-down situation represents a classic risk management decision. In the simplest sense, it is all about the magnitude and frequency of the resulting successes and failures. Whichever choice offers the highest resulting GWC is correct. Consider this simple example:

**Ball Position**: Fourth down on the opponent's two-yard line
**Clock:** One second remaining in regulation
**Score:** Trailing by two points

If we look at this from the perspective of a typical NFL team, we would expect the field goal attempt to succeed 98 to 99 percent of the time. A rushing attempt or a short pass attempt, by comparison, would succeed in the range of 45 to 50 percent on average. Let's compare the choices:

*Field Goal Attempt:*
>            Success = 100 percent GWC
>            Failure = 0 percent GWC
>   .985 x 100 percent = 98.5 percent GWC

*Touchdown Attempt*
>            Success = 100 percent GWC
>            Failure = 0 percent GWC
>   .475 x 100 percent = 47.5 percent GWC

There is little surprise in the result. Kicking the field goal wins approximately twice as much on average as a touchdown attempt. This example is essentially a binary problem. In reality, most fourth-down decisions involve a greater distribution of outcomes, each with its own associated GWC. The example above is like a decision tree with two branches. Earlier in the game, a fourth-down decision looks more like a giant oak with thousands of branches. The weighted average of magnitudes and frequencies for each branch ultimately determines the optimal decision.

The ZEUS model reliably assesses the probabilistic expectations of difficult critical calls in a matter of seconds. The simulation engine can accept any unique circumstance and play the game to conclusion in a virtual environment, beginning with the candidate play choices. Let's look at a more ordinary type of problem where risk aversion is prevalent among NFL coaches.

**Opponents:** Two identical teams with league average expectations
in every important category for offense, defense, and special
teams.

**Ball Position:** Fourth and three on the opponent's fifteen-yard line

**Score:** Tied

**Clock:** Ten Minutes remaining in the third quarter

**Timeouts:** Three each

**Simulations:** For this given situation, we run one hundred thousand game simulations to conclusion beginning with a field goal, a run, and a pass attempt. In total, we run four hundred thousand games in order to ensure statistical significance (i.e. rule out any material effect of random variation in the results). Each of those four hundred thousand games is a unique contest between two identical teams. The rates of rushing and passing successes are representative of NFL averages. The frequency of turnovers is also representative of NFL expectations, as is every other nuance of an actual game. In fact, if we lined the virtual teams up for an opening kickoff and played the game to completion millions of times, we would get just what one might expect—essentially a 50/50 outcome.

**Results:**

| Play Ranking | Cost in GWC |
|---|---|
| 1. Pass | Optimum |
| 2. Run | –1.7 percent |
| 3. Field Goal | –2.2 percent |

These results provide a compelling argument for more aggressive action. While typical coaching wisdom favors taking the points and the lead, the model is "seeing" something else. The long-term utility of four incremental points is an important factor. The poor resulting field position for the opponent when a fourth-down attempt fails is also an important factor. The possibility that the field goal attempt could fail must be factored into the equation as well. The beauty of modern computing power is that all of these factors and many others can be captured in hundreds of thousands of simulations all in a matter of seconds. At the end of the analysis, expected GWC is all that really matters.

Despite this evidence, most coaches would kick the field goal every time in this circumstance. We suspect, as behavioral economists often suggest, humans value losses differently than gains. When facing a short field goal situation, most coaches have already accounted for the extra three points because they know they are a substantial favorite to realize them. A more aggressive action is seen as potentially squandering something that is already in hand. As a result, focus shifts to immediate risk rather than the more important goal of winning the game. There is almost no chance Kevin Kelley would have kicked a field goal in this situation and he would have been right. There may be some speculation whether he would choose to run or pass, but undoubtedly, he would have gone for it. If it is correct for an average NFL team to shun the field goal against another average team, we can only conclude it is even more correct for the powerful offense of the Pulaski Bruins. In fact, we can adjust the strengths and weaknesses of the opposing teams to stress test any of the model's recommendations. As expected, the gap between the field goal and the short pass only widens when we increase the proficiency of the offensive team.


## THE "BLUNDER" EVERYONE TALKED ABOUT...

To illustrate just how complex and controversial a fourth-down decision can be, we need look no further than the now infamous call Bill Belichick made against the Colts in November of 2009. In case you have forgotten, the Patriots were facing a fourth-and-two on their own twenty-eight-yard line with two minutes remaining in the game and a six-point lead.

When Melvin Bullitt of the Colts tackled Kevin Faulk just short of the first down and the Colts subsequently scored the game-winning touchdown, it was the beginning of a firestorm. In the minds of many fans and media analysts, Belichick had committed one of the great blunders in modern NFL history. How could he have just handed the ball back to Peyton Manning in that situation when a punt could have made the Colt's game-winning drive so much more difficult? Of course, Belichick had focused on the gain associated with converting the first down. He was certainly aware of the potential risk of failure, but he realized a successful conversion would have, for all practical purposes, put the game away.

When we analyzed this situation with the ZEUS model, we were able to input the custom characteristics of the Colts and Patriots (see Table 5.1). The result was seemingly clear. With very conservative assumptions, the Patriots were improving their chances by at least 2 percent GWC with the first-down attempt. However, this was not enough for the naysayers. They

TABLE 5.1    SCENARIO ANALYSIS: INDIANAPOLIS COLTS VERSUS NEW ENGLAND PATRIOTS, NOVEMBER 15, 2009

*New England Patriots*

|  | O: Low D: Low | O: Low D: Avg | O: Low D: High | O: Avg D: Low | O: Avg D: Avg | O:Avg D: High | O: High D: Low | O: High D: Avg | O: High D: High |
|---|---|---|---|---|---|---|---|---|---|
| O: Low D: Low | 1.9 | -1.0 | -2.4 | 5.7 | 2.8 | 0.7 | 8.1 | 4.7 | 2.0 |
| O: Low D: Avg | 1.3 | -0.3 | -5.1 | 2.2 | -0.6 | -2.2 | 6.4 | 3.1 | 0.6 |
| O: Low D: High | -7.7 | -8.4 | -7.9 | -2.5 | -4.1 | -5.1 | 1.9 | -0.5 | -2.1 |
| O: Avg D: Low | 5.1 | 1.8 | -0.6 | 9.8 | 6.0 | 3.1 | 11.7 | 7.8 | 4.6 |
| O: Avg D: Avg | 0.4 | -2.5 | -4.4 | 4.4 | 1.9 | -0.6 | 9.8 | 6.1 | 3.2 |
| O: Avg D: High | -5.9 | -7.2 | -7.8 | -0.4 | -2.4 | -4.2 | 4.9 | 1.9 | -0.4 |
| O: High D: Low | 7.4 | 4.3 | 2.3 | 12.4 | 9.7 | 6.2 | 15.2 | 11.7 | 7.9 |
| O: High D: Avg | 2.1 | -0.3 | -2.1 | 7.5 | 4.8 | 1.7 | 13.3 | 9.7 | 6.2 |
| O: High D: High | -4.0 | -6.7 | -7.9 | 1.2 | -0.7 | -2.4 | 7.7 | 4.7 | 1.8 |

*Indianapolis Colts* (vertical axis label)

wanted to know if we fully considered momentum, the Patriots' defense, and not least of all the prowess of Peyton Manning. Table 5.1 reveals why we were so confident that Belichick made the right call.

**Key:** The horizontal axis represents a broad range of custom characteristics for the offensive team (Patriots) and the vertical axis is similarly arranged for the Colts. The first indicator is the assumption for offensive strength (rushing and passing) and the second indicator for defense. The shaded cells represent positive GWC scenarios in which the Patriots should go for it on fourth down rather than punt the ball.

> **O or D = Low:** Low-end assumption (40 percent below NFL average)
>
> **O or D = AVG:** = NFL league average assumption
>
> **O or D = High**: High-end assumption (40 percent above NFL average)

The lows and the highs represent extreme ends of the spectrum. For instance, O = High and D =Low approximates the highest ranked offense in the NFL in all categories and the lowest ranked defense in all categories. In reality, no team actually rates this high or low. The point of the table is to provide some perspective on the model's recommendations. If the argument is that we did not account for the potency of Manning's arm, the truth is we accounted well beyond it. Of the eighty-one extreme scenarios we analyzed, forty-nine favored the first-down attempt and thirty-two favored the punt. The average cost of the punt across all scenarios is 1.87 percent GWC. When the generic case, the custom case, and the cumulative case all point in the same direction, it becomes far more plausible that the first-down attempt was correct as opposed to the punt.

One interesting observation from this analysis, as represented in the last three columns of the matrix, is that a high-powered offense would benefit from a first-down attempt in virtually every scenario.

## ...AND THE BLUNDER EVERYONE ELSE MISSED

Often, situations arise when there is unanimous consensus for the model's recommendation. During the 2011 playoffs, we witnessed the most costly fourth-down decision to date. In the wild card playoff game between Indianapolis and New York, the Colts faced a fourth-and-six on the fourteen-yard line of the Jets while trailing 14-10 with 4:41 remaining in the game. To our surprise, the Colts kicked a field goal to close the gap to a single point. Even more surprising is that the first-down attempt was apparently not even considered by the Colts or the television analysts. With the custom characteristics of the Jets and the Colts fed into the model, the field goal turned out to be a whopping 15 percent GWC error. If we construct the strongest argument against the model's recommendation (i.e. the Colts are the worst team in the league at converting fourth downs, the Jets are the strongest defense in the league, and the Jets are impotent on offense), it scarcely changed the result.

To see why this is true requires a realization that if you assign the Colts a very weak offense, this will be the same group that is trying to win the game on a final drive, if they are fortunate enough to get the ball back after the field goal. Regardless of how we construct the characteristics of the Jets and Colts, the model overwhelmingly favors the fourth-down attempt.

To put this blunder in proper perspective, the GWC cost to the Colts is equivalent to handing the ball over to the Jets on the game's first play from the Colt's own twenty-yard line and letting the Jets walk unmolested into the end zone for a touchdown.

## THE LIMITS TO CONTRARIANISM

What about those contrarian strategies that are quickly becoming the lore of Arkansas high school football? As we have seen, aggressive actions on fourth down can often pay great dividends, but it is not always the case. The following tables provide some insight into when a punt can become more effective than a fourth-down attempt. In each instance, we are assuming a tie score and full timeouts at the start of the fourth quarter. The results are in GWC from the perspective of the offensive team attempting to convert a first down.

In the three tables (Tables 5.2, 5.3, 5.4), the offense (Team 1) is represented on the horizontal axis and the defense (Team 2) on the vertical axis. The lower left box in each matrix (i.e. O=High; D=Avg vs. O=Avg; D=Low) indicates a high-powered NFL offense opposing a very weak defense against both the pass and rush.* We are assuming NFL league averages in all other categories including punting. In each case, we performed one hundred thousand game simulations.

A couple of interesting conclusions arise from this study. It is quickly evident that going for it on fourth and one is often correct regardless of field position. In fact, for two equal and average teams, it is almost never correct to punt with very few exceptions, late in the second and fourth quarters. As seen in Table 5.2, even with various combinations of skill differences it is most often correct to avoid the punt.

---

* In Table 5.2, the Patriots' GWC for the lowest left hand box is 10.5 percent; in Table 5.3, 1.1 percent; and in Table 5.4, -5.0 percent. To interpret these results, we would say in the case of Table 5.2 that when a high-powered offense faces a low rated defense, the offense would improve its game-winning chance by 10.5 percent by going for it on fourth and one, even from the offense's own ten-yard line. In a scenario where the same offense is facing a fourth and twenty from the same spot against the same opponent, going for it on fourth down would reduce the offense's game-winning chance by -5.0 percent.

TABLE 5.2     SCENARIO ANALYSIS: FOURTH-AND-ONE FROM AN
              OFFENSE'S OWN TEN YARD LINE

### Team 1

|  | O:High<br>D: Avg | O: Avg<br>D: Avg | O: Low<br>D: Avg |
|---|---|---|---|
| O: Avg<br>D: High | 3.1% | -1.8% | -4.2% |
| O: Avg<br>D: Avg | 9.5% | 3.3% | -1.6% |
| O: Avg<br>D: Low | 10.5% | 9.3% | 2.9% |

*Team 2*

TABLE 5.3     FOURTH-AND-TEN FROM AN OFFENSE'S OWN TEN-
              YARD LINE

### Team 1

|  | O:High<br>D: Avg | O: Avg<br>D: Avg | O: Low<br>D: Avg |
|---|---|---|---|
| O: Avg<br>D: High | -3.1% | -4.4% | -4.4% |
| O: Avg<br>D: Avg | -1.0% | -3.3% | -4.2% |
| O: Avg<br>D: Low | 1.1% | -1.5% | -3.3% |

*Team 2*

TABLE 5.4     FOURTH-AND-TWENTY FROM AN OFFENSE'S OWN TEN-
              YARD LINE

### Team 1

|  | O:High<br>D: Avg | O: Avg<br>D: Avg | O: Low<br>D: Avg |
|---|---|---|---|
| O: Avg<br>D: High | -7.3% | -7.1% | -5.9% |
| O: Avg<br>D: Avg | -6.3% | -6.9% | -7.2% |
| O: Avg<br>D: Low | -5.0% | -6.7% | -7.2% |

*Team 2*

Rejecting the punt—even when a team is deep in their own territory when so much is at stake—seems to defy common sense. The problem is better understood when we consider that a successful punt generally does not knock the opponent back into its own territory. Punting from the back of the end zone, as is the case here, often provides the opponent a starting position no worse than the kicking team's forty-yard line. Converting the fourth-and-one, as scary as it may seem, is an enormous gain in opportunity. The team now has a new set of downs and most importantly retains possession while the clock continues to decay.

Table 5.2 reveals some situations where it is correct to punt on fourth-and-long when buried in your own territory. Interestingly, NFL coaches automatically punt in these situations at all score differences unless it is a final drive or last play desperation attempt. Only when a scoring deficit exceeds seven points, does the opportunity for aggressive action on fourth-and-long begin to gain credibility.

With respect to Kevin Kelley's hard line on fourth down, it seems likely that a considerable amount of game equity is being squandered in long yardage situations. Pulaski's skill advantage against some opponents may indeed exceed NFL high and low spreads. However, as represented in Table 5.3 and Table 5.4, even with the benefit of very favorable skill combinations, NFL teams would be making serious errors in rejecting the punt in certain circumstances.

To further examine Kelley's unique approach to success, we decided to analyze several blanket strategies with the model, which assumes that a team has a top-tier offense and an average defense.

**Strategy 1:** A strategy in which a team never kicks a field goal or punts

**Strategy 2:** A strategy that allows for punting but will never choose a fourth-down attempt over a field goal

**Strategy 3:** A strategy that allows for punting but will always go for it on fourth down instead of attempting a field goal

**Strategy 4:** A strategy that incorporates the common behavior of NFL teams on fourth down

Additionally, we adjusted the skill levels of the opposing team to examine the effects of various defenses as seen in Table 5.5.

TABLE 5.5     ANALYSIS OF BLANKET STRATEGIES AGAINST TEAMS
WITH AN AVERAGE OFFENSE AND EITHER A HIGH,
AVERAGE, OR LOW DEFENSE

*Team 1*

| | | *Never Kick (1)* | *Strategy 2* | *Strategy 3* | *Strategy 4* |
|---|---|---|---|---|---|
| | *O: Avg* *D: High* | -4.1% | -4.2% | -0.3% | BEST |
| Team 2 | *O: Avg* *D: Avg* | BEST | -1.0% | -0.4% | -1.2% |
| | *O: Avg* *D: Low* | BEST | -0.6% | -0.8% | -1.4% |

The first row essentially represents an average case, as the high-powered offense and high-powered defense have a somewhat cancelling effect. Not too surprisingly, the status quo strategy (Strategy 4) outperforms the extreme strategies (1-3) in matchups against an elite defense. Things begin to get interesting when we look at the case of the high-powered offense against an average or low-end defense (as displayed in the second and third rows). These conditions are closest in proximity to the case of the Pulaski Bruins playing against average high school competition. Kelley's convictions appear to trump the other blanket strategies.

Of course, this table only tells part of the story. If the conditions represented in the table are reasonable approximations of what Kelley is facing in Arkansas football, then we can conclude his strategy is the best of the blanket fourth-down approaches. However, we see no reason to adopt such a rigid strategy when each critical call requires its own unique assessment. Kelley certainly does well, but we believe he could do even better. The same can be said, albeit for somewhat different reasons, for his counterparts in the NFL.

## GWC, TURNOVER MARGIN, AND EXPLOSIVE PLAYS

*Rivals.com* recently published an interesting assessment of the statistics certain college coaches considered most important to their teams' success.[1]

The results are an insightful peek into the minds of these respected coaches. Eleven head coaches, seven offensive coordinators, and eleven defensive coordinators from different collegiate programs provided their opinions on the statistics that matter most to them. Turnover margin (twenty-two mentions), explosive or big plays (eleven mentions), third-down conversion (seven mentions), and scoring (five mentions) were among the leading candidates, followed by mention of eleven other statistics which various coaches believed were important.[2]

Turnover margin is particularly interesting, and undoubtedly very important in the outcome of a game. These coaches overwhelmingly selected turnover margin as the statistic that concerned them the most. The inherent challenge in evaluating turnover margin is the upside of the turnover risk. A sloppy snap is a raw blunder with a solidly negative expectation. Other turnovers, however, have potential outcomes that are favorable. Relinquishing possession in some situations is a natural component of the distribution of "explosive" plays (the second most popular statistic mentioned). Consider the following hypothetical example between two equal and average teams:

**Down and Distance:** First-and-ten on a team's own forty-yard line
**Play Choice:** Long Pass (thirty yards) attempt
**Score:** Tie
**Time Remaining:** Fifteen minutes
**Timeouts:** Three timeouts apiece

For simplicity, let's consider only three possible outcomes:

**Outcome 1.** Complete pass and five-yard continuation that results in first-and-ten on the opponent's twenty-five-yard line;
**Outcome 2.** Incomplete pass that results in second-and-ten on opponent's forty-yard line;
**Outcome 3.** Interception on thirty-yard line and a five-yard return that results in opponent starting first-and-ten on their own thirty-five-yard line.

The resulting GWCs (per 100,000 simulations) for each case can be seen in Chart 5.2.

Outcome 1: Completion (65.6 percent GWC)

Outcome 2: Incompletion (54.9 percent GWC)

Outcome 3: Interception (45.2 percent GWC)

Similar to pot odds in a poker game, attempting the long pass in this case is simply a matter of playing the odds. The incremental potential gain between a completion and an incompletion is 65.6 percent–54.9 percent or 9.7 percent. The potential loss between an incompletion and an interception is 54.9 percent–45.2 percent or also 9.7 percent. Therefore, if the completion (65.6 percent) is more likely to occur than the interception (45.2 percent), the play choice has a net positive incremental GWC. (Note that there might have been other play choices that had even higher incremental GWC expectations).

CHART 5.2    DECISION OUTCOMES

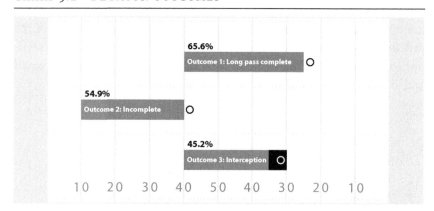

Again, this is a simplified example with other potential outcomes, but it serves to illustrate an important point. When an interception occurs at an important juncture of the game, it is indeed costly, but the potential reward may have justified the risk of a turnover. Turnovers are simply the cost of doing business.

Interestingly, among the twenty-nine collegiate coaches interviewed, not a single member of this fraternity mentioned fourth-down decisions or fourth-down conversions as an important statistical factor. Their comments suggest that not much seems to have changed since 2002 when we first started our analysis of fourth-down decision making. Their comments also indicate that the first mover advantage for the college football team that embraces our findings remains as high as ever.

# 6

# DETERMINANTS OF FBS HEAD COACHES' SALARIES

*An Economic Perspective*

BY BRAD R. HUMPHREYS,

BRIAN P. SOEBBING,

*and* NICHOLAS M. WATANABE

Brad R. Humphreys is a professor in the Department of Economics at the University of Alberta, where he holds the chair in the Economics of Gaming. He received his PhD in economics from the Johns Hopkins University. His research on the economic impact of professional sports, the economics of gambling, the economics of intercollegiate athletics, and the financing of the Olympic Games has been published in numerous scholarly journals. He is co-editor of Contemporary Economic Policy and associate editor of the *International Journal of Sport Finance*. His research has been featured in *Sports Illustrated*, the *Wall Street Journal*, *USA Today*, and numerous other media outlets worldwide. In 2007 and

2008, he testified before the United States Congress on the financing and economic impact of professional sports facilities.

Brian P. Soebbing is a PhD candidate in sport management at the University of Alberta. His main research interest is on the strategic behavior of professional and amateur sports leagues and teams. His dissertation, "The Amateur Draft, Competitive Balance, and Tanking in the National Basketball Association," examines the tanking phenomenon in the NBA and the various changes in the league's draft policy.

Nicholas M. Watanabe, PhD, is an assistant teaching professor of sport management in the Department of Parks, Recreation and Tourism at the University of Missouri. He received his PhD in sport management from the University of Illinois. His research interests are in sports economics, finance, and management. He is a contributor to the International Journal of Sport Finance Blog.

## INTRODUCTION

On January 3, 2007, Nick Saban became the head coach of the University of Alabama's football team. Saban received an eight-year contract paying him $4 million per season, which at the time made him the highest paid coach in college sports. Considerable criticism followed the contract's announcement, with news outlets like CNN noting that Alabama was "45th in Helping Kids, No. 1 in paying coach."[1] Saban's case is not unique; college football coaches earn large salaries and the size of their compensation frequently draws criticism or outrage. One common complaint is that the money paid to football coaches could be better spent on academics, research, or other activities that would improve universities.

The average salary of a Division I-FBS head football coach in 2010 was $1,361,791, and the highest paid coach, Saban again (whose salary increased by $2 million in just three seasons), earned nearly $6 million per year. Saban's salary increase was not particularly unique, and reflects broader trends in college football. All Division I-FBS head football coaches' salaries increased rapidly in recent years; the average salary of a Division I-FBS head coach grew by 10 percent in inflation-adjusted terms between 2006 and 2010.*

In 2009, the average salary for a full professor at a public university was just over $115,000. The *Chronicle of Higher Education*, a publication focused on issues in higher education, noted that the CEOs and presidents of universities were paid an average of $427,400 a year.[2] Compared to Saban's salary of nearly $6 million, the governor of Alabama, Bob Riley, earned just $112,859 in 2010, or 1.8 percent of Saban's salary. The president of the University of Alabama, Robert E. Witt, earned $604,161 in 2010, about 10 percent of Saban's salary. Not only are college football and basketball coaches the highest paid employees in many states, but in some cases they also are paid significantly more than other important government and university officials.

The compensation of a college coach generates a great deal of criticism and controversy. Critics argue that the money paid to coaches falls well short of the value of the services that coaches provide to the university, and that those funds could be better used elsewhere. Professors and administrators also believe that coaches are overpaid. For example, the Knight Commission has frequently criticized the salaries earned by college football coaches.† In 2009, the Knight Commission surveyed ninety-five university presidents from schools in the FBS. Eighty-five percent of the respondents, individuals who are all deeply involved in the hiring of athletic coaches, said they believed that college football and basketball coaches were being "excessively" compensated.[3] Curiously, the Knight Commission report also noted that many university presidents felt that spending for football and basketball coaches was excessive across the board at other academic institutions. However, when the presidents were asked about the compensation paid to coaches at their own university, the number who thought spending was excessive dropped, indicating that presidents were

---

* Division I-FBS is the highest division in college football (formerly called Division I-A). Division I-FCS is the next highest division in college football (formerly called Division I-AA).

† The John S. and James L. Knight Foundation created the Knight Commission in October 1989 to propose a reform agenda emphasizing academics in intercollegiate athletics. The Knight Commission consists of academics, journalists, and other stakeholders from intercollegiate athletics.

more likely to say spending was more excessive at other universities than at their own.[4] A final concern of the university presidents was the belief that that their authority had been diminished because of increases in private donations to athletic departments.[5] Just over half of them (56 percent) expressed this belief. In addition to these survey results, it is important to bear in mind that football coaches at public universities are public employees. Since public universities receive financial support from state governments, taxpayers often complain that their tax dollars support, directly or indirectly, the large salaries paid to college coaches.

Members of the media, academics, university and government officials, and taxpayers seem to object to the salaries paid to college coaches. Are these objections valid? The answer to that question, of course, ultimately lies in the eye of beholder. In this discussion, we evaluate the salaries earned by NCAA Division I-FBS football coaches, and try to place these salaries in context. A careful and objective assessment of the compensation of NCAA Division I-FBS head football coaches will provide an additional perspective for this conspicuous and contentious issue.

## THE IMPORTANCE OF MRP

Economics provides several perspectives for understanding how employees are compensated. The textbook economic model predicts that each employee will be paid a salary equal to his or her *marginal revenue product* (MRP).* According to this model, employees with higher MRP earn larger salaries while employees with lower MRP earn smaller salaries. Take, for example, a star pitcher and a middle reliever on a Major League Baseball team. The star pitcher earns more than the middle reliever does because the star pitcher generates more wins and attracts more fans to the stadium than the middle reliever attracts. A baseball team will likely pay the star pitcher more than the middle reliever because the star pitcher should play a more significant role in generating revenues for the team than the middle reliever. It is reasonable to expect that the star pitcher's MRP will likely be higher than the middle reliever's MRP, which is reflected by the different salaries.

---

* The MRP model also assumes that hiring entities operate in competitive output and labor markets in which the chief aim of those firms is to maximize profit.

MRP reflects two key factors determining employee compensation: the incremental output that can be attributed to each employee (called marginal product or marginal productivity) and the incremental revenues generated by this output (called marginal revenue).

Marginal productivity differs across employees because of differences in ability, experience, and other personal characteristics. Marginal revenue often differs across employees within the same firm based on the different output generated by each employee. Both marginal revenue and marginal product can explain variation in salaries within a firm and across different firms.

## ANALYSIS OF SALARIES

Over the past five years, *USA Today* has annually obtained the contracts of every Division I-FBS college football coach through Freedom of Information Act filings and published both summaries of the compensation and the full text of the contracts.[6] *USA Today* compiles information on the base salary, potential bonus payments, other income, and total compensation paid to each coach each season. For most of the coaches, *USA Today* also makes the official contract between the coach and the university available on the Web. The *USA Today* coaching compensation data contains 599 observations for Division I-FBS football teams over five seasons. Compensation data is available for 557 of these observations (93 percent).*We augmented these data with information on football team performance, along with coach and university characteristics from the College Football Data Warehouse (http://www.cfbdatawarehouse.com) and the NCAA Web sites. Taken together, these data provide a comprehensive picture of the compensation and performance of NCAA Division I-FBS head coaches.

Table 6.1 contains summary statistics for observations in which coaching salary data are available. Salaries were converted to constant 2010 dollars using the Consumer Price Index to make them comparable over time. From Table 6.1, the average salary paid to head coaches over this period was $1,205,388. Salaries ranged from $140,612 to almost $6 million.

Since our sample contains only Division I-FBS football programs, and NCAA rules permit these programs to play a limited number of

---

* Compensation data for most coaches at private schools, military academies, and in the state of Pennsylvania, are not made available to *USA Today*.

TABLE 6.1    SUMMARY STATISTICS (2006–2007 THROUGH 2010–2011)*

| Variable | Mean | Std. Dev. | Maximum | Minimum | Median |
|---|---|---|---|---|---|
| Salary | 1,205,388 | 943,029 | 5,997,349 | 140,612 | 1,012,787 |
| Wins | 6.679 | 3.038 | 14 | 0 | 7 |
| Winning Percentage | 0.518 | 0.219 | 1 | 0 | 0.538 |
| Tenure in Current Job | 5.750 | 5.910 | 45 | 1 | 4 |
| Years of Head Coaching Experience | 9.454 | 7.933 | 45 | 1 | 7 |
| Total Attendance | 290,790 | 191,721 | 882,115 | 25,080 | 250,997 |
| Average Attendance | 44,296 | 26,021 | 111,825 | 5,016 | 39,680 |
| Bowl Appearance, current season | 0.566 | 0.496 | 1 | 0 | 1 |
| BCS AQ Conference | 0.544 | 0.499 | 1 | 0 | 1 |

non-Division I-FBS teams, the average winning percentage in the sample is greater than 0.500.[†] Teams in the sample averaged about six and a half wins per season, although the standard deviation, minimum, and maximum indicate significant season-to-season variation in success.

Also in Table 6.1, we find that the head football coaches in the sample had been the head coach at their current institution for an average of six seasons, and the head coach at any level of college football for almost ten seasons. The average total regular season attendance at Division I-FBS universities is just under three hundred thousand for the season, which amounts to about 44,300 fans per regular season home game. Fifty-seven percent of the university-year observations played in bowl game, and 54 percent of the teams play in a conference in which its winner automatically plays in a Bowl Championship Series Bowl.

---

* The mean is the sum of the values a variable takes divided by the number of values, a measure of the center of the observations; the standard deviation is a measure of the variability of a variable; the median is the middle value when the values of a variable are ordered from lowest to highest.

† If Division I-FBS schools could play only each other, then the average winning percentage would indeed be 0.500.

## THE RICH GET RICHER

Table 6.2 summarizes the changes in salaries of Division I-FBS heads the past five years. The dollar values in Table 6.2 are expressed in constant 2010 dollars, which allows for a direct comparison of the salaries over time. In the 2006–2007 season, the average salary in Division I-FBS college football was just under $1 million. In the 2010–2011 season, the average salary was approximately $1.36 million. Salaries in 2010 were 47.5 percent higher than in 2006.

Over the past five seasons, notice the clear increase in both the lowest salary and the highest salary among Division I-FBS head football coaches. The lowest salary increased by just over 35 percent from 2006-2007 ($140,612) to 2010-2011 ($190,000). The maximum salary saw a larger increase, 61 percent, from $3,731,613 to $5,997,349 during the same period. The range, defined as the maximum value minus the minimum value, also increased from $3.6 million to over $5.8 million. Salaries at the upper end of the distribution increased faster than those at the lower end of the distribution over this period, but coaches across the salary distribution saw large increases over the period.

The overall price level in the US, as measured by the Consumer Price Index, increased by only 8 percent during the period measured here. The salary of the average Division I-FBS football coach, as well as the salaries of the lowest and highest paid coach, increased by more than four times the general price level over this period. In inflation-adjusted terms, football coaches saw significant increases in their salaries throughout the salary distribution, suggesting that the MRP of football coaches also increased substantially over this period. Since the largest increases came at the top of the salary distribution, the figures in Table 6.2 suggest that the most talented coaches, in terms of MRP, experienced the biggest salary increases. The US economy went through the worst economic downturn in decades during this period, and many workers saw their salaries fall in absolute value over the same period. Compared to the average worker in the US economy, college football coaches made out quite well over the past five years.

## MEMBERSHIP HAS ITS PRIVILEGES

Conference affiliation is an important factor within the structure of Division I-FBS college football. Conference affiliation affects MRP in a number

TABLE 6.2    AVERAGE SALARIES BY SEASON

| Season | Average | Std. Dev. | Median | Max | Min | Range |
|---|---|---|---|---|---|---|
| 2006 | 998,485 | 734,203 | 895,051 | 3,731,613 | 140,612 | 3,591,002 |
| 2007 | 1,092,749 | 823,446 | 978,056 | 3,807,057 | 151,678 | 3,655,380 |
| 2008 | 1,242,866 | 941,321 | 1,106,976 | 4,253,704 | 145,841 | 4,107,863 |
| 2009 | 1,322,857 | 1,030,230 | 1,016,692 | 4,458,605 | 162,624 | 4,295,981 |
| 2010 | 1,361,791 | 1,100,566 | 1,100,750 | 5,997,349 | 190,000 | 5,807,349 |

TABLE 6.3    AVERAGE SALARY BY CONFERENCE

| | ACC | B10 | B12 | Big East | CUSA | MAC | MWC | Pac-10 | SEC | Sun Belt | WAC |
|---|---|---|---|---|---|---|---|---|---|---|---|
| 2006 | 1,314,344 | 1,548,439 | 1,704,689 | 1,058,440 | 597,515 | 213,426 | 619,327 | 1,337,544 | 1,539,766 | 266,131 | 509,174 |
| 2007 | 1,490,694 | 1,493,402 | 1,715,302 | 1,246,080 | 683,117 | 238,178 | 678,994 | 1,379,761 | 2,041,941 | 278,171 | 574,748 |
| 2008 | 1,736,507 | 1,626,812 | 1,804,870 | 1,382,960 | 785,500 | 272,985 | 725,155 | 1,549,057 | 2,449,593 | 267,882 | 589,442 |
| 2009 | 1,874,448 | 1,793,624 | 2,125,133 | 1,387,639 | 821,194 | 347,282 | 883,798 | 1,820,629 | 2,680,863 | 286,267 | 615,609 |
| 2010 | 1,961,713 | 1,874,961 | 2,226,589 | 1,413,758 | 854,776 | 345,729 | 882,449 | 1,552,562 | 2,840,398 | 319,012 | 666,207 |
| % change | 49.25 | 21.09 | 30.62 | 33.57 | 43.06 | 61.99 | 42.49 | 16.08 | 84.47 | 19.87 | 30.84 |

of important ways. Teams in conferences that receive an automatic bid to the Bowl Championship Series (BCS) have many advantages over teams who are not in an automatic qualifying conference. In addition, teams in BCS conferences generally have larger, more popular football programs with larger fan bases than non-BCS conference teams. As a result, the salary structure differs by conference. Table 6.3 summarizes the average salaries of head football coaches by conference over the sample period. We exclude schools that are not affiliated with any conference due to the small number of schools and because many of those are private schools for which salary information was not available.

Notice the wide disparity in head coaching salaries between conferences (see Table 6.3). Non-BCS conferences like the Sun Belt have coaching salaries that average between $266,000 and $320,000, while BCS conferences like the Big 12, had an average salary between $1.7 and $2.3 million during the same period. Also in Table 6.3, we report the percentage change in average salary for each conference between the first season (2006-2007) and the last season (2010–2011). All conferences saw an increase in average salaries over the period. The Atlantic Coast Conference saw the largest percentage change in salary during the period at 49.25 percent. The smallest percentage change was in the Pacific-10 Conference, which experienced a 16.08 percent increase.

Economic theory provides some clear guidance about how to interpret the salaries of college football coaches. Salaries should reflect MRP, and coaches with higher salaries should have a higher MRP. In 2010, Arkansas head coach Bobby Petrino's salary was about $2.7 million while Arkansas State head coach Steve Roberts' salary was about $223,000. This disparity occurs because of differences in the marginal productivity of the two coaches, as well as differences in the marginal revenue generated by the output of the Arkansas football program compared to the marginal revenue generated by the output of the Arkansas State football program.

What observable factors can be linked to the MRP of a head football coach? Of course, one main goal of a head coach is to produce wins and championships. Often, public perception focuses heavily on game outcomes, and coaches are judged simply by how well they do in terms of wins, appearing in big games, bowl revenue, and winning championships. Winning games and championships along with appearing in bowl games clearly generates revenue and affects MRP.

Based on what we have discussed so far, calculating a coach's MRP and assessing whether a coach is "worth" his salary should be a straightforward exercise. The most successful coaches from a win/loss perspective who also play in the most successful conferences should receive the largest paychecks. Let's look at a few observations from the SEC—considered by many to be one of the most successful conferences in college football—to see if we can better understand the correlation between success on the field and coaching salaries.*

As we see from this small sample in Chart 6.1, in 2010 some coaches represented better value than others in terms of winning percentage. In 2010, the performance of coaches at Alabama, Florida, Georgia and Mississippi did not live up to the expectations reflected in the coaches' annual salaries. Auburn's Gene Chizik, who earns about one-third of Nick Saban's salary, won the national championship in 2010. Mississippi State's Dan Mullen delivered the most "value" when comparing salaries to winning percentage. In spite of being the lowest paid coach in the SEC (excluding Vanderbilt's coach whose salary is not available), Mullen had the fifth highest winning percentage. As this sample demonstrates, winning clearly is not everything. If a football coach's salary cannot be determined by success on the field, by what else might it be determined?

## FOOTBALL PROGRAMS ARE NOT PROFIT-MAXIMIZING FIRMS

The MRP model described earlier assumes that the employer is a profit-maximizing firm. Despite sharing many common attributes with profit-maximizing firms, universities and football programs clearly pursue different goals. Fortunately, economic models based on alternative organizational goals, for example revenue maximization, prestige maximization, or win maximization, generate similar predictions about the determinants of employee compensation. Let's look at those alternative organizational goals.

First, football programs produce multiple outputs, and some of these outputs are difficult to define, complicating the identification of both marginal

---

* College football teams from the SEC have won the past five national championships, six of the past ten national championships (LSU and USC were named co-national champions in 2003), and nine of the past twenty national championships.

CHART 6.1 SEC COACHING SALARIES AND WINNING PERCENTAGE IN 2010*

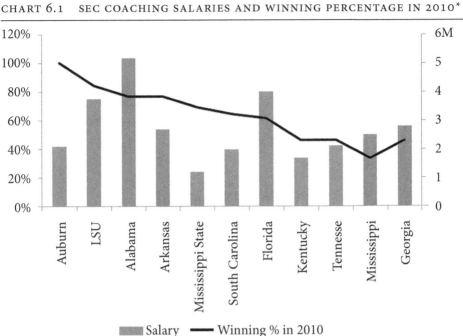

productivity and marginal revenue in this context. Football programs produce direct outputs including game day revenues such as ticket sales to
football games, concessions, programs, and parking. Successful programs
can also generate additional revenues from bowl appearances.† Football
programs in high-profile conferences also receive a share of lucrative tel-

---

* *USA Today*. Note that Vanderbilt does not disclose coaches' salaries, and is not
included in the chart.

† While all bowl teams generate additional revenues, they do not necessarily profit
from their efforts. In a *Sports Illustrated* article, written by Austin Murphy and Dan
Wetzel, entitled "Playoff: How (and Why) the BCS is Blocking What College Football
Needs," the authors note that "The $18.5 million [Ohio State received for making the
Rose Bowl last January] went to the Big Ten, where it was added to a pool of bowl revenue that was then sliced into twelve shares—one for each team, one for the league
office. That still left Ohio State with a tidy $2.2 million to spend, which the Buckeyes
did. Ohio State's team travel costs were $352,727. Unsold tickets ran the school a cool
$144,710. The bill to transport, feed and lodge the band and cheerleaders came to
$366,814. Throw in entertainment, gifts and sundry, and other expenses, and the Buck-
eyes lost $79,597."

evision contracts signed between their conferences and various television and media organizations, while programs in minor conferences generate much smaller television and media-related revenues.

Second, football programs also generate significant indirect benefits such as increased applications for enrollment and increased alumni donations.* Additionally (and most importantly in our view), football programs produce educated college graduates and very occasionally trained athletes for professional sports leagues.[†]

## EXPERIENCE AND SALARIES

Coaching experience should be an important determinant of compensation, because it affects human capital and MRP. Experience can be measured in two ways: the number of seasons a coach has spent at one institution and the total number of seasons coaching in college (regardless of level). The average head coach in this sample has been in his current job for just under six seasons. Overall, the coaches in the sample have almost ten years of experience as a head coach at the collegiate level. The standard deviation, minimum, and maximum values indicate significant variation in experience across coaches. Even though the average coach has almost six years of experience in his current position, there is also significant turnover in the coaching ranks in this sample. Coaches in their first year at a university account for almost 15 percent of the observations.

A look at the Big Ten conference provides a better sense of how Division I head coaching experience explains salary differences between coaches (see Chart 6.2).

There is a wide disparity in experience among Big Ten coaches. Wisconsin's Bret Bielema, age forty-one, has less than half the experience of college football's oldest coach Joe Paterno, who at the age of eighty-four

---

* Previous studies such as Chressanthis and Grimes (1993), Murphy and Trandel (1994), and McEvoy (2005) indicate that there is a statistically significant relationship between athletic team success and increased enrollment.

[†] According to Federal Graduation Success Rate measures (GSR), 64 percent of Division I football players who entered school in 2003 graduated from college within a four-year period (the GSR for the overall student population from those same schools was 63 percent).

---

CHART 6.2 DIVISION I COACHING EXPERIENCE AND SALARY

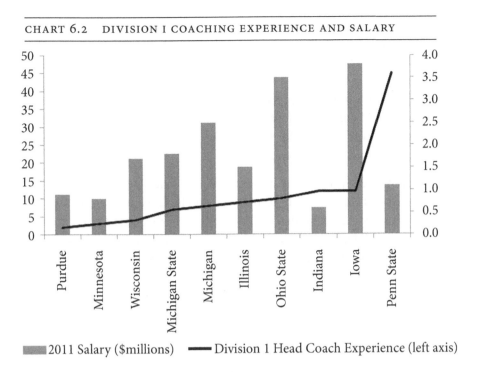

▬▬ 2011 Salary ($millions)  ▬▬ Division 1 Head Coach Experience (left axis)

will be coaching his forty-fifth season at Penn State. In Coach Paterno's case, despite his experience, his salary is among the lowest in the Big Ten. Indiana's Bill Lynch and Iowa's Kirk Ferentz both have twelve years of head coaching experience. Lynch's head coaching experience includes eight years at Ball State and four years at Indiana. All of Ferentz's Division I experience has been at Iowa. Despite having similar years of experience at the Division I level—Ferentz's winning percentage at Iowa is 54.5 percent while Lynch's record reflects a combined winning percentage of 40.3 percent at Ball State and Indiana—Ferentz's annual salary is six times that of Lynch. While the MRP model suggests that age and head coaching experience should play a role in determining MRP, we see in this sample that age and experience are not particularly useful for explaining observed variation in Big Ten football coaches' salaries.

## "I'M GLAD WE'RE NOT GOING TO THE GATOR BOWL."

—LOU HOLTZ, ON OPPOSING FANS THROWING
ORANGES AT HIS ARKANSAS TEAM
AT THE ORANGE BOWL.

Lou Holtz's comments may have been appropriate at the time, but those sentiments do not resonate as much when it comes time to pay a coach for success in the regular season. Access to the very lucrative Bowl Championship Series (BCS) bowl games in particular can generate significant revenues for a football program. Fifty-four percent of the observations from Table 6.1 come from football programs playing in automatically qualifying (AQ conferences) for the BCS, and 46 percent come from teams playing in non-AQ conferences.*

Nevertheless, postseason appearances have a negligible effect on MRP, because bowl eligibility is becoming less and less meaningful as the number of bowl games expands. In 2006, the NCAA introduced a rule change that would allow bowls to consider teams with a 6-6 record whereas previously teams had to demonstrate a greater than 50 percent winning record during the regular season. The NCAA also allows one victory per season over Division I-FCS opponents as part of the minimum six-win threshold. With these rule changes, teams can become bowl eligible simply by defeating five FBS opponents during the regular season. In response to the apparent shortage of available bowl opportunities, two new bowls, the TicketCity Bowl in Dallas, Texas, and the New Era Pinstripe Bowl in New York City were added in 2010, raising the number of bowl games to thirty-five matchups. In the 2010 season, seventy out of 120 Division I-FBS (58 percent of all Division I-FBS teams) played in a bowl game.

## ALUMNI RELATIONS

A coach's fund-raising prowess is another factor that arguably may affect a coach's MRP. As discussed in the Knight Commission survey, a large number of university presidents felt that they were unable to con-

---

* AQ conferences include the Atlantic Coast Conference (ACC), Big 12 Conference (Big 12), Big East Conference (Big East), Big Ten Conference (Big Ten), Pacific-10 Conference (PAC 10), and the Southeastern Conference (SEC). Although Notre Dame is not affiliated with an AQ conference, should it meet certain eligibility criteria, it too is eligible as an automatic qualifier to the Bowl Championship Series. Non-AQ conferences include Conference USA, the Mid-American Conference (MAC), Mountain West Conference (MWC), Sun Belt Conference, and the Western Athletic Conference (WAC). Independent teams, Army and Navy, are not affiliated with a conference and are considered non-AQ schools.

trol football and basketball coaches' salaries because of the significant donations from boosters attributable to these coaches. Without high profile football and basketball programs, and in some cases their high profile coaches, many boosters and donors might not give the money to the athletic department or university. Universities tend to believe that a coach who can draw interest to a program by increasing donations or attracting other revenue should be rewarded. Many stipulations can be found in the contracts of head football coaches that require or encourage the head coach to foster stronger relationships with donors (country club memberships, booster club appearances, etc.), in the hopes of attracting more donations to the athletic department.

Despite the emphasis on increasing alumni contributions, evidence supporting the benefit of cozy relationships between coaches and alumni boosters is rather thin. According to the Congressional Budget Office (CBO) in a report entitled, "Research on Certain Benefits of Intercollegiate Sports," the CBO notes that research on the relationship between athletics and donations has used a variety of measures of athletic success and has come to conflicting conclusions. One study, for example, found that winning percentages in the major sports did not have a significant effect on donations.[7] A larger study reached a similar conclusion regarding winning records, but the authors did document a positive relationship between giving and appearances in championship games.[8] Using a panel data set of 320 institutions, a third study (co-written by one of this article's authors) concluded that postseason success in football and basketball leads to increased gifts restricted for the use of the athletic department for some schools, but no increase in unrestricted giving to the university.[9] Another study, using detailed data from a single large university, found little relationship between teams' general success and donations, but found a significant increase in donations for some alumni when a sport in which they had participated was successful.[10] Overall, those studies seem to indicate that postseason success may slightly increase restricted donations to the athletic department by particular alumni, but that the effect on total giving to the university is likely to be small.

As we see from the above discussion, neither winning, experience, bowl appearances, nor alumni contributions attributed to a football program's success can adequately account for a coach's MRP, and cannot fully explain observed variations in earnings.

## SALARIES AND ATTENDANCE

Attendance is another factor to consider when determining the MRP of a coach. While wins are certainly nice, filling the stadium on game day may be more important, as more fans attending games usually results in more revenue generated for the football team and the athletic department. Teams in this sample average 290,000 fans per season. On a per home game basis, teams average 44,216 fans.

If a football coach has drawing power, attracting more fans increases MRP. Attracting more fans to games is clearly rewarded by some athletic departments. For example, the contract of Missouri head football coach Gary Pinkel shows that he receives compensation at different levels for the number of season tickets sold, as well as the average attendance per game in each season. For Pinkel, if there are forty thousand season ticket holders for football home games during a season, he is entitled to $125,000. For forty-five thousand season tickets holders the number increases to $150,000 in compensation. A final clause indicates he can also collect $150,000 if average attendance is sixty thousand or more in a season (Pinkel can collect only one of these attendance benefits).*

So just how important is attendance as a factor when it comes to determining a coaches salary and MRP (and is Missouri actually undervaluing the contribution of attendance in Pinkel's contract)?

## COACHING SALARIES AREN'T ABOUT WINNING

Having examined the negligible impact of age, coaching experience, fundraising ability, and bowl appearances in determining a coach's salary or MRP, we focus our analysis on success and attendance. In the following analysis, we only examine the strength of the relationship between success and salaries and attendance and salaries (not conditional measures of association or the causal relationship between success and compensation).† In order

---

* Details from Pinkel's contract, available at http://www.usatoday.com/sports/college/football/2010-coaches-contracts-database.htm.

† Remember correlation does not imply causation. A and B might be related somehow and the degree of that relationship may vary, but such an association does not necessarily imply that A causes B or that B causes A.

to assess the strength of the relationship between salaries, success, and attendance, we calculate correlation coefficients among these variables. Correlation coefficients measure the strength of association between variables and take on values between -1 (perfect negative correlation) and 1 (perfect positive correlation). For example, since high temperature and sales of ice cream cones are positively related, the correlation coefficient between the temperature and the number of ice cream cones sold at an ice cream shop would be a positive number near one; if one additional cone were sold for each increase in temperature of one degree, the correlation would be 1. The closer the coefficient is to 1 (or -1), the stronger the positive (or negative) relationship between two variables.

We can measure success for a single season or over multiple seasons. We look at the win/loss record for three different intervals: the current season, the previous season, and over the previous four seasons. In terms of attendance, we examine the attendance in the current season. Table 6.4 contains the correlation coefficients for the four variables.

Notice on Table 6.4 that all of the on-field success variables (i.e. winning percentage in the current season, winning percentage in the previous season, and winning percentage in the previous four seasons) have correlation coefficients between 0.41 and 0.56. These figures indicate a moderately strong positive relationship between success and salary. Similarly, a head coach's record over the previous four season has a slightly higher correlation with a coach's salary than a coach's performance over the most recent and current season. What stands out in this analysis is the relatively strong positive relationship between salary and average home game attendance (represented by a coefficient of 0.79).

The University of Michigan's recent performance provides an interesting example of the discussion above (see Table 6.5). In 2010, the final year of former head football coach Rich Rodriguez's three year tenure, the University of Michigan suffered its third straight disappointing season finishing 3-5 in the Big Ten, and 7-6 overall. Rodriguez's 2010 record came after two straight losing seasons. In the 2008-09 season, Rodriguez's first season, his team finished 3-9, resulting in Michigan's first losing season in forty-one years. Rodriguez's team finished the following season with another losing record of 5-7 marking the first time the school had endured back-to-back losing seasons since 1962–63 and 1963–64.

TABLE 6.4    CORRELATION COEFFICIENTS

|  | Average Salary | Attendance | Current Win % | Previous Win % | Previous 4 Win % |
|---|---|---|---|---|---|
| Coach's Salary | 1.00 | | | | |
| Average Attendance Per Game | 0.79 | 1.00 | | | |
| Team Winning Percentage, Current Season | 0.41 | 0.46 | 1.00 | | |
| Team Winning Percentage, Previous Season | 0.46 | 0.46 | 0.55 | 1.00 | |
| Team Win Pct: Previous 4 Seasons | 0.56 | 0.57 | 0.55 | 0.76 | 1.00 |

Michigan Stadium's official seating capacity is 109,901 which makes it the largest stadium in the United States. Over Rodriguez's three subpar seasons, Michigan Stadium sold out virtually every game. What is interesting about Rodriguez's case is that despite the team's poor performance, the crowds came anyway.

Rich Rodriguez's contract entitled him to an annual salary of over $2.5 million, making him the twelfth highest paid coach among Division I-FBS head coaches despite his 15-22 record over three years (40.5 percent winning percentage). In examining the attendance data, it appears that the only financial setback Michigan might have faced during Rodriguez's tenure was the program's inability to generate additional revenues from appearing in significant bowl games. Those revenues would have been marginal at best, as Big Ten schools share bowl revenues with other conference members in any case. This example demonstrates that Michigan, in spite of Rodriguez's woeful record, faced almost no financial harm during Rodriguez's tenure. So long as attendance remained high, the school and the football program were virtually shielded from any financial damage related to the football team's performance.

Similarly, despite leading Boise State to two BCS championship bowl appearances in five years and guiding his team to a remarkable 61-5 overall record (92.4 percent winning percentage) over that period, the Broncos' head coach, Chris Peterson, receives an annual salary of $1,489,053 (about

TABLE 6.5   UNIVERSITY OF MICHIGAN PERFORMANCE AND
            STADIUM CAPACITY

|  | *2008-09* | *2009-10* | *2010-11* |
|---|---|---|---|
| Team Record | 3-9 | 5-7 | 7-6 |
| Number of Home Games | 7 | 8 | 7 |
| Total Attendance | 759,997 | 871,464 | 782,776 |
| Average Attendance per Game | 108,571 | 108,933 | 111,825 |
| Capacity Utilization | 98.8% | 99.3% | 102.0% |

60 percent of Rodriguez's salary). Stadium size offers an explanation for Peterson's and Rodriguez's salary differential. Peterson's teams play in Bronco Stadium, which hold 33,500 fans, while Rodriguez's teams play in a stadium which holds more than three times that number. This comparison also underscores that when it comes to explaining coaches' salaries, winning might not be everything, but outputs such as revenues generated from home attendance are more useful in explaining a coach's MRP.

Attendance also reflects factors that influence MRP. The nation's largest football programs, for example, are predominantly affiliated with the nation's most prestigious football conferences. These conferences generate significant revenues from selling broadcasting rights to television networks regardless of the performances of the conferences' teams. Whether or not a university's football team in a prestigious conference finishes the season 12-0 or 0-12, it will still generate the same revenue from television contracts. For example, in 2009, the SEC signed a fifteen-year television contract with ESPN valued at $2.25 billion, which is in addition to an $825 million contract the SEC signed with CBS earlier in the same year (these contracts include the rights to televise primarily football and men's basketball games). Here we see once again that factors other than winning contribute to determining a coach's salary.

This analysis of head coach salaries suggests that their salaries depend on MRP, consistent with the predictions of economic theory. Observed variation in NCAA football coaches salaries can be explained by observed variation in factors related to MRP. The salaries earned by college football coaches, to some extent, reflect the ability of the coaches and the value that society places on the products of their labor. While on-field success is an important factor to consider when evaluating coaching salaries, a school's structural advantages that come from having a large committed fan base (which generate consistently high attendance figures), and belonging to a major conference (particularly a conference which has attractive agreements with major television networks) may actually be more important in understanding coaching salary variations.

## CONCLUSIONS

Although negative public sentiment about high salaries earned by college football coaches exists, a number of factors need to be considered when assessing these salaries. First, as we have seen, the salaries earned by football coaches depend on MRP, which in turn reflects, to some extent, their ability and the value that certain constituents place on the output of college football teams.

Second, Division I-FBS head football coaches possess a relatively rare skill set. A football coach could be compared to a leader of a company who is both the chief executive officer and the chairman of the board of directors.[11] They must be able to run a relatively large operation that involves significant logistical complexity and planning. Coaches must manage specialized employees and convince talented seventeen- and eighteen-year-old high school students to commit to play football for a period of three to five years. Head football coaches must provide long-term strategic guidance for the football program, devise game plans, scout opponents, coach their players, mentor their assistant coaches and graduate assistants, make sure that their players meet academic eligibility standards and stay out of legal trouble, deal with intense media coverage, maintain a close relationship with donors, alumni and fans, interact with the university administration, and be the articulate, friendly, passionate public "face of the football program." This is a multifaceted job requiring mastery of a large number of skills and extremely long work hours. Relatively few individuals possess the ability, drive, and energy to be a successful Division I-FBS football coach. The earnings of workers are determined by MRP and by market forces, summarized by the demand for NCAA Division I-FBS head football programs and by the supply of individuals with the ability to perform the job effectively. Demand grows with the number of Division I-FBS programs, as well as with growth in other job opportunities for college football coaches, primarily in the NFL, which have both increased over time. Increasing demand places upward pressure on the salaries of all coaches. The supply of individuals with the requisite skills and ability is quite limited, which also places upward pressure on salaries. The twin forces of increasing demand and a limited supply of potential coaches act in concert to push salaries above marginal revenue product.

Analogies comparing coaches to CEOs should not be pushed too far. In 2010, JPMorgan Chase CEO Jamie Dimon received a total compensation package worth $20.8 million, which included salary, bonuses, other compensation, and stock and option awards.[12] In 2010, JPMorgan Chase generated $104.8 billion in revenues.[13] Dimon's salary represented 0.02 percent of JPMorgan Chase's overall revenue. In 2007-08, the Texas Longhorns generated $72.95 million in revenues, more than any other team in college football.[14] Prior to the 2007–08 season (based on the most recent data available), Texas Longhorns' head coach Mack Brown's contract paid him over $2.8 million (Brown's contract has since increased by 79 percent to over $5.1 million).[15] Brown's contract at the time represented 3.8 percent of the Longhorns' overall 2007–08 revenue. On a relative basis, Brown's MRP at Texas would be considered 190 times higher than Dimon's MRP at JPMorgan Chase. This comparison suggests that some coaches receive a disproportionate share of revenues relative to CEO's of public companies.

Third, as we discussed above, universities and college football programs are not profit-maximizing firms. There are no stockholders or owners eager to see the maximum return possible on their financial investment. This lack of a clear "residual claimant"—the owner of a firm in profit-maximizing businesses—to the net revenues generated by a college football program greatly reduces the incentives for the people who set Division I-FBS football coaches' salaries. Unconstrained by the same pressures of owners of profit maximizing firms, the athletic director, university president, and university board of trustees are more likely to pay "whatever it takes," to retain a coach's services.

Fourth, a component of a head football coach's salary comes from outside the university, which allows a football coach to be paid well beyond the budgeting constraints of a university. In the Knight Commission survey, many university presidents reported that they were often unable to control the salaries of football coaches because large portions are paid through private funding, by booster organizations and other similar groups.

So are Division I-FBS head football coaches overpaid? Again, their salaries reflect their MRP, which depends on their ability and the value that sports fans place on the results of their work. Their salaries also reflect the fact that relatively few individuals possess the skills, ability, and drive to be a successful Division I-FBS head football coach. Many Division I-FBS head football coaches earn more than the governor of their state. Does that make the football coach overpaid? Anyone who meets the age and residence requirement with enough money and name recognition can be elected governor of a state, including former professional wrestlers, action movie actors/weightlifters, and individuals with surprisingly bad haircuts. The supply of individuals qualified to run a US state probably exceeds the supply of individuals qualified to run a Division I-FBS football program by a wide margin.

Are football coaches overpaid compared to teachers, firefighters, or any other socially important occupation that critics of college football harp on? The supply of teachers, firefighters, and other professions far exceeds the supply of Division I-FBS football coaches, so even if the MRP of workers in these jobs exceeded the MRP of college football coaches, economic theory tells us that workers in the professions with the most limited supply of potential employees receive higher pay.

One important institutional factor in college football suggests that coaches may be overpaid. Unlike professional sports, intercollegiate athletes are not paid a salary; instead, they receive scholarships (full or partial), room and board, textbooks, and a small stipend referred to as "laundry money." Collectively, this compensation is called a "grant in aid." College athletes are not paid, but many who participate in revenue generating sports like football clearly help produce revenue that goes to the NCAA, the athletic department and the university. Economists refer to the money earned by NCAA student-athletes as "rents." In this sense, rent refers to the difference between the MRP generated by student-athletes and the value of the grant in aid that players receives from the athletic department for their services.

In a paper published in 1993, economist Robert Brown estimated the amount of rent generated by premium college football players.[16] In this paper, Brown projected that a premium college football player with the skills to be drafted into the NFL generated over $500,000 in annual revenues for his college team. Based on data from 1988, that is roughly equivalent to $921,000 in 2010 dollars. The estimated salary derived from such revenues would be consistent with the salaries earned by many professional football players, who, according to economic theory, should receive a salary equal to their MRP, absent factors like salary caps. This means that a premier college football player who plays for four years while in college could generate almost $4 million in revenue for his school. Other research finds similar rents generated by premium male and female basketball players.

Brown's study suggests that premium college football players are exploited, in that they generate revenues for the football program and university far in excess of the value of the grant in aid they receive as compensation for their services. Where do the rents generated by premium college football players go? Some finance the operation of nonrevenue sports; others support the extensive, palatial practice facilities common on college campuses. And some of the rents generated by premium college football players finance the salaries of college football coaches. If college football players were paid more than the current grant-in-aid, then athletic departments would have less money to pay college football coaches. The result would be that college coaches would likely be paid less.

# UNDERSTANDING THE COLLEGE-TO-NFL TRANSITION

*The (Cautionary) Tale of Mike Williams*

BY WARREN K. ZOLA

The author is the assistant dean for graduate programs in the Carroll School of Management at Boston College. He has been a dean at Boston College since 2002, where he serves as the chief operating officer responsible for providing strategic direction and integration of non-academic and operational functions for the graduate management programs. He is responsible for the development and implementation of long-term strategic and tactical plans for the graduate programs, including the financial operational management of all budgets and the management of a twenty-four person team.

In addition to his administrative duties, Mr. Zola is an adjunct faculty member in both the Business Law and Operations & Strategic Management departments at the Carroll School, where he developed and teaches two courses—

Essentials of Sports Law and Business of Sports. He has served as an expert reviewer of several textbooks in both the areas of sports law and sports management. He most recently served as a panelist at the annual meeting of the Association of American Law Schools discussing "American Needle v. NFL and the Single Entity Defense: A New Frontier for Sports and Antitrust Law." In addition, he has served as a frequent expert panelist and/or lecturer on these topics at a variety of colleges and universities including Harvard Law School, Boston College Law School, Southwestern Law School, Suffolk Law School, and Tulane Law School among others.

Mr. Zola was appointed by university President Father William P. Leahy as the inaugural chair of the University's Professional Sports Counseling Panel in 2005, but has served informally in that capacity for over a decade. During that time, he has worked with student-athletes that have had the opportunity to pursue a career in professional athletics—with a particular emphasis on assisting the football, men's and women's basketball, baseball, men's soccer, and men's ice hockey teams. He has counseled over three dozen current professional athletes in a variety of sports. In this role, he often serves as the university's primary liaison with professional sports leagues and their players' associations.

Mr. Zola received his bachelor of arts with honors in economics from Hobart & William Smith College in 1989, where he was also a varsity student-athlete; a JD degree from Tulane University in 1992, where he founded the Sports Law Society; and a master's in Business Administration with concentrations in Finance and Strategic Management in 1995 from Boston College. He is a member of the Massachusetts Bar, and is currently a member of the advisory board of Athlete Advisory Services, British School of Boston, and Tulane Sports Law Program. Zola lives in Dedham with his wife, Amy, and daughter, Gabrielle.

Mr. Zola's publications include *"Going Pro in Something Other than Sports: Improving Guidance for Student-Athletes in a Complicated Legal and Regulatory Framework."* He is a frequent contributing writer to *The Sports Law Blog* (http://sports-law.blogspot.com/), honored by *Fast Company* as one of three best sports business blogs and by the *American Bar Association Journal* as a Top 100 Law Blog. Zola is also a contributing writer to the *Huffington Post*.

---

In 2003, Mike Williams, a sophomore wide receiver, caught ninety-five passes for 1,314 yards and sixteen touchdowns for the BCS Champion USC Trojans.* He averaged 101.1 receiving yards and 7.3 receptions per game. Williams also threw two passes for thirty-eight yards (including one touchdown) and even blocked a field goal. He was honored as a First Team All-American, First Team Pac-10 selection, 2003 Biletnikoff Award finalist (awarded to the nation's top receiver), and finished eighth in the Heisman Trophy voting. *CBSSportsline .com* recognized him as the National College Football Player of the Year.

As a freshman and as a sophomore, Williams played in all twenty-six of USC's games. Williams' sophomore campaign followed a stellar freshman season in which Williams broke several USC and Pac-10 freshman receiving records—eighty-one receptions, 1,265 receiving yards and fourteen touchdowns. After his first year, he was named to the First Team All-American Freshman team by a number of news services. Williams was by almost all measures one of the brightest young stars on the college football landscape.

As far as Mike Williams must have been concerned, playing professional football was not just a dream, but for all practical purposes, a foregone conclusion. Having more than proven his football abilities in two stellar years as a collegian, he was ready to move on. The only obstacle blocking Williams' path to the professional ranks was a rule, adopted by the NFL in 1990, which requires all prospects to wait at least three years after graduating from high school, to become eligible to enter the NFL draft.†

---

\* LSU and USC "split" the national title that year. Both USC and LSU finished the season with 11-1 records. BCS #3 USC defeated BCS #4 Michigan 28-14 in the Rose Bowl. BCS #2 LSU defeated BCS #1 Oklahoma 21-14 in the Sugar Bowl. USC was ranked #1 by the Associated Press. LSU was ranked #1 in the BCS standings.

† "A player may only apply for eligibility in the NFL draft three years after his graduation from high school or graduation of the class with which he entered high school, whichever is earlier. If a player chooses to enter the draft after only three NFL regular seasons have begun and ended following his high school graduation or graduation of the class with which he entered, he must apply for *early eligibility*, i.e., 'opt in.'" NFL Collective Bargaining Agreement.

The rationale for the NFL's age restriction rule seems mainly a pragmatic one. The NFL determined that players coming out of high school, no matter how physically mature, require several more years of physical, emotional, and mental development before they are able to participate in the more demanding world of professional football.

The NFL's age restriction requirements also serve a practical purpose. College football provides an environment where the laws of natural selection ultimately determine which players are able to demonstrate the skills and talent required to play in the NFL. Every year the NFL holds a seven-round entry draft, whereby thirty-two teams select just 224 players, for which Division I-FBS football provides a candidate pool of 10,200 athletes.*,† Assuming half of these athletes are eligible juniors and seniors, approximately four percent of eligible Division I-FBS players will be drafted in any given year.‡ These draft day realities are in contrast to the expectations of many incoming freshman. A recent survey of incoming student-athletes found that 44 percent of incoming African-American college football players and 20 percent of non-African American players expected to become professional athletes.[1] After three years in a college football system, the reality of being able to achieve those dreams is by then hopefully more than apparent to the vast majority of college football players.

It is easy to understand why Mike Williams might have believed that the NFL's eligibility restrictions, while perhaps suitable for most athletes, did not apply to his circumstances. As a sophomore, Williams had already received virtually every college football accolade imaginable. Based on his achievements during his freshman and sophomore years, he very reasonably might have believed that he had nothing left to prove in college. He also very reasonably might have believed that the NFL's age minimum requirements were anachronistic considering the tremendous professional success of younger athletes and the minimum age requirements observed

---

* With supplemental picks provided under NFL free agency rules this number changes slightly every year.

† There are 120 Division I-FBS schools each of which may carry 85 players. The 10,200 estimate reflects the product of these two figures.

‡ This estimate is somewhat generous. Division I-FBS candidate also compete for draft spots with Division I-FCS candidates as well as Division II, Division III and NAIA candidates. Players from these lower divisions are historically even less likely to be drafted than Division I-FBS candidates.

in other sports. Professional baseball and hockey players, for example, are eligible to be drafted directly out of high school. Three time Grand Slam winner Maria Sharapova turned pro at the age of fourteen, and nine months later became the youngest girl ever to reach the final of the Australian Open junior championship. In 1978, the fledgling World Hockey Association signed Wayne Gretzky as a seventeen-year-old.[*] The following season, the NHL recognized Gretzky, in his first year with the Edmonton Oilers, as the league's most valuable player at the age of eighteen. Most sports allow players to be drafted or signed directly out of high school. The International Federation of Association Football (FIFA), the world governing body for soccer, does not impose any minimum age requirements on its players or clubs (see Table 7.1).

Like the NFL, the NBA also has a minimum age requirement, although the NBA's position on this subject has shifted over the years. Prior to 1971, NBA bylaws had long provided that "no person was eligible to be drafted until four years after he had graduated or four years after his original high school class had graduated." Spencer Haywood, an All-American basketball player, challenged this rule in 1971, claiming it violated the Sherman Antitrust Act (Haywood v. The Denver Rockets, 325 F.Supp. 1049 (C.D. Ca. 1971).[†,2]

Haywood was a junior college All-American during the 1967–68 season. In 1968, he led the U.S. Olympic Basketball team to a gold medal. As a sophomore he played for the University of Detroit, where he was again recognized as an All-American after averaging 32.1 points per game and leading the NCAA with 21.5 rebounds per contest. In 1969, he left school early to sign with the Denver Rockets of the now defunct American Basketball Association where he played for just one season. In 1970, as his contemporaries were about to embark on their final year of playing college basketball, Haywood signed a contract to play for the NBA's Seattle Supersonics. The NBA commissioner disallowed the contract because Haywood was still not four years removed from his high school graduation as stipulated in NBA bylaws.

Litigation ensued after which the United States District Court ruled in favor of Haywood. The court found that NBA teams conspired not to deal

---

[*] The World Hockey Association folded one year later in 1979.

[†] The term "Antitrust" refers to anti-competitive practices.

TABLE 7.1    MINIMUM AGE REQUIREMENTS BY SELECTED
            PROFESSIONAL SPORTS LEAGUES

| Pro Sports League | Minimum Age Requirements | Waiver Option |
|---|---|---|
| National Basketball Association | Nineteen years old and a minimum of one year removed from high school graduation. Adopted in 2006. | No |
| National Football League | Minimum of three years removed from high school graduation. Adopted in 1990. | No |
| National Hockey League | For North American males, minimum of 18 years old by September 15 in the year in which they are drafted<br><br>For non-North American males, minimum age of 20 | Yes |
| Major League Baseball | No age minimum.<br><br>To be eligible for the MLB draft, players from the US, Canada, US Territories, and Puerto Rico must be at least 18 years old<br><br>International players may not be signed before the age of 16. | Yes |
| Women's Tennis Assoc. (WTA)* | Minimum age is 14. Annual appearances are limited for players between the ages of 14-18. | No |
| Assoc. of Tennis Professionals (ATP)† | Minimum age is 14. Annual appearances are limited for players between the ages of 14-18. | No |
| FIFA (soccer) | No age minimum | NA |

* The WTA is the governing body that presides over the women's professional tennis tour.

† The ATP is the governing body that presides over the men's professional tennis tour.

with players whose high school classes were not four years beyond graduation. According to the federal district court, this concerted refusal to deal constituted a group boycott in violation of the Sherman Antitrust Act.

The NBA appealed the US District Court ruling; however, the US Supreme Court upheld the District Court's decision and ruled against the NBA in a 7-2 decision.*

In response to the Supreme Court's ruling, the NBA began allowing underclassmen to be drafted as long as they could demonstrate financial "hardship." While a number of college underclassmen applied for the draft under the hardship exception, over the next twenty-four years, NBA teams would only draft two players directly from high school on such basis— Darryl Dawkins (drafted in 1975), the fifth overall pick by the Philadelphia 76ers, and Bill Willoughby (also drafted in 1975), the nineteenth overall pick by the Atlanta Hawks.† After Dawkins and Willoughby were drafted, not a single NBA team drafted a player directly from high school for another twenty years.‡ That practice changed in 1995 when the Minnesota Timberwolves selected Kevin Garnett, a high school phenomenon, with the fifth overall pick. The Charlotte Hornets followed suit in 1996 by selecting Kobe Bryant with the thirteenth overall pick (and immediately traded his rights to the Los Angeles Lakers). The same year the Portland Trail Blazers selected Jermaine O'Neal with the seventeenth overall pick. In 2001, the Washington Wizards' selection of Kwame Brown marked the

---

* The very first NBA player to be recruited directly out of high school was Reggie Harding, who was drafted by the Detroit Pistons in the fourth round in 1962. He did not begin playing until 1963. Harding's basketball career and life was marred by substance abuse and prison. Harding was shot and killed in 1972 on a Detroit street corner.

† Dawkins would go on to become one of the NBA's most popular players. After retiring from playing professional basketball, he coached in various semi-professional leagues and is the current coach of the Lehigh Carbon Community College Cougars. Dawkins remains involved with the NBA participating in promotional activities. Willoughby later graduated from Fairleigh Dickinson University in 2001. The NBA fully paid all of his college expenses. Willoughby is now a special adviser for the NBA where he counsels high school and college players who are considering early entry into the NBA.

‡ Lloyd Daniels and Shawn Kemp never played college basketball, although Daniels was enrolled at UNLV and Kemp first enrolled at the University of Kentucky before later transferring to Trinity Valley Community College in Texas.

first time that a high school player would be chosen as the draft's number one overall pick.* From 1995 to 2005, thirty-nine players were drafted directly out of high school.

In response to this relatively sudden influx of high school players, the NBA changed its minimum eligibility rules in 2006, which now required incoming players to be nineteen years old and at least one year removed from high school graduation.† NBA President Joel Litvin argued in a letter to Congress that the purpose of the minimum age requirement was to promote the league's business interests by "increasing the chances that incoming players will have the requisite ability, experience, maturity and life skills" to perform at a high level.[3]

Not surprisingly, some NBA players disagreed with the ruling. NBA forward Jermaine O'Neal, citing recent achievements of NBA players who did not play in college, argued that "in the last two or three years, the [NBA] rookie of the year has been a high school player. There were seven high school players in the [NBA] All-Star Game, so why [are] we even talking [about] an age limit?"[4] O'Neal further added, "As a black guy, you kind of think [race is] the reason why it's coming up. You don't hear about it in baseball or hockey. To say you have to be twenty, twenty-one to get in the league, it's unconstitutional. If I can go to the US Army and fight the war at eighteen why can't [I] play [professional] basketball for forty-eight minutes?"

Former University of Michigan Wolverines and current San Diego State head basketball coach Steve Fisher was also highly critical of the minimum age requirement. "I don't think it's American," he said. "I'm shocked that some way, somehow, somebody hasn't said, 'How can we do that?' If we had one senator's son who fell in that category, that would be the end of it."[5] Fischer added, "My head differs from my heart. If you said a kid had to remain in college for two years, it would benefit [college basketball]. But

---

* Kwame Brown has since been followed by LeBron James (2003, Cleveland Cavaliers) and Dwight Howard (2004, Orlando Magic), who were also overall number one selections in the NBA draft.

† The agreement states that in order to be eligible for the NBA draft, a player must be one year removed from the graduation of his high school class and must turn nineteen years of age during the calendar year of the draft. Foreign players must only meet the requirement that they turn nineteen during the year of the draft "NBA Collective Bargaining Agreement Ratified and Signed," *NBA.com*, July 30, 2005.

if I'm a dad, if I'm a parent of a sensational basketball player, I'm saying, 'Who's the best attorney I can get to file a lawsuit?'"

The senator (or in this case representative) to whom Coach Fisher may have been referring was Rep. Steve Cohen of Tennessee who, during a congressional hearing about the NBA's revised collective bargaining agreement, similarly argued that players should have "economic freedom."*

The debate about the transition from college football to professional football is not a particularly new one. In the 1920s, the NFL was overshadowed by the more popular (and more respectable) NCAA. In these early days of the NFL, NCAA traditionalists argued, "Players who turned professional disgraced the sport, one that should remain an amateur bastion... College coaches fretted the NFL would draw spectators away from Saturday games."[6] In 1924, the tension between the two sports erupted when Howard Edward "Red" Grange announced that he would be leaving the University of Illinois after his senior season to sign with the NFL's Chicago Bears for a then unheard of salary of $100,000 at a time when other professional football players were earning less than $100 per game.[7] Grange left the University of Illinois before completing his degree and joined the Bears for the final two games of the 1924–25 season. "Grange's decision touched off a national debate...by abandoning his studies for a blatantly commercial career, he openly flaunted the myth of the college athlete as a gentleman-amateur who played merely for the fun of the game and the glory of his school. Grange himself put it more succinctly, 'I'd have been more popular with the colleges if I had joined Capone's mob in Chicago rather than the Bears.'"[8] In the wake of public criticism, the NFL passed a rule known then as the "Grange Rule," which prohibited NFL teams from "signing players before their college class graduated."

NFL owners resolved at the time that the league "places itself on record as unalterably opposed to any encroachment upon college football and in preserving the amateur standing of all college athletes...it is the unanimous decision of this meeting that every member of the National Football

---

* An outstanding article, "Legality of Age Restrictions in the NBA and the NFL," by Michael McCann and Joseph Rosen addresses this issue in further detail and is available at http://papers.ssrn.com/sol3/papers.cfm?abstract_id=881710.

League be positively prohibited from enducing [sic] or attempting to induce any college player to engage in professional football until his class at college shall have graduated, and any member violating this rule shall be fined not less than One Thousand Dollars, or loss of its franchise, or both."[9]

Over the next sixty-six years, the NFL observed the Grange Rule virtually to the letter, allowing just two exceptional cases over that period.

The first exception came in 1964, when the NFL granted Andy Livingston hardship status, which allowed him to be drafted directly into the NFL by the Chicago Bears. Although Livingston attended Phoenix Junior College, he had never actually graduated from high school. At the age of twenty years and fifty-three days, Livingston became the youngest player in NFL history to score a touchdown (a record that stands to this day). Livingston played for six years before retiring from the NFL in 1970.[10]

Clarence Reece's signing with the Houston Oilers in 1975 marked the only other instance in which the NFL allowed an exception to the Grange Rule. Reece, a wide receiver for the USC Trojans, withdrew from USC after his sophomore season in 1974 and signed with the Canadian Football League. He spent one season in Canada before signing a three-year deal with the NFL's Houston Oilers in 1975. Then NFL commissioner Pete Rozelle initially disallowed the contract because Reece had not yet completed his minimum college eligibility requirements. Reece filed suit against the NFL, and Rozelle eventually allowed Reece's contract to stand.

In 1990, in response to Barry Sanders' 1989 petition to enter the NFL draft following his junior year, and as part of its revised collective bargaining agreement with the NFL Players' Association, the NFL reduced it minimum age requirement. Instead of requiring prospective players to complete their college eligibility prior to being allowed entry into the NFL, the revised standard required that players would now be eligible for the draft three years after graduating from high school.

Since that time, according to the NFL Players' Association, the draft outcomes for early entrants have been somewhat mixed. From 1990 to 2010, nearly 30 percent of the 808 underclassmen declaring for the draft were not selected.[11] Among the 578 early entrants who were drafted, about sixty percent were drafted after the first round.[12] The average draft guarantees for first-round draft picks in 2006 was $10,267,000 (a sum that includes base salary and signing, roster and option bonuses). These guarantees dropped nearly six-fold to $1,683,000 for second-round draft picks, and fell even further to $643,000 for third-round draft picks.[13]

The NFL's early entry rule stood unchallenged until 2003 when Maurice Clarett filed suit to enter the NFL draft following his freshman season at Ohio State.

As the *USA Today's* 2002 high school football player of the year, Clarett was arguably the most distinguished high school football player in the country.[14] That year, Clarett accepted a scholarship to play for Ohio State University. In his first season at Ohio State, Clarett rushed for 1,237 yards, scored eighteen touchdowns, and helped lead the Buckeyes to a 14-0 record and the 2002–03 BCS National Championship.[15] Clarett even scored the go-ahead touchdown against the Miami Hurricanes in the championship game.

Later that year, Ohio State suspended Clarett for filing a false police report in which he claimed that more than $10,000 in valuables had been stolen from a car he borrowed from a local dealership. After conducting an internal investigation into the matter, Ohio State's athletic director stated that Clarett had accepted thousands of dollars of inappropriate benefits and misled investigators.* In spite of his suspension from athletics, Ohio State still allowed Clarett to retain his scholarship. Clarett opted to leave school altogether.

As a freshman one year removed from high football, Clarett was nowhere close to meeting the NFL's minimum eligibility requirements. Nevertheless, Clarett was determined to enter the NFL draft in April 2004 —two years, rather than three years, after his high school graduation. To that end, on September 23, 2003, Clarett sued the NFL in federal district court arguing that the league's minimum age restrictions constituted a "restraint of trade" under federal antitrust laws.

Clarett's side argued that "had Clarett been eligible for the 2003 draft, it is almost certain he would have been selected in the beginning of the first

---

* On January 14, 2004, Clarett eventually pleaded guilty to misdemeanor charge for failing to aid a law enforcement officer, a lesser charge than lying on a police report. Clarett was fined $100 and was not required to serve any jail time. The misdemeanor charge would not appear on his criminal record.

round and would have agreed to a contract and signing bonus worth millions of dollars," according to the lawsuit.*,[16,]

In public statements, the NFL responded by saying that it would contest any challenge to the minimum age rule.[17]"We do not believe that this lawsuit serves the best interests of Maurice Clarett or college football players generally, but we look forward to explaining to the court both the very sound reasons underlying our eligibility rule and the legal impediments to the claim that was filed."

In her preliminary ruling, federal district court judge Shira Scheindlin agreed with Clarett's side and ruled on February 5, 2004, that the NFL's rule that barred underclassmen from entering their draft was illegal. "One can scarcely think of a more blatantly anticompetitive policy than one that excludes certain competitors from the market altogether," she wrote.[18] As a result of the court's ruling, Clarett was free to apply for the 2004 draft.[19] The NFL responded to the decision by appealing the federal district court's initial ruling.

On February 24, 2004, three weeks after the federal district court's ruling, Mike Williams declared himself eligible for the NFL draft in spite of the continued uncertainty surrounding the outcome of Clarett's case. In a press statement following William's announcement, former Trojans head football coach Pete Carroll noted, "We gave Mike all the information we could to help him make this decision. We believe he might be missing out on a tremendous financial opportunity by not staying another year, but he wants to go play in the NFL now. He knows all the ends of this decision."[20]

In making his announcement, Williams also acknowledged that he had been thoroughly advised on his decision, "To get right to it, it was a very, very difficult decision. I used all my resources, both at the university and my family, plus some outside resources to come to this decision. I realize there are a lot of pluses and minuses to this decision. I realize it's

---

* Because of the federal appeals court's ruling, Clarett was eligible to participate in the NFL's 2005 draft at the earliest. That year he was selected in the third round (#101 overall) by the Denver Broncos. Clarett did not play in a single preseason game and was released by the Broncos on August 28, 2005, just one month removed from signing his contract. No other team expressed interest in signing Clarett. He would never play in a single NFL exhibition or regular season game.

a decision that you can argue either way. I received a lot of valuable input from so many people. But it ultimately came down to me making my own decision and doing what's best for me. This was not a decision based on money. Playing in the NFL has always been a dream of mine. The opportunity is there now to pursue that dream."[21]

Williams went on to say, "I received calls from a number of guys, mostly Trojans. Guys like Carson Palmer and Tony Boselli. I heard so many things this past week. I think Coach Carroll was the biggest influence, though. He told me, 'If you are going to do this, you need to go all out now.' That's what it came down to. It didn't come down to money. It came down to Coach Carroll telling me that whether I went or stayed, I would have to work harder than I ever had before. That was probably the most important thing I was told throughout the whole process."[22]

Williams further added, "Football is not like basketball or baseball. An injury can be detrimental to a career. Not that the injury factor was the main reason, but there are no guarantees in life. I have a chance to fulfill a life's dream. I didn't break the rule [regarding the NFL draft]; I just took advantage of it."[23]

When asked if he was aware of the ramifications should the courts reverse the initial Clarett decision, Williams acknowledged that he was aware of the risks, "That was definitely something that had to be considered. It made the decision difficult. But either way, I was going to make a decision to affect the rest of my life. If it turned out bad, I would have to take it on as a man. Wherever it takes me, it's my decision. I have no choice but to live with it."[24]

Over the past ninety years, only one other university has had as much experience sending college players to the NFL as has the USC football program. According to the athletic department's Web site, over the football program's history, "USC has produced 464 NFL draft picks—second to Notre Dame's 466—along with twenty-eight by the AFL before it merged with the NFL and 437 players who since 1920 played in the NFL (or its sister leagues, the AFL or All-America Football Conference)."[25] At the start of the 2010 season, fifty-four ex-Trojan football players represented USC across twenty-six different NFL teams. A 2010 ESPN.com survey ranked USC as "the most fertile NFL draft pipeline" from 1979 to 2009.[26] In 2009,

ESPN's NFL draft analyst and former NFL head coach Herm Edwards enthused, "If you want to play pro football and you're a young high school athlete, you know going to USC is going to give you the best opportunity system-wise and competitive-wise on the field. That's what USC brings to the table. That's why historically, year after year, you see all these players coming into the league."[27]

USC offers its student-athletes access to its Professional Sports Counseling Panel (PSCP), which it describes as an organization that "provides practical information, learning opportunities, and services to student-athletes interested in pursuing a professional athletic career upon leaving the university. Workshops, resource people, and materials are available to assist student-athletes and their families to be informed and responsible decision makers as they explore or pursue professional athletic opportunities and prepare for life as a professional athlete."[28] Members of the PSCP program are mainly well-respected members of the USC academic community who are appointed by the university president.

On February 3, 2004, three days after Williams made his NFL intentions public, the *Los Angeles Times* reported that Williams hired an agent, Mike Azzarelli, from Williams' home town of Tampa Bay, Florida.[29] Shortly thereafter, Williams signed separate promotional agreements with various trading card companies reportedly worth $175,000 to $200,000, and an endorsement deal with athletic apparel company Nike, reported to be worth $100,000 per year.* Furthermore, Williams withdrew from classes in the spring semester of his of his sophomore year to focus his attention on preparing for the NFL's supplemental draft.[30] While Clarett's case was under appeal and because Williams' announcement came after the January 15 early entrance deadline, the NFL determined that Williams would not be eligible to participate in the 2004 NFL draft. In the event that the federal appeals court upheld the Clarett decision, both Williams and Clarett would be eligible to participate in the August 2004 supplemental draft.

---

* These agreements were described by Steve Rosner, a partner in 16W Marketing, who was retained by Azzarelli to handle Williams' marketing endeavors; Darren Rovell, "Williams' Marketing Deals Now in Limbo," *ESPN.com*, April 20, 2004; accessed March 11, 2011.

On May 24, 2004, three months after Williams' officially declared his intent to play in the NFL, the Second US Court of Appeals formally and unanimously ruled against Clarett overturning the federal district judge's initial ruling. In its ruling the appeals court was critical of Clarett's argument:*

> Clarett…stresses that the eligibility rules are arbitrary and that requiring him to wait another football season has nothing to do with whether he is in fact qualified for professional play. But Clarett is in this respect no different from the typical worker who is confident that he or she has the skills to fill a job vacancy but does not possess the qualifications or meet the requisite criteria that have been set. In the context of this collective bargaining relationship, the NFL and its players union can agree that an employee will not be hired or considered for employment for nearly any reason whatsoever so long as they do not violate federal laws such as those prohibiting unfair labor practices or discrimination.

Because of the court of appeal's ruling, Mike Williams would not be allowed to participate in the 2004 supplemental draft and would have to wait another year to be eligible for the 2005 NFL draft.

Williams now found himself in the unenviable position of not only being barred from entering the NFL for another year, but also being ineligible to return to USC for his junior season. According to Trojan spokesperson Tim Tessalone, "At the time he made his decision, he was acting under the law of the land. In this new era of the NCAA looking out for the good of the student-athlete, we hope they'll allow him to return to school."[31,†] Williams' agent, Mike Azzarelli, blamed Williams' predicament on the NFL.[32] "By virtue of what the NFL told him and got him to do, he's violated every major [NCAA] rule there is. So some people are talking about, 'Gee, if they forgive all of those sins you can tee it back up.' You're academically ineligible, you've been out of school, you've signed with an agent, money—everything."

---

* Maurice Clarett versus National Football League. United States Court of Appeals for the Second Circuit. Argued April 19, 2004.

† Tessalone's comments are a bit hyperbolic. Clarrett's case was under appeal at the time Williams declared for the draft, and could hardly have been considered established law at the time.

TABLE 7.2    SUMMARY TIMELINE OF KEY DATES

**September 23, 2003**

Maurice Clarett sues NFL to gain early entry into the NFL draft

**February 5, 2004**

Federal District Judge allows Clarett to make himself eligible for the NFL Draft

**February 27, 2004**

*Los Angeles Times* reports that Williams has hired Mike Azzarelli as his agent.

**August 24, 2004**

NCAA denies Williams' request to reinstate NCAA eligibility

**January 15, 2004**

Early Entry Deadline for NFL Draft. NFL determines that Clarett and Williams are eligible for supplemental draft, subject to the outcome of Clarett's case.

**February 24, 2004**

Mike Williams declares his intent to enter into the NFL draft.

**May 24, 2004**

Second US Court of Appeals rules against Clarett, overruling the Federal District Court.

SEPTEMBER, 2003

AUGUST, 2004

Following the Clarett ruling, Williams severed ties with his agent, re-portedly returned monies he had received from Azzarelli, and re-enrolled in summer classes at USC. Citing the unique circumstances of his case, Williams filed an appeal with the NCAA seeking to restore his college foot-ball eligibility.[33]

On August 24, 2004, the NCAA formally denied Williams' request to rejoin the Trojan football team. The NCAA explained in a press release that, "due to the uniqueness of the case and the complexity of issues, follow up was required in order to provide Mike Williams with a fair and thoughtful analysis…There were two obstacles facing Mike for eligibility: one related to academics and one related to amateurism, and sports agents in particular. Either one was sufficient to prohibit participation in compe-tition. In this case, neither obstacle could be cleared."

With that ruling, Mike Williams would never play college football again.

---

## THE ROLE OF THE NCAA

College athletics has evolved considerably in the past century as have the rules governing them. During the fall of 1905, three college players died as a result of game-related injuries. President Theodore Roosevelt was so concerned about the game's increasing violence, that he convened a series of meetings at the White House where he urged the presidents of Harvard, Princeton, and Yale to address growing violence and other issues.* The In-tercollegiate Athletic Association of the United States (IAAUS) was borne out of these discussions on March 31, 1906, and in 1910 was renamed the National Collegiate Athletic Association (NCAA).[34]

The NCAA serves as the governing body for intercollegiate athletics and, as such, determines under what rules student-athletes are able to

---

* There appears to be some dispute among historians about President Roosevelt's motivation for seeking reforms to the game. Some argue that Roosevelt was a respond-ing to a public health concern. Others argue that Roosevelt was motivated by personal concern over a broken nose suffered by his son who was playing football as a freshman at Harvard. Still others note that Roosevelt was concerned that the game might be ir-reparably changed or even abolished by the sport's more ardent critics.

participate in college football. Unlike other major domestic professional sports leagues, there is no established minor league for professional football; playing in college is virtually the only path for a career in the NFL and, thus, the NCAA becomes a necessary door through which hopeful professional football players must pass.

## Eligibility

The NCAA has comprehensive rules regarding student-athletes eligibility. Over fifty pages in the NCAA manual are dedicated to eligibility regulations for student-athletes.

Athletic departments are responsible for ensuring that their institution complies with all of the NCAA rules and regulations as detailed in the 453-page *NCAA Division I Manual*.[35] This charge is usually given to the Office of Compliance within an athletic department.

Once a student-athlete enrolls in college, he or she must maintain minimum eligibility standards. The NCAA requires student-athletes to demonstrate that they are enrolled on a full-time basis; pass a minimum of six credits each semester and eighteen credits each academic year; declare an academic major by the start of their junior year; meet a school's minimum GPA requirements; and remain in "good academic standing"—a standard that varies by academic institution.[36]

When applying the NCAA's minimum academic eligibility requirements to the Williams' case, for example, it is clear that Williams' decision to withdraw from school during the spring semester of his sophomore year was in breach of those requirements, specifically because he failed to pass at least six credit hours during the spring semester.* Williams' subsequent re-enrollment in summer school was ultimately deemed an insufficient step by the NCAA. To maintain his academic eligibility, Williams would have had to remain continuously enrolled at USC.

---

* In order to be eligible at the start of the third year, the NCAA requires players to pass six credits the previous term (summer term excluded), pass 18 credits during the previous academic year (fall and spring), declare a major, while maintaining a minimum GPA. NCAA Bylaw 14.4.3. 2003–04 NCAA Division I Manual. August 1, 2010 (effective August 1, 2003).

## Amateurism

The NCAA has long defined itself as the protector of amateurism. While the NCAA bylaws do not specifically define the term "amateur," the bylaws state that there must be a "clear line of demarcation between college athletics and professional sports."[37] These rules also extend to the player's family and anyone else who may hold themselves out as representatives of the individual. Failure to follow these rules can end a career before a player's football skills can be developed and evaluated.

The NCAA defines a professional athlete as "one who receives any kind of payment, directly or indirectly, for athletics participation except as permitted by the [NCAA]."*,[38]

NCAA bylaws list several activities that would cause the loss of a student-athlete's amateurism, including:

- accepting a promise of pay prior to completing collegiate eligibility
- signing a contract to play professional athletics
- receiving any kind of financial assistance from a professional sports organization without NCAA permission
- competing on any professional athletics team
- entering into a professional draft
- entering into an agreement with an agent[39]

The definition of "pay" per NCAA bylaws is also quite broad, encompassing all the various benefits a student-athlete might receive because of his or her athletic skill.[40]

When the NFL determined that Mike Williams was not eligible to participate in the 2004 supplemental draft, Azzarelli, was critical of what he characterized as the NFL's duplicitous treatment of Williams claiming that the NFL had misled Williams by virtually "inviting" him into the league. Azzarelli's comments might have been interpreted by some as nothing more than sour grapes, but Azzarelli's criticisms seem to have some merit

---

\* The situation often occurs when European players come to play college basketball in the United States. The NCAA ruled Enes Kanter ineligible to participate in NCAA Division I men's basketball after he agreed to play for the Kentucky Wildcats due to concerns about his amateur status. http://www.cbssports.com/collegebasketball / story/14522271/ncaa-rules-kentuckys-kanter-ineligible-for-second-time/rss, accessed March 12, 2011;Division I Manual, Supra note 8, Bylaw 12.1.2.

at least with respect to the NFL Players' Association's (NFLPA) actions. Prior to signing with the trading card companies, the NFLPA allowed Williams to sign its Group Licensing Agreement (GLA), which pools the rights of the players so that their names and images can be used in conjunction with NFL products such as trading cards and video games.[41] Once Williams signed the GLA, he was able to begin signing endorsement deals with trading card companies and others.

Gene Upshaw, then head of the NFLPA, defended his organization's actions by noting, "When the courts said [Williams] was eligible for the draft, we had an obligation to treat him like any other player who was coming into the league. We had to treat him like any other rookie."[42]

Unlike the NFL Players' Association, which may have acted hastily—after all Williams did not participate in the 2004 NFL draft, and his entry status was still subject to an appeal—the NCAA was under no obligation to recognize the ambiguity of Williams' circumstances.

When Mike Williams signed with an agent, he clearly violated the NCAA's amateurism bylaws. When Mike Williams accepted funds from his agent, even though he later reportedly returned those funds, he clearly violated the NCAA amateurism bylaws. When Mike Williams agreed to accept payment from the likes of Nike and the trading card companies, even though those agreements were contingent on Williams making an NFL roster, he clearly violated the NCAA amateurism bylaws.

## ROLE OF AGENTS

Sports agents, particularly experienced agents with strong prior track records, offer a number of valuable services. Agents provide future NFL players with legal and commercial advice and personal guidance. The NFL Players' Association requires all agents to become registered and certified. NFL clubs will only deal with agents certified by the NFL Players' Association of which there are over eight hundred active agents on its roster.

The NFLPA caps the commissions for an agent at 3 percent of a player's post-tax net income, and while this is negotiable, it is fairly standard. Additionally an agent will offer marketing and/or endorsement assistance.

The agent's key role is to help clients negotiate and manage their NFL employment contracts. Agents may also offer services in a number of other areas, which include financial planning, community service, charitable endeavors, tax advice, media relations, legal matters, and estate planning. The compensation percentages for these services vary greatly and are not governed as of yet by the NFLPA.[43, 44] Each athlete must ultimately determine the right level of service and support he is seeking when selecting the appropriate agent.

Agents also assist athletes to train and prepare for the NFL's annual scouting combine, which is regarded by many participants as "the biggest job interview of their lives." Agents often pay ten to twenty thousand dollars in training and preparation expenses on behalf of the players they represent, including expenses for many candidates who ultimately go undrafted.

A potential first-round pick may have several dozen agents and/or firms offering their services. Potential middle round picks will also receive dozens of inquiries. Someone who may be on the bubble of being drafted or fall under the "priority free agent" category may receive only a few inquiries, while some student-athletes may actually need to convince an agent to represent them.

Many of the agents an athlete will consider are competent and trustworthy. Becoming a professional athlete can be an overwhelming process, and agents are able to provide sound counsel and advice. Because competition to represent players is fierce, players must also be wary of less than scrupulous agents. Players are advised to do their homework and research agents' track records, speak to players represented by those agents, and seek advice from their coaches and their school's athletic departments.

Typically, each college football program will determine a period, before, during, or after the season, in which it allows student-athletes to conduct agent interviews. Each school and football program may have their own rules that govern when and how student-athletes may meet and interview with potential agents. Some schools allow student-athletes to interview and speak with agents at any time. Others seek to restrict access during the football season. Some schools will formally host "agent days." While other schools will retain outside consultants to help student-athletes navigate the NFL entry process.

Contrary to popular belief, the NCAA does not restrict contact between student-athletes and agents, and there are no provisions in the NCAA's regulations that prohibit direct discussions at any point during a student-athlete's career. The NCAA and member institutions have no direct regulatory power over agents. Agents are instead regulated by the players' associations of various professional sports leagues.*Additionally, both state and federal laws help to regulate agent conduct.[†] Ultimately, the onus falls upon the client for selecting appropriate representation.[45] This decision, while difficult and filled with potential pitfalls, is the responsibility of the student-athlete. A student-athlete's duty is to use the resources available to determine his or her unique needs and to determine which potential agent is the best match.

Most players will want to sign with an agent as soon as their collegiate eligibility has expired. While the NCAA rules prohibit a student-athlete from indicating that he or she will sign with a particular agent while the player still has remaining eligibility, in practice, a player will "invite" the agent to the team's last game, and then sign with the agent immediately after the game when his or her eligibility has formally expired.

To many people inside and outside the world of sports, agents are considered a leading cause of problems relating to eligibility and amateurism violations. Agent misconduct is well documented, litigated, and remains problematic. Nevertheless, agents play a critical role during the NFL transition process and beyond. In spite of the impression offered by lurid headlines, most agents adhere to legal and regulatory guidelines and place the interests of their clients first.

A student-athlete loses his amateur status once he or she agrees, either orally or in writing, to accept representation from an agent or similar party

---

* Only the NFLPA makes its Agent Regulations publicly available on its Web site, www.nflplayers.com. Other regulations can be viewed by members of the Sports Lawyers Association at www.sportslaw.org, or by directly contacting certain professional sports associations.

† The Federal Law is the Sports Agent Responsibility and Trust Act (SPARTA), 15 U.S.C.A. § 7801 (2004). Some states have their own legislation but 39 states have passed some form of the Uniform Athlete Agents Act. See Uniform Athlete Agents Act (UAAA) History and Status at www.ncaa.org > Legislation and Governance > Eligibility and Recruiting > Agents and Amateurism > UAAA; accessed May 4, 2010.

prior to completing his or her final intercollegiate contest. This rule also applies to contingency agreements (i.e. agreements which are "not effective" until after an athlete finishes his final game). In 2009, Andre Smith, an All-American offensive lineman for the Alabama Crimson Tide, ran afoul of this NCAA regulation. As a result, the NCAA declared Smith ineligible to participate in his team's bowl game because he entered into an agreement with an agent before the game rather than afterward.[46]

Players also will lose their amateur status if they receive benefits of any kind (expenses, gifts, meals, transportation) from any agent or financial adviser. In another recent case, the NCAA declared three North Carolina Tar Heels players permanently ineligible for receiving improper benefits from a potential agent.[47]

In 2010, following these well publicized incidents and a few others, the NCAA formed an Amateurism Cabinet to look into ways that student-athletes could properly engage with agents without forfeiting their eligibility.[48]

## NCAA SUPPORT PROGRAMS

[Editor's Note: Some of the material in this section has been taken from a prior article co-written by Glenn Wong, Warren K. Zola, and Chris Deubert, entitled *"Going Pro in ~~Something Other than~~ Sports: Improving Guidance for Student-Athletes in a Complicated Legal and Regulatory Framework,"* which was published in the winter of 2011 in the *Cardozo Arts & Entertainment Law Journal.*][49]

In 1984, the NCAA allowed universities to establish Professional Sports Counseling Panels (PSCPs) to help educate future prospects about the transition process into the professional sports ranks.[50] This legislation "was intended to encourage member institutions to provide guidance to their student-athletes regarding future professional athletics careers."[51]

PSCPs consist of at least three panel members, only one of which may be a member of the athletics department. Sports agents or individuals affiliated with sports agents may not serve on these panels. [52,53]

PSCPs are permitted to advise student-athletes about a future professional career; help them with purchasing disability insurance, review professional contracts, meet with prospective agents and representatives of prospective professional teams; assist players secure professional tryouts; aid in the agent selection process; and help prospective professional athletes determine their market value.[54]

Colleges and universities were expected to embrace PSCPs and take advantage of this opportunity to assist student-athletes. In practice, however, the majority of Division I-FBS colleges and universities do not place significance on PSCP programs due to competing priorities, lack of demand, limited resources, and lack of appropriate expertise. Even among those that do, some panel members lack the specific expertise needed to be truly helpful to athletes.[55]

In the absence of organized PSCP programs, guidance to student-athletes is offered haphazardly across many schools. Players will seek advice from their coaches who may have limited experience with the NFL transition process. Some schools will invite NFL or NFLPA representatives to speak to athletes. More recently, a variety of specialized private consulting firms have emerged, which schools hire to provide individual counseling to transitioning players. Other players rely on the experience of alumni who are either current or former NFL players.

## THE NFL AND THE NFLPA

The NFL and the NFLPA recognize the importance of educating transitioning athletes. The NFLPA travels across the country hosting seminars entitled "Pipeline to the Pros," which provides an overview of the NFL transition process. The NFLPA also uses these forums to emphasize the importance of education and obtaining a degree. The NFL has recently developed a road show designed to educate potential players. The scope of the NFL and NFLPA presentations is generally limited to providing an overview about the transition process, but the programs are not substitutes to well-planned PSCPs.

After meeting the NFL's minimum age requirements, transitioning athletes who are considering early entry may also request a formal evaluation from the NFL's College Advisory Committee about their potential draft prospects without jeopardizing their NCAA eligibility. The committee consists of general managers, personnel directors, and various NFL scouts. Candidates are required to apply for an evaluation from the College Advisory Committee between the end of the regular football season and early January. The committee will then provide an NFL hopeful with a confidential assessment of his professional prospects and project the round in which the player is most likely to be selected.[56] The committee's evaluation is non-binding and certainly does not guarantee that the player will be selected in a specific round. Nevertheless, the assessment provides a potential early entry candidate with an informed view about his likely draft position.*

Early entry candidates must declare for the NFL draft typically by January 15. However, within seventy-two hours of this date, a student-athlete may formally remove himself from the draft and declare his intention to resume his college career so long as he has not signed with an agent or violated other regulations related to maintaining his amateur status.[57]

For some college football players there may be circumstances whereby an individual might be better off leaving early to enter the NFL. However, unless the individual is clearly a top prospect, there should be a genuine bias toward returning to school. NFL players who graduate from college tend to have longer playing careers and earn more than early entrants.† A college degree has tremendous value and passing it up should occur only in rare circumstances.

In Williams' case, because he had not yet met the three-year eligibility requirement, he was not able to benefit from the NFL's draft advisory service. Once Williams had given up his eligibility, he might have had informal discussions about his likely draft selection with team representatives, but it is difficult to imagine that these discussions amounted to the "invitation" described by Azzarelli given the contentious circumstances of Clarett's appeal at the time.

---

* For some good background on this committee refer to http://www.nationalfootballpost.com/Inside-the-NFL-College-Advisory-Committee.html, accessed on March 12, 2011.

† As reported by the NFLPA in its 2010 "Pipeline to the Pros" presentation.

## RISK OF INJURY

Risk of injury and the subsequent harm such injury may have on a player's future professional prospects is often cited as a reason why prominent student-athletes should leave school early. Indeed, Williams himself noted risk of injury as one of many reasons to forego his junior season.

To ease Williams' and others' concerns, the NCAA created the Exceptional Student-Athlete Disability Insurance (ESDI) program.* This program allows potential professional athletes to take out insurance policies against possible injury while in college.[58] The program, offered for the first time by the NCAA in 1990 for football and men's basketball, has subsequently been expanded to include men's ice hockey, baseball, and women's basketball.[59]

Student-athletes who have demonstrated that they have the potential to be selected in the first three rounds of the NFL or NHL draft, or the first round of the NBA, MLB, or Women's National Basketball Association (WNBA) drafts are eligible for the program.[60] The policy provides the student-athlete with a lump sum payment in the event that he or she suffers from permanent total disability while in college.[61] Student-athletes are eligible for loans to pay the premiums without jeopardizing their amateur status.[62]

The NCAA's ESDI program, administered through HCC Specialty Underwriters Company, caps coverage at $5 million for projected first-round NFL and NBA draft picks.[63] Coverage for baseball, men's ice hockey, and women's basketball is capped at $1.5 million, $1.2 million, and $250,000, respectively.[64] The annual premiums cost between $10,000 and $12,000 for each $1 million of coverage, which is a few thousand dollars cheaper than a private policy.[65] Reportedly, some eighty to one hundred athletes

---

* For more information on the ESDI program, see www.ncaa.org > About the NCAA > Budget and Finances > Insurance, accessed May 5, 2010, [hereinafter NCAA ESDI Program] and DI Manual supra n. 17 at Bylaw 16.11.1.4. Also see Glenn M. Wong and Chris Deubert, "The Legal and Business Aspects of Disability Insurance Policies in Professional and College Sports, 17 VIII." *Sports & Ent.* L.J. 473 (Spring 2010).

participate in the ESDI program each year, and approximately 75 to 80 percent of those participants are college football players.[66]

## WHAT SHOULD WILLIAMS HAVE DONE?

Although certain elements of Mike Williams' story are unique, his case in many ways illustrates common issues that college football players must navigate when transitioning to the professional ranks. All student-athletes must follow NCAA eligibility and amateurism guidelines.

Williams made a fundamental miscalculation when he declared for the NFL draft. He and presumably some of his closest advisers anticipated that the federal court's initial decision in favor of Maurice Clarett would be upheld on appeal. Given the uncertainty of the outcome, Williams' decision was a high-risk gamble, which ultimately did not pay off. While Williams' bet cost him a shot at participating in the NFL's 2004 season, his decision to declare for the draft did not also require him to forfeit his NCAA eligibility.

Williams' key mistakes were to hire an agent, drop out of class, and accept money for endorsements. Having committed these errors, Williams denied himself a chance to resume play in the NCAA. Williams very easily could have explored his NFL options while remaining enrolled at USC. He needed only to pass a minimum of six credit hours in the spring term. Williams could have waited to hire an agent. Also, he could have waited to sign endorsement deals and the like until after the Clarett appeal had been resolved.

USC officials do not seem to have misadvised Williams. His comments and the comments of USC officials indicate that Williams' decisions were carefully considered. USC officials indicated sympathy with Williams' circumstances at various times—first, when he declared for the NFL draft, then when the NFL denied Williams' petition to participate in the supplemental draft, and once again after the NCAA denied his reinstatement—but sympathy should not be confused with failing to provide adequate advice. USC appears to have done everything in its power to assist Williams prior to his early declaration and after his early entry prospects had been denied.

Williams and his agents might have received indications from NFL scouts and other draft services about his potential draft position, but such conversations would have been at best highly speculative, especially considering that Williams was not invited to attend the NFL Combine or participate in other types of formal evaluation workouts.

The NFL Player Association's decision to allow Williams to sign its General License Agreement appears questionable in hindsight. While Upshaw notes that the NFL Players' Association was acting in accordance with the law—however temporary—when it allowed Williams to sign the agreement, Williams had not yet been drafted, had not been signed as a free agent, and was in no other way contractually bound to any NFL team. The NFL disallowed Williams' participation in the NFL draft pending the outcome of Clarett's appeal. The NFL Players' Association should have exercised similar restraint.

While Williams' may arguably have felt misled by the NFL Players' Association, the NCAA was not required to recognize the actions of the NFL Players' Association when applying its own bylaws. Williams clearly breached NCAA rules governing amateurism and eligibility in spite of the extenuating circumstances he claimed. USC officials would later protest that the NCAA's investigation into the Williams affair took too long, and was unfair to both Williams and to the USC football program. The NCAA denied USC's charges pointing out that it needed time to gather all available facts before making its final determination on Williams' eligibility.

## WILLIAMS' ROAD BACK

The season following Williams' NCAA eligibility saga, the Trojans went undefeated to claim yet another National Championship following the 2004-05 season. As for Williams, he would go on to become the tenth overall pick in the 2005 draft signing with the Detroit Lions. One and a half years later, the Lions would trade him to the Oakland Raiders which released him after he played in just six games. The following season, Williams signed with the Tennessee Titans where he was cut again after playing two games in which he did not catch a single pass. Williams sat out the entire 2008–09 and 2009–10 seasons over which period not one NFL team signed him. In 2010, he rejoined his former college coach, Pete Carroll, who had recently become the head coach of the Seattle Seahawks, where Williams recorded the best performance of his NFL career so far—sixty-five receptions in fourteen games for 751 total yards and two touchdowns. In January 2011, Williams and the Seahawks agreed to a three-year contract extension. As Williams' winding road since leaving college indicates, even the most stellar college football career is no guarantee of future NFL success. Future early entry candidates are urged to proceed wisely.

CHAPTER **8** CHAPTER

# THE NO-HUDDLE OFFENSE

*A Championship Formula*

## BY G. MARK MCELROY

Mark McElroy, EdD, is the head football coach for the Saddleback College Gauchos in Mission Viejo, California. Since arriving at Saddleback, Mark has accumulated an 84-28 record over a ten-year period, advancing to bowl games in each of those seasons (2001–10). He was named the Region IV coach-of-the-year in 2004 and 2006, and has had eight former players advance to the NFL. Ninety-three of his players have transferred into Division I-FBS and FCS programs and over two hundred players have transferred to four-year institutions during his tenure.

Coach McElroy is a graduate of California State University—Chico, where he received his bachelor's degree in physical education in 1982. He completed two master's degrees, one in leadership and human behavior from the United States International University in San Diego, California, and another in physical education from Azusa Pacific University. He earned a doctorate in physical education from Brigham Young University in 1990.

In addition to his coaching duties, Coach McElroy loves to teach and is very active in physical education. He wrote the curriculum for the surfing program at Saddleback and also coached the Saddleback Surf Team to the National Scholastic Surfing Association State Championships in 2002. He has served as a professor in physical education at the graduate level at Azusa Pacific University for over twelve years.

Coach McElroy was vice president of Boys' and Men's' Athletics for the California Association for Health Physical Education Recreation & Dance from 2000 and 2001. He authored a book titled *Coaching the No-Huddle Offense*, produced six instructional videos for football, has presented at numerous clinics over the past fifteen years, and wrote the initiative to change the high school tiebreaker system in California in 1997. He believes strongly in teaching character to his athletes and helping them to become not only better football players, but also better people.

———————

The 2011 BCS Championship game featured two undefeated teams each representing the season's highest rated college football teams.

The Oregon Ducks finished the season with the number one ranked offense in all of football, tallying 6,899 yards of total offense over thirteen games during which the Ducks averaged 530 yards per game.* Oregon generated 286 rushing yards (ranked fourth nationally) and 244 passing yards per game; averaged 6.74 yards per play and scored forty-seven points per contest, making it the top scoring offense among Division I-FBS teams. Statistically speaking, the Auburn Tigers' offensive output closely mirrored Oregon's performance. The Tigers accumulated 6,989 yards over their fourteen-game season by gaining 499 yards per contest, making it the sev-

———————

* Ranking is based on Total Offense, and recorded by the NCAA.

enth best offense in the country.*,† Like Oregon, Auburn was effective running the ball. The Tigers averaged 285 yards per game (one yard shy of Oregon's performance), and generated 214 passing yards per game, averaging an astonishing 7.37 yards per play. Like Oregon, Auburn's offense was also able to score in bunches posting 41.2 points per game (good for seventh overall among Division I-FBS teams).

That two of the best offenses in the country ended up meeting in the national championship game should not be particularly surprising, except that—at least during the BCS era—it rarely happens. The game marked just the second time since 1998 that two top ten offenses had met in a national championship game.‡ What actually makes Auburn's and Oregon's national championship game unique is that it marked the first time that two teams with no-huddle offenses had met in a BCS national championship game.§

This accomplishment did not occur in isolation, and it is not the product of random events. The no-huddle offense has become a significant part of the college football landscape over the past twenty-five years. In 2010, seven of the top ten offensive teams, as measured by total offense, employed a no-huddle system as part of their attack. The combined record of those teams was 82-13 (86.3 percent winning percentage).

Auburn's and Oregon's success merely marked a coming out party for an offensive philosophy, which started at the fringe of the sport and has now become a prominent feature of dominant offenses throughout the country. The no-huddle offense has also gained prominence in the NFL where teams such as the Atlanta Falcons, Cincinnati Bengals, New England Patriots, Indianapolis Colts, and Pittsburgh Steelers have embraced the no-huddle system as part of their offensive attack.

---

\* Ranking is based on Total Offense, and recorded by the NCAA.

† Auburn played fourteen games while Oregon played in thirteen contests. Auburn's fourteen game season includes the SEC Championship game. Oregon's conference, the Pac-10, does not have a conference championship game, but will sponsor an inaugural conference championship game in 2011 following the additions of Colorado and Utah to the newly named Pac-12 conference.

‡ The other instance came in 2005 when Texas and its third ranked offense (as measured by Total Offense) defeated USC and its first ranked offense.

§ In this chapter, an offense that employs the no-huddle system as a key component of its overall offensive attack is considered to be a "no-huddle" offense.

The preoccupation with whether or not a team is a rushing team or a passing team is becoming an increasingly irrelevant argument. Teams and coaches will execute offenses that best fit their knowledge and talent. The decision to embrace the no-huddle is increasingly differentiating elite offenses from the rest of the pack.

As this chapter will explain, teams that adopt the no-huddle offense become *no-huddle teams*. The no-huddle system not only transforms offenses, but the character of the entire team.

## HISTORY OF THE HUDDLE

In college football's earliest incarnation, teams did not use huddles. Once a play ended, players would return directly to their positions at the line of scrimmage. The quarterback would then yell out signals that would describe the ensuing play.* Quarterbacks would code their signals to confuse the opposition. For example, a quarterback might yell out a series of numbers, but perhaps only the third number would actually mean something.† In those days, there was no coaching from the sidelines. Coaches could not send in plays. If the officials found a coach guilty of actually "coaching," his team would be penalized.‡

Most college football historians credit Paul Hubbard with the invention of the huddle. In 1892, Hubbard played quarterback for Gallaudet University, which also happened to be America's first college for the deaf.⁵ Since Hubbard and the rest of the Gallaudet Bison were deaf, Hubbard had to call plays using sign language. Hubbard realized that opposing teams, especially opposing teams whose players were also deaf, had become adept at intercepting his hand signals. Expressing commands to

---

* Interview with Kent Stephens, historian at the College Football Hall of Fame, April 22, 2011.
† Kent Stephens interview.
‡ Kent Stephens interview.
⁵ Gallaudet University, based in Washington, D.C., is named after Edward Miner Gallaudet, a renowned educator of deaf students.

ten teammates in the heat of physical competition is not something that is best conveyed subtly. Whether expressing those commands verbally or using sign language, play calling requires a certain intensity to ensure that teammates receive and understand the communication. In sign language, that intensity is conveyed by strengthening the execution of the hand signals. Hubbard realized that if his teammates could see the play calls, so too could the opposing team. To remedy this problem, in between plays, Hubbard would organize his teammates in a tightly enclosed circle while their backs were turned to their opponents. In this fashion, he was able to clearly communicate with his teammates without exposing the team's signals to the other side.

Over the next twenty years or so, there were various cases in which the huddle was reportedly utilized. In 1894, two years after Hubbard was credited for forming the first huddle, Alfred E. Bull, a center for the University of Pennsylvania who was reputedly hard of hearing, is said to have asked that his team form a circle around him, because he was unable to hear plays called on the line of scrimmage.* In an 1896 contest against the University of Michigan, Amos Alonzo Stagg had his University of Chicago players form a circle ten yards behind the line of scrimmage because the crowd noise made signal calling too difficult to hear (Staggs' use of the huddle probably helped popularize its usage).†,‡ In 1918, H.W.

---

*Alfred E. Bull was named to the 1895 All-America Team. Bull later served as the head football coach at the University of Iowa (1896), Franklin & Marshall College (1896–1897), Georgetown University (1900), Lafayette College (1903–1907), and Muhlenberg College (1908–1910), compiling a career college football record of 62–34–15. After retiring from coaching, Bull practiced dentistry for thirty years.

† Kent Stephens interview, historian at the College Football Hall of Fame, April 24, 2011.

‡ Amos Alonzo Staggs was the head football coach for Springfield College (1890–1891), the University of Chicago (1892–1932), and the College of the Pacific (1933–1946), where he compiled a career college football record of 314–199–35, including two national titles in 1905 and 1913. He was inducted into the inaugural College Football Hall of Fame class in 1951. Arguably the most prolific innovator in the history of college football, Staggs is credited with inventing the forward pass, center snap, onside kick, Statue of Liberty play, man in motion, line shift, linebacker position, hip pads, lateral pass, and many other innovations.

"Bill" Hargiss, then the head football coach for Oregon Agriculture College (now Oregon State), claimed that he was the pioneer of the huddle:[1]

> While coach of the Oregon Aggies in Corvallis in 1919, I refereed a high school game. For three periods, the game was scoreless. Near the end of the last quarter, the McMinnville team started a drive and carried the ball to their opponents' ten-yard line. All this time the cheering was deafening. The quarterback...unable to make himself heard above the din, pulled off his headgear, threw it on the ground and yelled "Come back here, you guys, and I'll tell you what the play is." . . . This gave me an idea. In the spring of 1920, during the few weeks practice for the next fall [sic], I tried it out at the Aggie school. At first it was awkward, but eventually it became better and I have been using it ever since.

The University of Illinois' legendary head football coach Bob Zuppke was the first coach to use of the huddle on a frequent basis beginning in 1921. He was criticized for slowing down the game at the time, but when Illinois won its first of four national championship titles in 1923, the huddle concept became even more popular. By the end of the 1920's, most college football teams had adopted the huddle.[2] By the time Winston Churchill saw his first football game at Columbia University in 1930, he famously remarked, "Actually, it is somewhat like rugby, but why do you have to have all those committee meetings?"[3]

## THE RISE OF THE NO-HUDDLE OFFENSE

The first "no-huddle" offense is likely to have emerged out of necessity when teams were confronting desperate circumstances. A team faced with a deficit and little time had to improvise and do without a huddle in an effort to save time. On the first play of such a drive, several plays would be called in the initial huddle, until the clock could be stopped with an incompletion, penalty, or a player going out of bounds.

Glenn "Tiger" Ellison is credited for being the first coach to include the no-huddle strategy as a key feature of his offense. Tiger Ellison, then a high school coach from Middletown, Ohio, pioneered the run and shoot offense, which relies heavily on a no-huddle system.[4] In 1963, Ellison was hired as a quarterbacks' coach for the Ohio State Buckeyes by head coach Woody Hayes.

Hayes first allowed Ellison to occasionally run the "Gangster Series" from Ellison's playbook, which was executed out of a no-huddle attack.[5] In this formation, the quarterback, prior to taking the snap, would first look to determine if he could make a quick short throw to one of four different receivers. If those immediate options were not available, and the defensive backs were instead lined up tightly across from the receiver, the initial play call would often develop into longer pass plays in which the wide receiver would try to run past the opposing defensive back.

Rex Kern,* Ohio State's quarterback from 1968-1970, recalls that the Buckeyes "used a predetermined set of plays in the no-huddle. In 1968 against Michigan State, [the Buckeyes] used military code names such as Duffy One, Duffy Two, and so on [representing] three play [sequences which could be] run without using a huddle."[†]

In the second half of a 1968 midseason contest against the number one ranked Purdue Boilermakers, the Buckeyes broke a scoreless halftime tie game by running a no-huddle offense for the entire second half of the contest. Ohio State ultimately prevailed in that game 13-0. Ohio State also ran the no-huddle offense extensively in its 27-16 national championship victory over the USC Trojans in the 1969 Rose Bowl.[‡]

As hard as it might be for many football fans to believe, Woody Hayes, who is much better known for his ultra conservative offenses, was actually

---

* Rex Kern played defensive back for the NFL's Baltimore Colts and Buffalo Bills from 1971 to 1974. He was inducted into the College Football Hall of Fame in 2007. Kern earned his baccalaureate, master's degree, and doctorate of philosophy in Education from Ohio State University.

† Telephone conversation between Rex Kern and Kent Stephens, historian at the College Football Hall of Fame, April 28, 2011.

‡ That game also marked the last of three national championships for Woody Hayes. Hayes would coach another ten years finally retiring in 1978.

one of the first early adopters of the no-huddle system.[*,†] Tiger Ellison's retirement from coaching after that 1968–69 season raises the intriguing possibility that Woody Hayes' legacy might have been different had Ellison remained on board and had Ohio State embraced the run and shoot offensive philosophy more fully. Kern notes that Ellison "had a great influence on Woody (Hayes)."[‡]

Many football historians credit Portland State's former offensive coordinator and head coach Darrel "Mouse" Davis as being the first coach to implement the run and shoot system on a full-time basis.[ⁱ] Davis' teams, then led by SMU's current head football coach June Jones and retired NFL (and two-time Pro Bowl) quarterback Neil Lomax, employed the no-huddle offense as a key feature of its offensive attack. The run and shoot offense was considered by many coaches to be a fringe concept, which might have worked in the lower college football divisions, but was considered too gimmicky to be effective against the faster and more athletic teams in Division 1-A.

The run and shoot offense, along with the full time use of the no-huddle offense, was introduced to Division 1-A football in 1987 when Jack Pardee

---

* The phrase "three yards and a cloud of dust" was used to describe Woody Hayes' offenses. Hayes has also been famously quoted for saying "only three things can happen when you pass and two of them are bad."

† "Would I say Woody was a great football genius? No, Woody was not a great football genius. Woody was not great with the x and o's of innovation. But Woody was a great strategist. And he was a great planner. He was a great preparations person and repetition. And all of those elements put together made Woody a great football coach." Former Ohio State Quarterback Rex Kern as quoted in a 2002 interview for the film "Beyond the Gridiron – The Life and Times of Woody Hayes," accessed April 28, 2011. (http://www.duncanentertainment.com/interview_kern.php)

‡ Telephone conversation between Rex Kern and Kent Stephens, historian at the College Football Hall of Fame, April 28, 2011.

ⁱ Mouse Davis was the offensive coordinator and head coach for Portland State from 1975 to 1980. He is currently the wide receivers coach at the University of Hawaii at Manoa. Davis has also been a head coach with the Denver Gold of the United States Football League (1985), the New York/New Jersey Knights of the World League of American Football (1991–1992), the Detroit Fury (2001–2002), and the San Diego Riptide (2003) of the Arena Football League. He served as Offensive Coordinator for the University of California – Berkeley (1981), CFL's Toronto Argonauts (1982), USFL's Houston Gamblers (1984), NFL's Detroit Lions (1988-1990), and again at Portland State (2007-2008).

became the new head football coach for the Houston Cougars. John Jenkins, who was considered the architect of the school's run and shoot offense, joined Pardee as offensive coordinator. Pardee took over a moribund Houston program that had gone 1-10 the season prior to his arrival. In his first season, Pardee's team finished with a 4-6-1 record. At one point in the 1987 season, the Cougars held a miserable 1-6 record, before finishing the season with three victories and one tie—a late season run which included a wild 60-40 home victory over the Texas Longhorns, and a sign of things to come.

From 1988 to 1990, the Cougars' explosive offense became the most dominant in college football. Over that period, the Cougars won its games by incredible margins—Louisiana Tech (60-0), Tulsa (82- 28), Texas (66-15), UNLV (69-0), Temple (65-7), Baylor (66-10), SMU (95-21), TCU (55-10), Texas (47-9), Rice (64-0)—on the way to a combined 28-6 overall record.

The run and shoot eventually gave way to a West Coast offensive system, which features different combinations of running backs and tight ends. Pardee's and Jenkins' offense, however, demonstrated the potency and effectiveness of the no-huddle approach that remains a prominent feature of today's spread offenses.

June Jones remains the only coach in college football who still runs the run and shoot as Mouse Davis probably intended. The run and shoot allows receivers and quarterbacks to make multiple decisions on any particular play. Coaches who are able to employ the run and shoot have to be comfortable with this more extreme form of offensive fluidity. Few coaches possess this degree of comfort, but because June Jones has a deep understanding of the offense, first as a quarterback under Mouse Davis at Portland State, and later after twenty-seven years as an offensive coordinator and head coach, he is more confident about allowing his players to exercise that kind of freedom on the field.* The spread offenses that are more prevalent today offer fewer decision-making options to players, and can be better controlled by an offensive coordinator.

---

* June Jones has coached in the USFL (Denver Gold, Houston Gamblers), CFL (Ottawa Rough Riders), NFL (Houston Oilers, Detroit Lions, Atlanta Falcons, San Diego Chargers), and in the NCAA (Hawaii, SMU).

Sam Wyche deserves special mention for being the first coach to use the no-huddle system as a standard part of his offense in the NFL. Wyche was the first coach in the NFL, initially as head coach for the Tampa Bay Buccaneers and later with the Cincinnati Bengals, to demonstrate that the no-huddle offense could be used as a weapon when utilized over long stretches during a game. Prior to Wyche, no one else in the NFL used the no-huddle to a similar extent. Most teams used the no-huddle offense as a time saving device. Wyche used the no-huddle in an attempt to gain matchup advantages. By operating out of a no-huddle offense, defenses were unable to replace linebackers with defensive backs in obvious pass situations. If Cincinnati decided to employ a group of running backs on a particular play, defenses were unable to bring in extra linemen in run situations. Some opposing defenses were so overwhelmed by the game's speed they would fake injuries in order to gain a stoppage in play. Some teams today still employ this illegal technique when facing no-huddle offenses.

## ANALYZING THE NO-HUDDLE OFFENSE

"Defense wins championships" is a familiar refrain, and it is certainly true that a good defense is a key component for any successful team. Dating back to the beginning of the BCS championship era in 1998, a typical national champion was more likely to be a team whose defense was statistically better than its offense.

As the data in Table 8.1 shows, in most cases, one could predict the outcome of the national championship game simply by examining which of the two teams had a stronger defense. In nine out of thirteen cases, the teams with top ten defenses won the contest. In contrast, teams with top ten offenses won just three out of thirteen contests.

How then can one explain the rather unchampionship-like defenses of Oregon (ranked thirty-fourth in Total Defense) and Auburn (ranked sixtieth in Total Defense), when so many past national champions had won with top ten defenses? If one relies solely on defensive rankings as an indicator, neither of those defenses appeared to be particularly elite.

To better understand Auburn's and Oregon's defensive performance in 2010, it is important to understand how adopting a no-huddle system

TABLE 8.1    TOTAL OFFENSE AND DEFENSE RANKINGS FOR NATIONAL CHAMPIONSHIP GAME PARTICIPANT (1998-2011)

| | Winners | Losers | Winner's Total Offense Rank | Loser's Total Offense Rank | Winner's Total Defense Rank | Loser's Total Defense Rank |
|---|---|---|---|---|---|---|
| 1998 | Tennessee | Florida State | 32 | 31 | 17 | 1 |
| 1999 | Florida State | Virginia Tech | 12 | 9 | 19 | 3 |
| 2000 | Oklahoma | Florida State | 18 | 1 | 8 | 6 |
| 2001 | Miami | Nebraska | 8 | 12 | 6 | 8 |
| 2002 | Ohio State | Miami | 70 | 6 | 23 | 7 |
| 2003 | LSU | Oklahoma | 31 | 19 | 1 | 3 |
| 2004 | USC | Oklahoma | 12 | 8 | 6 | 13 |
| 2005 | Texas | USC | 3 | 1 | 10 | 48 |
| 2006 | Florida | Ohio State | 19 | 26 | 6 | 12 |
| 2007 | LSU | Ohio State | 26 | 62 | 3 | 1 |
| 2008 | Florida | Oklahoma | 15 | 3 | 9 | 68 |
| 2009 | Alabama | Texas | 42 | 29 | 2 | 3 |
| 2010 | Auburn | Oregon | 7 | 1 | 60 | 34 |
| | **AVERAGE RANKING** | | **22.8** | **15.3** | **12.2** | **17.2** |

impacts not just the offense, but the defense as well. One of the benefits of using a no-huddle attack is that a team has the opportunity to run more plays during a game since they are using less time in between plays. Instead of jogging back to the huddle after a play is over, no-huddle teams will line up in a formation and either snap the ball quickly or freeze the defense to catch the defense off guard. Opposing defenses have less time to substitute players or lineup, which can lead to either a mismatch or a blown coverage for an offense.

Table 8.2 compares the allocation of time between a conventional offense and a no-huddle offense.* Assuming a conventional offense holds the ball for thirty minutes in a sixty-minute game, and utilizes each second

---

* This is a theoretical construct. Actual time of possession varies based on number of plays and time per play.

TABLE 8.2    ILLUSTRATION OF TIME ALLOCATION PER PLAY IN
             HUDDLE OFFENSE VERSUS NO-HUDDLE OFFENSE

|  | *Huddle* (seconds) | *No-Huddle* (seconds) |
|---|---|---|
| Line up and get set | 5 | 5 |
| Execute a play | 5 | 5 |
| Recover from a play | 10 | 10 |
| Return to the Huddle | 5 | 0 |
| Call a play | 10 | 10 |
| Proceed to line of scrimmage | 5 | 0 |
| | | |
| **Total Time per Play (seconds)** | **40** | **30** |
| **Total Number of Plays per Game**\* | **45** | **60** |
| **(with 30 minutes of possession)** | | |

\* Divide Time of Possession by Total Time per Play to solve for Total Number of Plays per Game.

of a forty-second play clock, it would be expected to run forty-five plays per game.[†]

In this example, the no-huddle system allows an offense to reduce the time per play from forty seconds to thirty seconds. This ten second difference reflects the time it takes to return to the huddle after a play ends, plus the time it takes to proceed to the line of scrimmage after a play call has been exchanged in the huddle. By eliminating these ten seconds, a no-huddle offense is able to run sixty plays per game— thirty-three percent more offensive plays per game than a conventional offense is able to execute.[‡]

While a huddle allows an offense time to catch a quick breather between plays, that time is essentially unproductive and provides little benefit to an offense. In fact, those additional ten seconds can often benefit the opposing

---

[†] For the purpose of simplifying terms in this chapter, the term "conventional offense" is shorthand for a team that utilizes a huddle-based communication system.

[‡] Calculation for 33 percent = $((60 \div 45) - 1) \times 100$

defense more than the offense. Defenses have an opportunity to make key substitutions, introduce more defensive looks, rest, and emotionally prepare themselves for the next play.

By "eliminating" those additional seconds, in this example, an opposing defense "loses" seven minutes and thirty seconds of rest and transition time to which it is normally accustomed (representing 25 percent of the time defense normally spends on the field).*

No-huddle offenses, of course, operate in real game conditions. Even though no-huddle offenses are able to generate more plays per game, they do not hold the ball as long as conventional offenses. The top ten no-huddle offenses in 2010 on average held the ball for less than thirty minutes per game (see Table 8.3).

Oregon's top-ranked offense held the ball for just 28:09 per game (ranked 106 out of 120 Division I-FBS teams). Auburn's time of possession per game was 29:31 (ranked sixty-seventh out of 120 Division I-FBS teams).

Table 8.4 helps to illustrate the overall impact that a no-huddle offense can have on a team. The key observation to be made from this table is that despite the decline in Auburn's overall defensive statistics, its scoring output soared. By 2010, Auburn had increased its scoring output by 68 percent more than what it had been able to achieve as a conventional offense. In 2007, Auburn's offense generated 335 yards and gave up 297 yards, yielding a net productivity gain of thirty-eight yards per game.† That season, Auburn's defense was ranked sixth best in the country. Although Auburn's 2007 offense was able to maintain a time of possession of 30:23 minutes per game, it was not particularly productive, finishing the season ranked 97 out of 119 Division I-FBS teams.

The 2010 numbers tell a different story. In 2010, Auburn generated 499 yards on offense while surrendering 368 yards per game. Although Auburn's 2010 defense allowed significantly more yards relative to its 2006 and 2007 teams, Auburn's offensive gains were so great that it was able to

---

* Seven minutes and thirty seconds is arrived at by multiplying forty-five plays with ten seconds per play.
† Calculation for 38 yards per game = 335–297.

TABLE 8.3    2010 TOP TEN TEAMS BY TOTAL OFFENSE AND
            TIME OF POSSESSION

| Total Offense Ranking | Team | Passing Percentage* | Time of Possession | Time of Possession Ranking |
|---|---|---|---|---|
| 1 | Oregon | 38.6% | 27:55 | 106 |
| 2 | Boise State** | 46.6% | 30:38 | 42 |
| 3 | Oklahoma State | 54.2% | 27:41 | 109 |
| 4 | Nevada | 35.9% | 32:48 | 7 |
| 5 | Tulsa | 46.6% | 30:35 | 43 |
| 6 | Hawaii | 66.7% | 29:30 | 70 |
| 7 | Auburn | 31.2% | 29:18 | 73 |
| 8 | Michigan** | 40.9% | 27:10 | 113 |
| 9 | Arkansas** | 52.5% | 30:22 | 49 |
| 10 | Oklahoma | 52.3% | 30:22 | 50 |
| | **Averages** | **46.5%** | **29:44** | **65.4** |

* The passing percentage statistic reflects the percentage of plays teams pass instead of run. Hawaii passed the most frequently, while Auburn passed the least frequently. These figures demonstrate that whether a top no-huddle offense employs a rushing or a passing based scheme, the time of possession on average was less than thirty minutes per game.

** Conventional Offenses are excluded from the above calculation

TABLE 8.4    AUBURN TIGERS' NET OFFENSE AND DEFENSE PRODUCTION
            (2006–2010)†

| | 2006 | 2007 | 2008 | 2009 | 2010 |
|---|---|---|---|---|---|
| **Total Yard Gained** | 321 | 335 | 303 | 432 | 499 |
| Change from previous year (yards) | | +14 | -32 | +129 | +77 |
| Percent Change (Offense) | | 4.4% | -9.6% | 42.6% | 15.5% |
| **Total Yards Allowed** | 292 | 297 | 317 | 374 | 368 |
| Change from previous year (yards) | | -5 | -20 | -57 | +6 |
| Percent Change (Defense) | | -2% | -6% | -15% | 2% |
| **Net Productivity Increase/Decrease** | +29 | +38 | -14 | +58 | +131 |
| **Offensive Point scored per Game** | 24.8 | 24.2 | 17.3 | 33.3 | 41.2 |

† Figures rounded to the nearest integer.

offset the defensive "decline," and generate a net productivity increase of 131 yards per game.*

Auburn's defensive statistics suggest that it underperformed compared to previous seasons, but these statistics are misleading. No-huddle teams generally require their defenses to play for longer stretches of time than conventional team's defenses because the no-huddle system increases the number of plays per game. As a result, no-huddle defenses will surrender more total yards and give up more points. When comparing a conventional team's defensive statistics to a no-huddle team's defensive statistics, the conventional team's defense will more than likely have better numbers. No-huddle teams accept a certain trade-off—suboptimal defensive statistics for more points which should produce more wins.

## WHY RUN THE NO-HUDDLE OFFENSE?

No-huddle offenses enjoy advantages, in part driven by opportunities created by the offense, and in part based on the added pressure a no-huddle offense places on opposing defenses. No-huddle offenses primarily offer quarterbacks the advantage of being able to spot opportunities for receivers and running backs prior to the snap while opposing defensive players are still settling into their defense. Playing against a no-huddle offense creates anxiety for opposing defenses. Defenses are more likely to become confused or suffer from fatigue in "up tempo" scenarios, increasing the likelihood that an opposing defense may miss an assignment or blow a coverage.

One of the main reasons to use the no-huddle offense is to reduce the defense's ability to call its own plays. Defenses are accustomed to a certain rhythm when playing against conventional offenses. The communication systems used by most defenses rely on the break in action while the offense is in its huddle—precisely the same time that defenses usually call their own plays, rotate personnel, and gear themselves up emotionally for the next play.

Adapting to no-huddle conditions within a single week's worth of practice time is challenging for most opponents. The no-huddle is an extra component for which defenses must prepare that takes time away from preparing for a no-huddle offense's scheme. Defenses often try to counter

---

* Calculation for 131 yards per game = 499 − 368.

a no-huddle offense by simplifying coverage and strategies, which plays right into the hands of a no-huddle offense's quarterback, who is able to more easily recognize mismatches and opportunities in the defense. No-huddle offenses tend to dictate the pace of the game, which in turn limits how an opposing defense can react: defensive substitutions are limited and defenses are less likely to blitz.

## THE COACHING STAFF

Good football teams, whether or not they employ a no-huddle offense, tend to be successful because they have strong coaching staffs. Football teams and their head coaches have unique identities and employ different philosophies. For a head coach to be successful, he must be able to hire assistant coaches who can coach a particular system well. When evaluating candidates for assistant coaching positions, head coaches must consider a candidate's skill sets, experience, talent, and enthusiasm. Head coaches must determine whether an assistant coach is open to new ideas, is willing and able to learn a new system, and is able to recruit well.

The no-huddle offense is a proven way to upgrade any offensive system, but a head coach, offensive coordinator, and defensive coordinator must first believe in a system, be able to coach that system, and then be able to apply the no-huddle philosophy in order to gain maximum advantage over an opponent. Hiring a defensive coordinator who buys into the no-huddle philosophy can be particularly challenging.

Defensive coordinators from no-huddle teams must accept from the outset that their defensive statistics will not be as impressive as the statistics produced by conventional teams. Most defensive coaches measure their success based on statistics such as points allowed, total yards allowed, passing and rushing yards allowed, number of first downs allowed, and so on. A no-huddle defense generally will record poorer defensive outcomes in these categories than conventional defenses because the no-huddle system increases the number of plays per game for a defense.*

Conventional statistics that reflect either the number of plays or time of possession do not accurately measure the performance of no-huddle de-

---

* In this chapter, defenses whose offensive counterparts utilize the no-huddle system are referred to as no-huddle defenses.

fenses. No-huddle defenses should instead focus on an alternative set of measurements that evaluate defensive efficiency such as: (1) first-down efficiency (holding opponents to less than four yards), (2) opponent third-down conversion percentage, (3) red zone conversion percentage, (4) average yard per offensive play, (5) scoring percentage per possession, and (6) points allowed. Defensive coordinators and their players must be willing to accept that their statistical performance may not actually reflect the quality of their effort, and buy-in to the overall advantages provided by no-huddle offenses.

The no-huddle style of play lends itself to quick transitions. The offense may score very quickly or a series may result in a "three and out," forcing the defense back onto the field without much rest. Teams featuring offenses that hold the ball for relatively short periods require their defenses to stay on the field for longer periods. Defenses that stay on the field longer experience additional fatigue, which affects a no-huddle team's overall defensive performance. No-huddle teams must be prepared to accept this trade-off.

## ANALYZING THE NO-HUDDLE IMPACT ON A DEFENSE

Auburn's defensive performance over the past five years illustrates the impact that implementing a no-huddle system can have on a team's defense (see Table 8.5).

When comparing Auburn's 2006 season with its 2010 season, Auburn's defense allowed over ten points more per game (a 73 percent increase), and still the team went undefeated. The 24.1 points allowed by Auburn's defense in 2010 was more than offset by its no-huddle offense that generated 41.2 points a game.

During the 2006–2007 seasons, Auburn's offense ran a "Gulf Coast" (run-oriented West Coast offense) under offensive coordinator Al Borges.* Auburn's offense converted to a no-huddle spread option attack in 2009, when current offensive coordinator Gus Malzahn joined Auburn's newly hired head coach Gene Chizik. Malzahn's new no-huddle offense reduced Auburn's time of possession from previous years requiring Auburn's defense to stay on the field for an additional two minutes and five seconds

---

* Al Borges is the current offensive coordinator for the Michigan Wolverines.

TABLE 8.5    AUBURN TIGERS DEFENSE (2006–2010)*

| Per Game Averages | 2006 | 2007 | 2008 | 2009 | 2010 |
|---|---|---|---|---|---|
| Yards Allowed | 292.31 | 297.72 | 317.75 | 374.08 | 368.36 |
| Opponent's Time of Possession | 29:51 | 28:37 | 29:48 | 31:56 | 30:42 |
| Number of Defensive Plays | 59.5 | 65.8 | 64.75 | 72.7 | 68.8 |
| Average Gain per Play | 4.9 | 4.5 | 4.9 | 5.1 | 5.4 |
| Additional Defensive Plays per game | | 6.3 | 5.3 | 13.2 | 9.3 |
| Offensive Point Allowed | 13.9 | 16.9 | 18.00 | 27.5 | 24.1 |

per contest.[†] That marginal change in time of possession masks a multiplier effect that reflects additional pressure placed on a no-huddle team's defense.

In spite of the change in time of possession statistics, the number of defensive plays increased significantly.[‡] Auburn defended an average of 8.1 more defensive plays per game in 2009–2010 than it did in 2006–2007 (reflecting an 12.9 percent increase), and gave up an average of seventy-six more yards per game over that period (reflecting a 20.5 percent increase).[¶, ‖, **, ††] Over the 2006–2007 and 2009–2010 periods, Auburn's

---

* Of course, the primary goal of an offense is to score as many points as possible. While it is helpful to evaluate statistics such as total yards, third-down conversion rates, etc., scoring points is the most important statistic.

† Calculated by subtracting the average opponent time of possession in 2006 and 2007 from the average opponent time of possession in 2009 and 2010 (the 2008 figures are excluded in this analysis).

‡ In 2008, Auburn implemented a new look spread offense. Auburn's offense struggled in its first six games, a stretch which included a 3-2 victory over an eventual 4-8 Mississippi State team and the program's first loss to Vanderbilt since 1955. The offensive coordinator was fired after the sixth game of the season, after which Auburn reverted to a more conventional offense. Auburn's offense finished the 2008 season ranked 104th in Total Offense and 99th in passing. The 2008 season is excluded in the comparison, but is included in this table for the sake of showing continuity. The 2008 season does not offer a particularly useful comparison as Auburn's offensive philosophy was altered mid-season because of the coaching change.

¶ Calculation for 8.1 defensive plays = ((72.7 + 68.8)÷2) − ((59.5 + 65.8)÷2)

‖ Calculation for 12.9 percent = [(((72.7+68.8) ÷2) ÷ ((59.5+65.8) ÷2)) -1)] x 100

** Calculation for 76 yards = ((292.31 + 297.72) ÷2) − ((374.08 + 368.36) ÷2)

†† Calculation of 20.5 percent = [(((292.31 + 297.72) ÷2) ÷ ((374.08 + 368.36) ÷2)) -1)] x 100

defensive strategy did not change significantly—relying primarily on a 4-3 defensive front—nor did the program bring in lesser caliber recruits. While the no-huddle offense affected Auburn's statistical defensive performance from previous years, those impacts were more than offset by Auburn's increased scoring output.

## TEACHING THE NO-HUDDLE OFFENSE

Amos Alonzo Stagg once famously noted, "It's not what the coaches know that counts, but rather what the players have learned." College football teams are able to work with players for up to five years. Over that time, offensive coaches have a large window in which to teach and implement an offensive system. Today's players virtually receive year-round instruction.

College football players have the benefit of practicing an offensive system during spring and summer football. They understand the game, and they get more film than they ever have before. Due to advances in technology, players have the ability to access and study game film anywhere and at any time. Players can upload game film onto their laptops, iPhones, iPads, Androids, and so on, and study film wherever they happen to be. Most football players are highly motivated to be successful. They are competitive. That motivation drives players to learn, making the teaching process more effective.

Teaching the no-huddle offense starts with teaching a communication system. Whether running a no-huddle system or not, all coaches must invest time with their players to teach terminology, which is necessary to relay information from the coach to the quarterback and from the quarterback to the other players. No-huddle communication is simply the ability to tell everyone on the offense what he is supposed to do while at the line of scrimmage without the opponents' defense being able to understand the communication.

Players can sometimes be involved in the development of the no-huddle communications system. This interaction helps establish communication processes that players can better adapt and memorize. For example, if all runs are named after cartoon characters, the players are given the opportunity to come up with the characters and hand signals. "Bugs" Bunny might be a blast or "Daffy" Duck might be a draw, and so on.

When creating terminology, coaches should encourage a positive environment and be open to any and all ideas. All coaches should be included and make every attempt to encourage athlete participation. The aim should be to include at least one idea from each coach. This process helps to further establish team and staff camaraderie and buy-in of the no-huddle offense. In subsequent years, the players and coaches who helped originate the initial terminology are able to assist the next wave of players. Subtle communication and scheme adjustments that enhance communication can also be adopted in the future.

Teaching the no-huddle communication system is similar to teaching any complex language system. The first teaching sessions illustrate the big picture and discuss why the communication system is used. Subsequent teaching sessions break down the communication into a series of modules that enable players to focus on particular aspects of a communication system. For example, coaches may have players draw certain hand signals and assign certain plays to those hand signals, and build on that process over time.

Coaches are encouraged to test players, just as a player would be tested in an academic setting to reinforce that the player is absorbing the communication system. Regular testing makes the players accountable for learning the system. This should occur in the spring and summer. Offensive coaches may administer written tests to players each week prior to game day to confirm that the players know their offensive responsibilities on each play. Coaches are similarly encouraged to make practice and playing time conditional upon learning the communication system.

Prior to the game, position coaches should also issue tests and correct any mistakes with the player. During practices, especially in spring and summer, an assistant coach, on an ad hoc basis, will require players standing behind the offense to interpret hand signals and terminology. This exercise puts players on constant alert and conditions them to focus on the signals and communication. Once offensive players have internalized a team's communication system, coaches can devote more time to teaching schemes and technical skills during practice sessions. When players transfer or coaches leave, the communication system has to be adjusted. A coach's ability to adjust communication to fit his players is critical. Coaches must be ready and willing to improvise and adapt according to the various situations that can occur.

## CONDITIONING

No-huddle teams are *fast* teams. Playing fast becomes part of the team's identity. They play fast and practice fast. No-huddle teams must pride themselves on being highly conditioned so that they can operate at a high tempo for an entire game. Hustle should be stressed at all times in all practices. Teams that feature no-huddle offenses tend to be better conditioned than their opponents are. A no-huddle team is accustomed to 25 percent more "game" than its opponents are.

No-huddle offenses are accustomed to executing more plays in practice and in games. Their defenses are accustomed to being on the field longer than their opponents are as well. Since the entire team must be prepared to play a game that is longer than what players are normally accustomed, conditioning must be an integral part of the preparation. Creating a practice environment that emphasizes conditioning as a way to gain an advantage over other teams increases the motivation of the athletes to perform well in all practice periods. Conditioning is essential from spring training through the summer. Linemen, for example, should be encouraged and rewarded for lining up quickly in a "ready" position waiting to receive the call between plays. No-huddle teams must practice fast and play fast on both sides of the ball.

## PRACTICING THE NO-HUDDLE OFFENSE

The practice structure for a no-huddle team is notably different from the practice structure of a conventional offense. During practice, conventional offenses usually follow a script of predetermined plays during various practice periods (inside run, blitz pick up, pass skelly, team, etc.). In the no-huddle offense system, such scripting in certain practice periods can inhibit tempo variations and decrease repetitions. Some no-huddle teams will employ either checklists or scripts, while others utilize a combination of scripts and checklists.

The checklists include plays that players practice in specific situations against specific fronts, coverages, and blitzes. Over the course of a practice period, a coach will review his checklist and make sure he has executed all of the plays and situations against various defensive scenarios. A checklist approach, as opposed to a scripted approach, helps make practices more similar to game conditions and flow.

The scout team must also be able to simulate an opponent's tendencies in practice. One way to run the scout defense is to attach basic grids to the wristbands of scout team players that tell the players what to do, so that practice can be conducted at a high tempo and better allow a team's offense to prepare for the game.

Coaches, like their players, also have to adjust to the no-huddle offense. This generally means that coaches have to learn how to "coach on the run" while players are returning to the line of scrimmage to maintain tempo and to meet repetition targets in practice. If a certain situation requires more time with a particular player or group of players, those players can be pulled from the drill and replaced with backups, ensuring that a coach still has ample time to correct mistakes and reinforce instructions. Most fast no-huddle teams receive coaching in video review meetings with players and coaches in attendance. In fact, almost all teaching is done from film to maintain a high level of tempo during practice. "Play the next play" is a common term used to keep the tempo going in practice; correcting mistakes is emphasized in meetings when watching film.

## PRACTICE FILM AND THE NO-HUDDLE

In the early 1950's, Paul Brown, the former head coach and namesake of the NFL's Cleveland Browns, pioneered the practice of filming and evaluating games. Digital video and film editing technology, which are commonplace today, were not available until the latter years of the 1990s. Many of the analytical innovations in film have developed over just the last decade.

While there is much popular emphasis on analyzing game film, practice film may be even more important. Most teams only play twelve to fourteen games per season, but they are allowed over one hundred practice sessions during the year. Practices offer more opportunity to refine skills, assess weaknesses, and improve. Practice film is especially critical for teams that run the no-huddle offense. Because no-huddle teams run highly disciplined, yet very fast-paced practices, coaches are not able to catch every mistake. The cameras act as another coach on the field. Practice film is comprised mainly of sideline and end zone shots. These two angles provide the coach with great vision in making sure players can learn from their mistakes and successes. "The big eye in the sky doesn't lie" is an old term referring to the fact that cameras capture "the truth."

Practice film provides a level of granularity that would surprise most football observers. Coaches are generally able to see obvious mistakes in practice—that is, when a lineman or running back misses a blocking assignment, a quarterback misreads a defense, or a wide receiver runs an improper route. Practice film allows coaches to see the nuances.

Coaches, for example, are able to see if an offensive lineman correctly executed a six-inch power step when the ball was snapped. Practice film enables coaches to see if linemen use their hands or feet properly or if a receiver responds correctly to a defensive back playing in press coverage.* Film can be customized to focus on specific positions for each player to watch as homework. In meetings, coaches can review film together with the players and teach them about certain techniques, and how to respond to various scenarios. They can download this film to portable devices that enable players to study their assignments in their dorm rooms, in between classes, or wherever they may happen to be. With new technology, players can also review telestrated plays with voiceovers recorded by their position coaches. These current technologies are revolutionizing the way players learn the game.

---

* Defensive backs in press coverage play a very physical game, and they will attempt to disrupt a passing route, particularly timing routes, by jamming a receiver at the line of scrimmage.

## GAME FILM

Game film enables coaches to evaluate the strengths and weaknesses of their opponents. Coaches evaluate a number of variables when assessing game film. Coaches study opposing personnel including particular individuals who are likely to have a big influence on a game's outcome. These observations are supplemented with player statistics, which can be gathered from various Internet sites. Offensive coaches can also gain a better insight into the structure and formations employed by opposing defenses. From there, coaches break down video by defensive fronts, line stunts, blitzes, and other common coverages favored by a defense. Game film also enables coaches to determine defensive tendencies by down-and-distance, by field position, situational, red zone, and so on. Game film is important for self-scouting, which helps an offensive coordinator adjust different things in the offense each week to break his tendencies. Video and computer software has enabled coaches to better understand their opponents and their own teams in great depth. Coaches can download data into software platforms that can calculate defensive probabilities based on these inputs. If an offense is in a third-and-short scenario, defensive tendencies can be determined from data that has been input from an opponent's previous games. The software helps coaches determine the probabilities of various defensive fronts and coverages that an offense is likely to face in certain scenarios. For example, on third down and four to seven yards to go, play calling software can predict, based on a defense's past tendencies, that 50 percent of the time, a defense is most likely to line up in two-deep zone, 25 percent of the time in man-free coverage, or 25 percent of the time in man-blitz. Offensive coordinators can then call a play based on these coverage probabilities.

Even armed with this information, the human element of decision making still comes into play, which surprises the best analytical tools. The information gathered from statistics and video produce probabilities, which provide coaches with a best guess, but are by no means predictive. There are a myriad of analytics that an offense coach can evaluate, but too much information can overcomplicate a coach's (and subsequently a player's) ability to make decisions during the course of the game. Coaches must not only decide which statistics are the most relevant, but also understand what those numbers are genuinely intended to convey.

BYU's third-down conversion rate offers a useful of example of a team whose success in one statistical area is explained by its success in another statistical category. In 2009-10, BYU recorded a 55.62 percent third-down conversion rate—the top performing Division I-FBS team in that category (the median conversion rate that season was 39.59 percent). BYU developed a successful methodology for achieving that conversion rate by self-scouting its tendencies not just in third-down situations, but also on first down and second down as well. The offensive staff identified several plays that it defined as "high success" plays, which could be utilized on first-and-ten and on third-and-medium. Those plays that worked best stayed in the package based on success rates, while those that did not were discarded. One of BYU's critical success factors is being able to generate at least four yards on first down. BYU's success on first down allows its offense more freedom to make aggressive second-down calls. If the second-down call is also successful, a team is under less pressure to generate large gains on third down to keep a drive alive.

Some coaches align their game plans along statistical probabilities and follow this order and structure in their game plan. The great play callers have no problem veering from the offensive game plan when the game circumstances dictate a change or adjustment. Coaches call plays from their game plan based both on statistical tendencies as well as reacting and making adjustments as circumstances change or if the defense is playing against their tendencies. Injuries also have a significant impact on play calling decisions. An offensive coordinator may modify a game plan if he determines that an opposing cornerback or defensive tackle is hurt. A coach is likely to modify his game plan if his own best player is hurt.

Defenses of course have access to the same software and film as their offensive counterparts. In order to "beat the probabilities," good offensive coordinators will self-scout to tweak and adjust formations with different movements or shifts to keep opposing defenses off balance. Offensive coordinators will try to make the plays look different or even vary their play calling in certain situations to keep the defense off balance.

In spite of offense coordinators' efforts to disguise an offense or a defense coordinators' efforts to run a stunt to confuse an offensive lineman, most coordinators, like most people, are creatures of habit. Just like people at church oftentimes sit in the same pew or go to the same restaurants and order the same food, offensive and defensive coaches also tend not to change their tendencies or approach very much.

## INNOVATION AND THE NO-HUDDLE OFFENSE

Offensive strategy in football evolves in different ways. In some cases, it is fresh and new. In other ways, the game embraces old ideas and adds new twists. The single wing formation, which lost favor after the World War II era, is back in vogue in the form of the "wildcat" offense, which is a modified single wing formation that uses different motions and movements. In the 1970s and 1980s, many considered the triple option wishbone to be the most innovative offense of its time. Coaches like Darrell Royal of Texas, Bear Bryant at Alabama, Gene Stallings at Texas A&M, and Barry Switzer at Oklahoma—coaches who dominated that era—all employed the triple option wishbone. Today, Georgia Tech, Navy, Army, and Air Force are the only remaining teams in Division I-FBS that employ a form of the traditional triple option offense (now known as the spread triple option attack).

Many teams now employ the triple option out of the shotgun—an old concept mixed with a new idea. In the 1970s, few coaches would have thought that the triple option could be run out of the shotgun. The spread option offense employs similar blocking principals to the wishbone offense, but with different timings, different players touching the ball, and different reads. Many more innovative ideas will emerge over time. Old ideas will be refreshed and made new in other contexts. The dominant offenses of yesterday are reappearing in different forms today.

The no-huddle offensive system surely must qualify as one of the most innovative developments in football over the past thirty years. The brief success enjoyed by the Houston Cougars in the late 1980s has given way to a plethora of spread offensive systems, which rely on the no-huddle as a key part of their strategy. High schools across the country have adopted no-huddle offenses. More coaches and players are gaining familiarity with the no-huddle offense, which is leading more teams to hire coaches who have experience running no-huddle systems. Some of college football's traditional powers, particularly those that are able to attract the best athletes in the country, continue to utilize a more conventional offensive approach, but are increasingly using more tempo in their offensive schemes. Other coaches remain concerned that employing a no-huddle offense will place too much strain on their defense.

Regardless of offensive scheme, the no-huddle system gives an offense many advantages. It keeps the defense in base defensive fronts, coverages, and blitzes, and limits defensive substitutions. No-huddle teams outlast opponents because they are better conditioned. No-huddle offenses are difficult to simulate and difficult to prepare for in practice. The no-huddle system requires coaches to be less concerned with traditional defensive statistical data and more concerned with the ultimate outcome: winning and losing.

Perhaps most importantly, the no-huddle system changes the mentality of the entire team. A no-huddle *offense* is actually a no-huddle *team*. The idea that a no-huddle team is in fact a "fast" team unites the offense and the defense. The offense executes more plays because it operates more quickly. The defense also tends to be on the field longer because the game has more plays. No-huddle defenses accept that their unit's statistics might not look as good as some other teams, but that their team's winning percentage will increase.

Finally, championship success far outweighs success in a particular statistical category. No-huddle offenses are just one part of a *fast team* that practices and plays differently as a whole team. This concept of a *fast team* changes the offense versus defense dynamic within a team and places the emphasis instead upon the ultimate goals of scoring points on offense and stopping opponents from scoring on defense. Ultimately, this philosophy will result in more wins per season and put teams in the best position for championship success as evidenced by the 2011 BCS championship game between two fast no-huddle teams.

Over time, one can expect that defenses will eventually adapt, ultimately diminishing the advantages offered by the no-huddle offense. However, until this equilibrium is reached, the no-huddle offense will continue to offer less talented teams a means to compete more effectively against opponents that are more talented. No-huddle offenses also offer elite teams the ability to separate themselves from their competition. As the recent fortunes of Auburn and Oregon may suggest, the combination of elite talent and a no-huddle system may also be the new formula for winning national championships.

# AVOIDING THE "CAN'T-MISS" PROSPECT

## BY DAN HILL, PHD

Dan Hill, PhD, founder and president of Sensory Logic, Inc., is a recognized authority on the role of emotions in consumer and employee behavior. Dan is inspired by breakthroughs in brain science that challenge traditional ideas of understanding human nature, and by facial coding as an aid in gauging people's decision-related motivations and behavior.

In 1998, Dan Hill started Sensory Logic, Inc., a scientific, research-based consultancy that specializes in measuring and helping to enhance companies' sensory-emotional connection with consumers.

Dan is a frequent speaker around the world and has appeared on CNN, FOX and MSNBC, as well as on NPR's Marketplace, CNBC and CNNfn. His work has been featured in the *Wall Street Journal*, the *New York Times*, *China Forbes*, *BusinessWeek* and *Business 2.0*.

Sensory Logic's unique research combines eye tracking and facial coding to measure consumers' split-second, intuitive reaction to advertising and products. Dan's research led him to publish three business books. *Body of Truth: Leveraging What Consumers Can't or Won't Say* (John Wiley & Sons 2003), was a *Fast Company* Book of the Month nominee, and rated as one of the three most important business books of 2004 by *DDI Magazine*. His second book has been published in over a dozen languages. *Emotionomics: Winning Hearts and Minds* (Kogan Page, 2007, 20008 and 2010), which explores both the marketplace and workplace and features a foreword by Sam Simon, co-creator of *The Simpsons*, was chosen by *Advertising Age* as one of the top ten must-read books of 2009 and won an AXIOM Business Books award. Dan's latest book is *About Face: The Secrets of Emotionally Effective Advertising* (Kogan Page, 2010).

Raised in Minnesota and Italy, Dan received his PhD from Rutgers University following studies at Brown University, Oxford University, and St. Olaf College. Dan and his wife, Karen, a women's clothing designer, live in St. Paul, Minnesota.

---

In sports, as in life, some mysteries seemingly cannot be solved. Take college football recruiting ratings as one example. According to David Biderman of the *Wall Street Journal*, only twenty-five of the sixty-four players selected in the first two rounds of the 2010 NFL draft were considered Top 100 college football recruits during their senior year in high school.[*,1] From 2003 to 2005, just 17 percent of the top one hundred high school football recruits were selected in the NFL's first two rounds.[2] Meanwhile, the NFL's first overall draft pick in 2010 draft, Sam Bradford from the University of Oklahoma, was not ranked among the top one hundred recruits as a high school senior.

There are numerous reasons why highly touted high school prospects do not succeed at the college level. Recruiters misevaluate players' actual talent level. Players suffer injuries. Other players are not able to adjust emotionally and academically to the rigors of being a college athlete. In almost

---

* Top 100 prospects are determined by Rivals.com, a college recruiting service.

all of these cases, fans fault the players for failing to live up to their billing or criticize a coach for failing to properly gauge a player's talents. Fans' judgements can of course be unforgiving. Injuries are unavoidable and poor evaluation of talent is somewhat understandable (college recruiting is, after all, a subjective business by nature). Players who fail to adjust emotionally or who experience discipline problems are likewise lumped into the broader category of athletes who fail to live up to their potential. Their failures are brushed aside as another unpreventable outcome —nothing more than the cost of doing business in high-stakes college football. It is this latter category of outcomes that attracts our interest.

In an effort to analyze the overall predictive quality of the high school recruiting services, we reviewed the college football career outcomes of the top fifty high school recruits from the classes of 2005 and 2006 as compiled by the college football recruiting service *Scout.com* (see Table 9.1). These prospects represented the top two percent of all players selected to play Division I-FBS football. As of the date of this writing, all of these recruits have either exhausted their college eligibility or dropped out of school. Many of these recruits participated in the NFL drafts in the years 2009, 2010, and 2011.* Among those one hundred players, we counted forty-nine players who were "correctly valued" (i.e. Top-50 high school recruits who significantly contributed to the universities that originally recruited them). We further counted fifty-one players whom we considered "over-valued" (i.e. players whose high school recruiting rankings were not validated at the college level).

We used a loose definition of "value" to determine whether a Top-50 recruit was correctly valued based on the following considerations:

- **Number of starts, number of games played:** We would expect a Top-50 recruit to start frequently, particularly toward the latter part of his college career.
- **Conference and national honors received:** We would expect a Top-50 recruit to garner various conference and national honors.

---

* We were unable to provide a precise draft participation figure. Many of the Top 100 players in the survey conducted individual workouts for NFL teams, but did not officially take part in the NFL draft.

- **Completion of junior or senior year in good standing:** We would expect a Top-50 recruit to at the very least complete his junior year of eligibility, indicating that the team which recruited the player was able to benefit from his abilities for a significant period of time.
- **NFL Draft participation:** We would expect a Top-50 high school recruit to be selected in the NFL draft.

Recruits who were highly rated, completed their minimum college eligibility requirements, performed well for the original team that recruited them, and went on to be drafted would meet the definition of being "correctly valued." The recruit's star billing in high school proved to be accurate at the college level and was further validated in the NFL draft. We place more weight on the player's productivity at the college level, presumably the league in which the player was drafted to play, and de-emphasize the player's NFL draft status—although a player's draft status provides some degree of endorsement for the player's high recruiting ranking. Among the forty-nine correctly valued players, forty-three went on to be drafted in the NFL while six players were high performers in college, but were not drafted.

We found in our study that among the fifty-one players whose rankings we considered overvalued, twenty-one of those players experienced disciplinary, legal or academic problems at the university that recruited them. Twenty-one recruits either transferred or withdrew from school prematurely prior to finishing their junior season (a list which overlaps with twelve of the players who exhibited discipline problems including one player who died of a drug overdose after he left the team). Injury problems hampered the playing abilities of just nine recruits.

This small sample suggests that from 2005 to 2006 over twenty percent (one in five) of the top one hundred high school football recruits in Division I-FBS college football failed at the college level due to disciplinary or academic reasons. The findings suggest that recruiters may have been getting the players' physical "measurables" mostly right, but were failing to properly evaluate the players' emotional maturity.

Some of the disciplinary and academic problems might very well have been predictable. Coaches spend a great deal of time researching the backgrounds of players. They can assign probabilities to certain recruits who

TABLE 9.1   RECRUITING OUTCOMES OF SCOUT.COM TOP 50 HIGH
            SCHOOL RECRUITS (2005 AND 2006 RECRUITING
            CLASSES)

| Recruiting Outcomes | | Early Transfers/Dismissals | | NFL Draft Round | |
|---|---|---|---|---|---|
| Discipline | 21 | Transfer (Fresh) | 7 | Round 1 | 15 |
| Injuries | 9 | Transfer (Soph) | 4 | Round 2 | 9 |
| Part-Time Starter | 21 | Ineligible as Fresh | 2 | Round 3 | 6 |
| Met Expectations | 49 | Dismissed | 8 | Round 4 | 3 |
| **Totals** | **100** | **Totals** | **21** | Round 5 | 2 |
| | | | | Round 6 | 7 |
| | | | | Round 7 | 4 |
| | | | | **Totals** | **46*** |

* Among the forty-six players drafted by the NFL, forty-three were considered correctly valued while the remaining three were drafted in spite of exhibiting discipline problems during their college careers.

were poor students at the high school level or who displayed disciplinary problems off the field. Some coaches believe they are taking a "calculated risk" based on how well they think they "know" these players. Other coaches opt to generally avoid such players altogether. Over the 2005 and 2006 recruiting periods, Florida signed three Top-50 players who later exhibited discipline problems, while Florida State, Georgia, Maryland, Michigan, Penn State, and Tennessee each signed two Top-50 players who later demonstrated disciplinary problems. Among the twenty-one instances in which players displayed problems, just seven of those recruits would complete their senior seasons. The NFL drafted three of these troubled players (a conversion rate of 14 percent compared to an overall conversion rate of 49 percent among Top 50 prospects). These outcome discrepancies suggest that coaches are better off avoiding troubled recruits altogether, and focusing instead on recruiting solid four-star or three-star players who are more likely to contribute to a team's success.

Some coaches believe that by offering discipline and structure they have the ability to turn around the lives of talented but troubled athletes. Troubled players offer solemn promises that they have the capacity to change their behavior in college. Coaches accept these promises; after all, they want to believe. Other players exhibit no evidence of discipline or maturity problems until after they arrive on campus. Recruits that lack the emotional capacity to succeed in college are often more disruptive to a team's success than a high profile recruit whose talent does not translate on the field. Disruptive players command valuable time from coaches, can damage team chemistry, diminish a football program's brand, and reflect poorly upon the head football coach responsible for recruiting the player.

Can any coach really know how a high school recruit will adjust at the college level? How many coaches later realize that they "should have known better" after a highly touted prospect fails to succeed due to off the field troubles? What if there was a technique that allowed coaches to "know better" simply by being able to look into the eyes of the player and make a much more informed judgment?

The answers to those questions can be provided by a technique known to professional interrogators in organizations such as the CIA and the FBI as "facial coding." These experts have been using facial coding for over twenty years as a method to determine the rectitude of various thieves, embezzlers, murderers, mobsters, and terrorists. One reason why these organizations have embraced facial coding has to do with human physiology. These experts draw upon scientific study and experience, which indicate that the face does not lie. The face is the only place in the body where the muscles attach right to the skin. Since the nineteenth century, researchers from Charles Darwin to Paul Ekman have helped to establish that emotionally encoded impulses generated by the brain are instantaneously delivered to the face via a single facial nerve that controls all facial muscles and resulting facial expressions. As a result, a person's face may betray what the person is actually feeling when he or she is being less than honest. Highly trained facial coders can observe these responses in real time and through careful video analysis. Over the past twenty to thirty years, facial coding has been extended to disciplines such as marketing, advertising, political campaigning, and even speed dating. As the practice of facial coding has become more established, researchers have determined that facial coding can be used to predict future outcomes by assessing a subject's answers to questions that reveal desirable and undesirable character traits.

This chapter will describe how facial coding can be applied to the high-stakes world of college football recruiting as a means of improving recruiting outcomes. We argue that facial coding can improve upon the failure rates associated with discipline problems of otherwise "can't-miss" high school prospects. Facial coding can also help determine which recruits have the emotional (and not just physical) capacity to succeed at the college level, and which players unfortunately do not.

## WHAT IS FACIAL CODING?

A famous NFL franchise owner once said before the 2010 NFL Combine in Indianapolis that he could tell in an interview which players had "what it takes" to be successful and claimed that he could see right through those who did not. Many people share his type of confidence, believing that they possess the innate ability to look into the eyes of another person and determine whether that person is telling the truth. The real truth is that only Secret Service agents assigned to protect the president of the United States have the ability to perform at levels above pure chance when it comes to detecting liars in real time.[3] They are trained to use facial coding and body language detection techniques—non-verbal signals—to spot signs of danger.

Facial coding is a process that interprets a person's facial expressions by analyzing the activity variance of facial muscles to determine how the person is feeling. These expressions typically last from as little as 1/10th of a second to no more than four seconds. Facial coding can be applied in real time, such as during a conversation; however, video offers the best tool with which to conduct proper analysis. Trained academic coders may take up to an hour to watch a single minute of video. Video can be slowed to frame-by-frame shots, each representing one-thirtieth of a second, which allows the coder to meticulously review a person's face and establish how that person is emoting. The forehead, eyes, nose, cheeks, mouth, and chin are the areas that command a coder's interest. On video, a straightforward look at a person's well-lit face is recommended to provide a facial coder with the best view of a subject. Software that helps to automate the facial coding process is in development, but at present, no system is considered sound enough to use on a stand-alone basis, although that time is surely coming.

## THREE PROPERTIES OF FACIAL CODING

Facial coding is based on three properties: universality, spontaneity, and abundance.

The first property of facial coding is universality. Facial expressions are such an innate part of humans' communication system that by nine months of age a child can display all of the seven core emotions with their face. Even a person born blind has the same facial expressions as a person who has sight. Across the globe—regardless of gender, race, or age—facial muscle movements reveal the same emotions. These expressions are not socialized or learned. They are hardwired into the brain.

That said, facial displays vary somewhat by culture. In Japan, emoting may be more muted. Emotional signals from the face may be briefer and less intense. Meanwhile, in Brazil, the expressions may be more dramatic, but the facial muscle activity involved in emoting in Sao Paulo is in essence no different than in Tokyo. As a point of contrast, body language is not universal. An "OK" sign with your fingers can mean "money" in China, is a derogatory symbol for homosexuality in Turkey, and is the Brazilian way of signalling displeasure to nonconforming motorists.

The second property of facial coding is spontaneity. As mentioned earlier, the face is the only place in the body where the muscles attach right to the skin. There is no one single "lying muscle" in the face. Interpreting facial expressions is not that easy. But because the brain generates emotionally encoded impulses that show up as facial expressions, it is nearly impossible for a person to hide their true feelings from a trained facial coder who can interpret what is being revealed emotionally, even if the coder is not necessarily sure of the underlying reason. Much as an ocean wave forms, builds, and dissolves, facial expressions also have an onset, a peak, and fade. Checking for that natural rhythm in an expression is one way to determine a person's veracity, also known as the say/feel gap. "Micro-expressions," the expressions with the shortest durations, are sig-

TABLE 9.2    SEVEN CORE EMOTIONS APPLIED TO SPORTS

| | Emotion | Performance Enhancers | Performance Inhibitors |
|---|---|---|---|
| *Positive Emotions* | *Happiness* | More open, creative thinkers | Happy-go-lucky, inattentive |
| | *Surprise* | More alert, seek to absorb more information | "Freezing." Unable to perform. |
| *Negative Emotions* | *Anger* | Determination, fortitude | Rigidity, resentfulness |
| | *Sadness* | Renewed focus | Listless |
| | *Fear* | High alertness | "Freezing." Unable to perform. |
| | *Disgust* | Seek to upgrade performance | Reject new input |
| | *Contempt* | Seek authenticity | Disrespectful |

nals that flit on and off the face in as little as one-tenth of a second. Facial expressions in effect provide an observer with real-time data. Facial coding's third property is abundance. Human beings have more facial muscles than any other species on the planet.

Facial coders analyze forty-three key muscles in the face. These muscles combine to form movements that Paul Ekman and his research colleague, Wallace Freisen, cataloged into "action units." Twenty-three of these action units correspond to one or more of the seven core emotions of happiness, surprise, sadness, fear, anger, disgust, and contempt. Each emotion has its own positive and negative meaning, depending on the scenario in which it appears, including within the context of sports (see Table 9.2).

## FACIAL CODING IN THE FIELD

Facial coding is used in many other disciplines. For example, my work has been applied in politics, marketing, advertising and sales force hiring. Facial coding can be used to assess a politician's personality and his or her likely appeal to voters. During the recent 2008 presidential election, my firm developed conclusions about a candidate's likelihood of success by watching hours of televised debates and speeches, as well as observing the candidates live in Iowa and New Hampshire.[4] On the Republican side, we were able to use facial coding to predict Mike Huckabee's ascent, as well as Rudy Giuliani and Fred Thompson's early demise. Our research predicted that Mitt Rom-ney was likely to draw lukewarm responses. On the Democratic side, we foresaw that Barack Obama could pose as the one actual threat to Hillary Clinton. We also projected that Clinton might have the capacity to come back and win the New Hampshire primary because her interactions with voters improved after her setback in the Iowa primary.

My firm's work has been applied to employee performance evaluations to help assess the factors that can be attributed to successful employees.[5] For instance, we have applied facial coding techniques to evaluate school teachers' abilities in the classroom.[6] Those studies helped to establish the relationship between teacher enthusiasm and teaching ability. As you might suspect, our research found a clear emotional divide separating good teachers from more mediocre ones.

We were also able to use facial coding to determine why certain salespeople outperformed others.[7] We created a questionnaire designed to elicit particular emotional responses. The first question sought to assess career satisfaction. The subjects' responses verified that above-average salespeople demonstrated more happiness than their mediocre counterparts did. The second question asked interviewees to describe specifics about their jobs. Poorer performers tended to feel more sadness and frustration than their more successful peers did. The third and fourth questions had to do with closing the deal. Our results showed that better salespeople feel more frustration when "speed bumps" occur in closing a deal because these are the salespeople most eager to make something happen.

Facial coding can also be applied to predicting relationship outcomes. As captured in Malcolm Gladwell's book, *Blink*, psychologist John Gottman from the University of Washington, Seattle, spent two decades studying couples talking to each other during marriage counseling.[8] By viewing only fifteen minutes of video, he could predict with 90 percent accuracy whether a couple would still be married fifteen years later based on observing their facial expressions and non-verbal signals.[9] Romantic chemistry is not necessarily very different, in essence, from the chemistry between a coach and player, or between players on a team. In reality, human beings are all naturally facial coders. We like to have important conversations in person because we know by instinct—and by research—that in ambiguous situations an estimated 55 percent of communication is received by viewing the face of the other person, while only 6 percent of communication is derived from the actual words spoken.[10] During conversations a part of the brain is devoted exclusively to reading the faces of others, which is as much as eight times more sensitive than the part of the brain that reads objects.[11]

Before the start of a recent NFL season, a *USA Today* headline considered whether a highly drafted quarterback would finally justify the team's faith in him. Out of curiosity, I went on YouTube and watched some video footage of interviews with the quarterback. I concluded that the answer would prove to be an unfortunate no. What concerned me about the quarterback was really twofold. First, the player appeared less prepared to field questions than most other high-quality quarterbacks I had studied. Moreover, the quarterback in question betrayed an anxiety level well above that of good quarterbacks in the NFL.

But that is not all. Next, I went in search of video to see how the quarterback's current coach was responding to the player. The coach was saying all the right things: "this quarterback is my guy; he's ready to step up to replace so-and-so," and so forth. But that's not what the coach's face showed. Instead, while he was verbally expressing his confidence that the quarterback would be able to overcome a recent series of on-field disappointments, the coach's face demonstrated contempt toward the player. I was not surprised when the season opened and the quarterback's results were not good. If the player's coach was not convinced after getting close up looks in practice every day, why should I be? I was also not surprised that the quarterback eventually found himself traded.

## ORIGINS OF FACIAL CODING

The story of facial coding begins with Charles Darwin, an encounter with an orangutan named Jenny, and the birth of Darwin's first child. In March of 1838, Darwin observed his first ape, Jenny an orangutan that being held in captivity at the London Zoo. Jenny had a significant impact on Darwin:

> One of the keepers was teasing her—showing her an apple, refusing to hand it over. Poor Jenny "threw herself on her back, kicked & cried, precisely like a naughty child," Darwin wrote in a letter to his sister. Darwin was speculating about evolution from every angle, including the emotional, and he was fascinated by Jenny's tantrum. "What is it like to be an ape? Does an orangutan's frustration feel a lot like ours? Might she cherish some sense of right and wrong? Will an ape despair because her keeper is breaking the rules—because he is just not playing fair?[12]

Darwin's first child, a son, was born about a year and a half later on December 27, 1839, prompting Darwin to muse "at once [I commenced] to make notes on the first dawn of the various expressions which he exhibited, for I felt convinced, even at this early period, that the most complex and fine shades of expression must all have had gradual and natural origin."[13]

Over time, Darwin expanded his research to include correspondence with scientists conducting similar studies from around the world. Darwin concluded that animals undergo emotions comparable to human beings, and that people could physically observe these emotions. Darwin's research convinced him that human expressions were innate and therefore universal. After an extensive amount of research (and thirty-four years after his first encounter with Jenny), Darwin published *The Expression of the Emotions in Man and Animals* in 1872, which helped lay the foundation for modern biological anthropology. In this book, Darwin provided evidence that the facial expressions of humans correlate to those of other primates.

Ten years before the release of Darwin's *Expressions*, Duchenne de Bologne, a French neurologist, published "The Mechanisms of Human Facial Expression." Duchenne defined expressive gestures on the human face and associated each with a specific facial muscle or muscle group. To stimulate the facial muscles and capture these "idealized" expressions of his patients, Duchenne applied shock treatments through electrified metal probes pressed upon the surface of the various muscles of the face. Having applied the electrical shocks, Duchenne would then immediately capture his patients' expressions by utilizing the then recent technological innovation of

---

FIGURE 9.1　PHOTOGRAPHS FROM DUCHENNE THAT ARE INCLUDED
IN DARWIN'S *EXPRESSIONS*

---

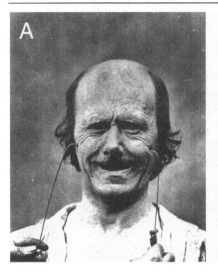 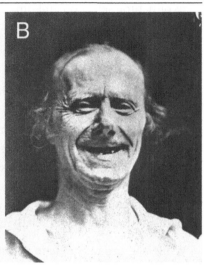

*The photographs depict the same person. The picture on the left depicts a man smiling because of electrical shocks applied to his face. The picture on the right depicts the same man smiling spontaneously.*

photography. Darwin displayed some of these photographs in *Expressions* (see Figure 9.1).

After Darwin and Duchenne had completed what would become facial coding's foundational work during the mid-nineteenth century, the technique of facial coding basically lay fallow. Part of the explanation was due to the Victorian era's resistance to the notion of evolution, which helped to somewhat inhibit the influence of Darwin's ideas. Another part of the explanation, however, lay in what happened next. Adolph Hitler, the founder of the German Nazi party, adopted Darwin's works to help provide scientific justification for the systematic execution of over six million Jews and four million other people who belonged to what Hitler regarded as "inferior races."

Because of the mayhem wrought by Hitler during World War II, Darwin's work was to a certain extent tainted by its association with Hitler's atrocities, causing it to fall out of favor with many prominent thinkers. The great social thinkers of the post-World War II era were anxious to better understand and put the horrors of Hitler and the holocaust behind them, including those ideas, which, at least, notionally, were based on Darwin's ideas of natural selection and universality. In some disciplines such as social anthropology, Darwin's ideas, while not completely discredited, were subject to extreme criticism.

Among social anthropologists, including notably Margaret Mead, the idea of cultural relativity began to hold sway instead.* Cultural relativity is a broad field with many variations, but in essence, the theory holds that human values, far from being universal, vary a great deal according to different cultural perspectives. Two distinct cultures, for example, may practice the same religion, but introduce their own cultural norms, which are not necessarily condoned or practiced in the underlying religion. Darwin's focus on emotions universally felt and consistently expressed was at odds with this notion of cultural relativity.

While the broader debate about cultural relativity and universality raged on in academic circles, the U.S. government was channelling research dollars into learning more about the human brain, particularly the brains of the thousands of GIs who had suffered head wounds during World War II.

During these studies, Paul MacLean, a government scientist, discovered in 1949 that the human brain is actually comprised of three-parts that evolved over a long period.[14] MacLean's findings revealed that the sensory or reptilian brain first evolved an estimated five hundred million years ago. The emotional or mammalian brain followed, most likely coming into existence about two hundred million years ago. The final part of the brain, the rational, cognitive component came afterward: a mere one hundred thousand years ago. MacLean's findings suggested, at least from an evolu-

---

* Margaret Mead was a cultural anthropologist who popularized anthropology in American culture, and whose work informed the feminist movement in the 1960s. She received the Presidential Medal of Freedom posthumously from President Jimmy Carter. The medal's citation read, "Margaret Mead was both a student of civilization and an exemplar of it. To a public of millions, she brought the central insight of cultural anthropology: that varying cultural patterns express an underlying human unity. She mastered her discipline, but she also transcended it. Intrepid, independent, plain spoken, fearless, she remains a model for the young and a teacher from whom all may learn."

tionary perspective, that human beings feel before they think. In fact, our emotional responses happen five times more quickly than our cognitive responses and these emotions inevitably color our rational responses.[15]

From 1965 to 1978, Dr. Paul Ekman, a clinical psychologist (considered by many to be the father of modern facial coding), working together with his colleague Wallace Friesen, conducted the bulk of his foundational work on facial coding. Ekman took Darwin's initial studies and systematically figured out which muscle movements corresponded to specific emotions. In time, Ekman would even go so far as to visit the Fore Tribesmen in the jungles of Papua, New Guinea, to determine whether people who had never been exposed to Western civilization would display similar facial expressions. Ekman's research revealed that the tribesmen exhibited similar facial expressions to those of civilized people. He also determined that the tribesmen could interpret pictures of Westerners' facial expressions correctly. From his research, Ekman defined core emotions that are universal to all human beings: anger, disgust, fear, happiness, sadness, and surprise. He would later add contempt to this list.

In the early 1990s, Ekman's findings were bolstered by the introduction of functional MRI (fMRI) brain scanning technology that enabled scientists to link neural activity to changes in blood flow and blood oxygenation in the brain.* The changes in blood flow observed through the fMRI provided physiological evidence that tied the centrality of emotions to people's decision-making process. Ekman's decades' worth of research on facial coding, which was likewise predicated on human beings' instinctive reactions to stimuli, suddenly began to find a much wider audience as a consequence of this observable validation.

The core of Ekman and Friesen's methodology is known as the Facial Action Coding System (FACS).[16] In a manual of some two hundred pages in length, they laboriously identified what they term as Action Units (or AUs), assigning a variety of muscle movements that together form a unit of analysis (AU1, AU2, AU3 and so forth). Many AUs are signifiers of response, but not specifically of emotions. Those AUs that correspond to emotions form a separate, subset methodology known as EMFACS. For

---

* Collectively known as hemodyamics.

years now, Ekman and others have used EMFACS primarily in the field of psychology and for the purposes of training law enforcement officers.

## APPLYING FACIAL CODING TO COLLEGE FOOTBALL

Facial coding can help provide insight into such variables as a player's passion for the game, capacity to overcome adversity, ability to focus when the game is on the line, receptiveness to coaching, ability to coexist in a team environment, and his or her will to win. These qualities can be assessed in structured settings, similar to the interviews that take place at the NFL Combine.

In preparation for an interview with an NFL club, a former starting college quarterback was conducting a series of mock interviews with former NFL coaches. These practice sessions are designed to help players respond to questions which address matters ranging from the most mundane to those designed to better understand weaknesses, discipline and maturity issues.

> *Interviewer A:* "Considering everything that you hold dear in your heart, where does football rank?"
>
> *Player:* "Football has always been y'know, number three to me. I've put faith always, always first and foremost and getting me here is family. Without my family, I wouldn't be here where I'm at today. And right behind that is football."
>
> *Analysis: Statement is mere boilerplate, pat answer. No emotion behind it. Lack of conviction*
>
> *Interviewer B* asks if the player has ever been in trouble with the law.
>
> *Player* says: "No sir," shaking his head no. On repeated questioning, he says "no" twice more (third time the player finally shows slight anger).
>
> *Analysis: Good response. What you want to see. Resents doubts about his character, but isn't quick to anger (not hot-headed).*
>
> "Were you pissed off at your coach for leaving you? Or did you understand?"
>
> *Player* says: [Anger, Fear, Sadness] "At a point, y'know, you're a little upset just because of the way it happened. Y'know, you're at

your sports banquet and you're celebrating, y'know, 12 and 0 [Weak Smile] and you find out you're playing (team name redacted). So you're all geared up for that, and then y'know [Weak Smile] all of a sudden the news breaks. And at that point y'know [Anger] it was almost a team divided. A lot of guys were y'know, Screw this. I'm not doin' this [Anger, Fear, Sadness] and, if he's gonna bail on us, we'll be back and... [Surprise]."

**Interviewer A:** "What was your stance personally?"

**Player** says: "My stance [Surprise] is that (coach's name redacted) is an unbelievable coach, and I owe him a lot and I told the guys, y'know, we're an exceptional bunch of players."

*Analysis: Player expresses a range of emotions, consistent with what would be expected following a coach's departure. The player does not acknowledge his anger at the coach's departure. The player describes the other players as being angry (i.e. "a lot of guys") because he is still angry. The player's answer raises concerns that the player might be slow to accept that NFL football is a business in which coaching turnover is high.*

**Interviewer** asks player to draw up his favorite play

**Player** reacts [Weak Smile, Anger] when told to go to the white board. Player is then asked to remember as much as he can from the play Interviewer A drew up earlier in the interview, and Player attempts to do so. When asked if the player remembers what play was called, he says "Jet drive or something" [Anger, Fear, Sadness] before he smiles [True Smile].

*Analysis: This is not a player who is highly confident about his mental abilities. There is some anger exhibited in response to the request to go to the white board. The player seems to almost expect failure after he suggests what the name of Interviewer A's favorite play might be. The player then follows with a big smile, in an attempt to win over the interviewers.*

From the video available of that mock interview, Sensory Logic's facial coders were able to determine the player's emotional profile (see Figure 9.2). The percentages indicate the distribution of emotions exhibited during the interview across ten different emotional states. The face expresses four types of smiles: true  smile, robust social smile, weak soc-

FIGURE 9.2    EMOTIONAL PROFILE OF NFL QUARTERBACK PROSPECT

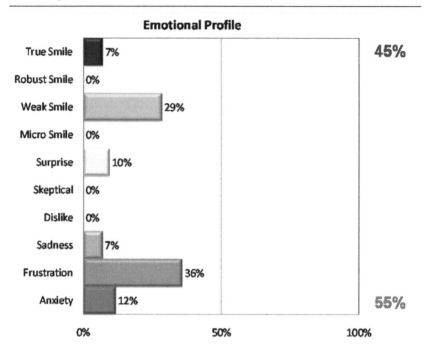

ial smile and brief micro-smile. Based on an analysis of the player's verbal responses in relation to the player's facial response, some interesting insights emerge. Fifty-five percent of the player's facial reactions were associated with negative emotions, while 45 percent of the player's facial reactions were associated with positive emotions. Coaches, in general, whether they are aware of it or not, like to see players smile, which they associate with happiness. That is because strong levels of happiness have been correlated to being the innovative, open-minded problem-solving type of player who gets to superior solutions quickly—qualities a coach is looking for in the quarterback position. On balance, players that emote more—authentically so—tend to be more engaged. A higher level of engagement is, in turn, advantageous because the engaged player is typically more likely to be motivated to perform.

In the case of the prospective quarterback's emotional profile, the AUs shown on the ex-college quarterback's face during the interview are categorized into the particular emotion(s) to which they correspond. These occurrences are recorded as frequencies (percentages)—as shown in Figure 9.2 —that can be used to develop a player's overall emotional profile.

Facial coders will prepare a list of questions designed to elicit the emotions needed to evaluate key characteristics. The filmed interview can be broken down to analyze the emotions demonstrated in order to score/rank each player by position. Different coaches may wish to emphasize certain characteristics more than others. Questions can be structured to account for this particular emphasis. We advise that the questionnaires be designed to assess a player's drive, his ability to handle stress, his ability to cope with setbacks, and his ability to build chemistry with teammates and coaches.

Facial coding also allows the observer to determine if a player has a predominantly positive or negative disposition. In some instances, coaches may want to see more negative emoting when assessing a player's dislike of losing. In other instances, coaches may want to see more positive emoting when answering questions about being receptive to coaching advice and guidance. Facial coders can compare data recorded from multiple players. On average, a more intense and engaged player is most likely to perform better than a casual, lackadaisical player is (although the latter might enjoy the virtue of remaining calm under duress).

Facial coding can also predict an individual's ability to perform when the game is on the line. Facial coding can be used to determine if a tennis player is more likely to lose a close match or assess which NBA players lack the confidence to make crucial shots late in playoff games. Facial coding can be used to improve player-coach relationships by recording interactions between players and coaches. Coaches and players often come from different generational, racial, ethnic, and socioeconomic backgrounds. As current NBA head coach Erik Spoelstra noted a recent article profiling the team chemistry of the Miami Heat, "Probably what I've learned from Pat [Riley] the most is that coaching in this league is about managing personalities, more than about managing Xs and Os."[17] In a similar fashion, facial coding can assess team chemistry within a particular roster. Facial coding may be used to determine which players are more likely to be "bad apples" and can even be used to decide on optimal personnel combinations based on personality traits.

Facial coding provides a disciplined methodology that can be used to assess human emotions. On an instinctive level, all coaches are facial coders. As former president Lyndon Baines Johnson once said, "If you can't walk into a room and know who's with you and who's against you, you ain't worth spit as a politician." The same thing can be said of a college football coach entering a locker room at halftime of a big game or while he is pacing the sideline during a game. The best coaches have an instinctive feel for the emotional state of their teams. Good coaches can tell if such and such a player is emotionally up to the challenge of being inserted into the game, or if he should keep a player in the game rather than allowing another player to take his place. Those spontaneous decisions can be partially informed by facial coding based on looking at a player's face. Relying on one's ability to look a recruit in the eye to predict if he has the emotional maturity to succeed at the college level, on the other hand, is an entirely different matter.

This chapter suggests that when it comes to recruiting, rather than trying to judge a book by its cover, coaches would be better off applying modern techniques of facial coding instead. Facial coding techniques provide coaches with an ability to rigorously assess the emotional readiness of high school recruits and can help predict how likely a player will be successful at the college level. It is not enough to know how fast a high school football player runs, how high he jumps, how far or fast he can throw a ball, or anything else that is physical in nature. Virtually any college recruiting staff can do that. The benefit of recruiting a five-star prospect can be negated if that player proves to be disruptive to a team's chemistry and has disciplinary problems that keep him off the field. College recruiting is an imprecise discipline, but facial coding offers the ability to improve outcomes by reducing the likelihood that a team recruits a player who later becomes prone to discipline related problems. There will always be coaches who are so enamored by a player's physical potential, that they are willing to ignore any behavior or emotional problems. Facial coding can provide a necessary check that dissuades a coach from allowing the potential of a tantalizing, yet troubled, prospect to override the better interests of the team.

# SPECIAL THANKS

The editors would like to thank all of the authors for sharing their ideas and spending their time with us to develop the book. We also thank Seth Jungman for his friendship and support, and wish Seth, his wife and the soon-to-be addition to his family well. Special thanks goes out to Kent Stephens, the historian at the College Football Hall of Fame, whose research and advice greatly enhanced our understanding of the huddle's origin; Tony Athersmith, former head coach of the University of Birmingham Lions; and Andy Fuller, the British American Football Association (BAFA) director for Student Football Development for opening our eyes to a new world. We would also like to thank our families for humoring us while we entertain the idea of having literary careers alongside our day jobs. Last, but hardly least, we send a note of sincere thanks to our fathers for doing what fathers do best.

# NOTES

### CHAPTER 1

1. Excerpted from "Two Step Shuffle for Texas QB," Inside the Big 12 Column, *CNN Sports Illustrated*, December 21, 1999, accessed May 15, 2011, http://sportsillustrated.cnn.com/football/college/1999/bowls/news/1999/12/21/big12_insider/.

2. American Council on Education. Accessed April 30, 2011. http://www.ace net.edu/Content/NavigationMenu/ProgramsServices/CPA/Executive_Summary .htm

### CHAPTER 3

1. Associated Press, "Blocked field goal secures Appalachian State's upset of Michigan," *ESPN.com,* September 1, 2007, accessed January 28, 2011, http://scores.espn.go.com/ncf/recap?gameId=272440130.

2. Jack Carey, "For Small Schools, There's A Big Payoff To Road Trips," *USA Today,* September 3, 2009, accessed January 28, 2011, http://www.usatoday .com/sports/college/football/2009-09-02-smallschool_payoffs_N.htm.

3. "What's the Difference between Divisions I, II and III?" *National Collegiate Athletic Association,* last modified February 7, 2007, accessed January 28, 2011, http://www.ncaa.org/wps/portal/ncaahome?WCM_GLOBAL_CONTEXT =/ncaa/NCAA/About+The+NCAA/Membership/div_criteria.html.

4. Congressional Budget Office, *Tax Preferences for Collegiate Sports* (Washington, DC: US Government Printing Office, 2009).

5. Amy Daughters, "College Football: Should FBS vs. FCS Games be Banned Permanently?" *Bleacher Report,* September 28, 2010, accessed January 28, 2011, http://bleacherreport.com/articles/475339-college-football-should-fbs-vs-fcs -games-be-banned-permanently.

6. "Goliath Hasn't Gone Anywhere," *Wall Street Journal,* September 21, 2010, accessed January 28, 2011, http://online.wsj.com/article/SB1000142405274870 3556604575501740109812272.html.

7. Daughters, "College Football."

8. Daughters, "College Football," ¶ 16.

9. Adrian Bouchet and Matthew Scott. "Do BCS Schools Have an Advantage Over Non-BCS Schools in APR Rankings? An Early Examination," *The Sport Journal*, 13:2 (2010), accessed January 28, 2011, http://www.thesportjournal .org/article/do-bcs-schoolshave- advantage-over-non-bcs-schools-apr-rank-ings-early-examination.

10. "Goliath Hasn't Gone Anywhere," *Wall Street Journal*, September 21, 2010, accessed January 28, 2011, http://online.wsj.com/article/SB100014240 52748703556604575501740109812272.html.

11. "2009-10 Revenue Distribution Data," *Bowl Championship Series* (January 25, 2010), accessed April 15, 2011, http://www.bcsfootball.org/news/story ?id=4856975.

12. Curtis Eichelberger, "BCS Conferences Receive $145 Million, Six Times Paid to Other Leagues," January 25, 2011, Bloomberg.com.

13. Edward Aschoff, "Scheduling Games Part of Business," *Gatorsports.com*, September 10, 2009, accessed April 11, 2011, http://www.gatorsports.com/ar-ticle/20090910/ARTICLES/909109920?p=2&tc=pg.

14. Tim Tucker, "Georgia Adds Florida Atlantic to 2012 Football Schedule – At Cost Of $1 Million," *Atlanta Journal Constitution*, November 30, 2010, accessed April 11, 2011, http://blogs.ajc.com/uga-sports-blog/2010/11/30 /georgia-will-pay-1-million-for-2012-football-game-vs-florida-atlantic/.

15. Jack Carey, "For Small Schools, There's A Big Payoff To Road Trips," *USA Today*, September 3, 2009, accessed April 11, 2011. http://www.usatoday .com/sports/college/football/2009-09-02-smallschool_payoffs_N.htm

16. Adam Jacobi, "Boise State Wanted $1 Million To Play Nebraska?," *CBS Sports.com*, September 9, 2010, accessed April 11, 2011, http://college-football .blogs.cbssports.com/mcc/blogs/entry/24156338/24447857

17. Chad Cripe, "National Title Is Not On Boise State Football Team's Goal List; Redskins Expect 86,000 Fans for Boise State-Virginia Tech," *Idaho States-man*, September 3, 2010, accessed April 11, 2011, http://voices.idahostatesman .com/2010/09/03/ccripe/national_title_not_boise_state_football_teams_goal _list_redskins.

18. Yuri Hanin, "Fear Of Failure In The Context Of Competitive Sport: A Commentary," *International Journal of Sports Science & Coaching* 3 (2008): 185-189.

19. Johnmarshall Reeve, Bradley Olson, and Steven Cole, "Motivation and Performance: Two Consequences of Winning and Losing in Competition," *Motivation and Emotion* 9 (1985): 291-297.

20. Jim Polzin, "UW Officials Insist FCS Opponents Are Here To Stay," *Madi-son.com*, September 15, 2009, accessed April 11, 2010, http://host.madison .com/sports/college/football/article_a1f81f9a-a274-11de-b121-001cc4c002e0 .html

## CHAPTER 4

1. Tom Dienhart, "Coaches pick the most important statistic," Rivals.com, accessed May 22, 2011, http://rivals.yahoo.com/ncaa/football/news?slug= rivals-1222359.

2. Dienhart, "Coaches pick the most important statistic."

## CHAPTER 6

1. Wieberg, S., Upton, J., Perez, A.J., & Berkowitz, S. (November 10, 2009). "College Football Coaches See Salaries Rise in Down Economy," *USA Today Online,* accessed February 19, 2011, http://www.usatoday.com/sports/college /football/2009-11-09-coaches-salary-analysis_N.htm.

2. "Special Reports: As Economy Sours, Presidential Pay Draws Increased Scrutiny," *The Chronicle of Higher Education Online,* accessed February 19, 2011, http://chronicle.com/article/As-Economy-Sours-Presidential/7891.

3. Wieberg, S., et al., "College Football Coaches."

4. Report of Findings from Quantitative and Qualitative Research for Knight Commission. Knight Commission – FBS Presidents Study, accessed February 27, 2011, http://www.knightcommissionmedia.org /images /President_Survey_APPENDICES.pdf.

5. Report of Findings, Knight Commission.

6. USA Today Web site: http://www.usatoday.com/sports/college/football /2010-coaches-contracts-table.htm.

7. Paul W. Grimes and George A. Chressanthis, "Alumni Contributions to Academics: The Role of Intercollegiate Sports and NCAA Sanctions," *American Journal of Economics and Sociology,* 53:1 (1994): 27–40.

8. Robert Baade and Jeffery Sundberg, "Fourth Down and Gold to Go? Assessing the Link Between Athletics and Alumni Giving," *Social Science Quarterly* 77:4 (1996): 789–803.

9. Brad R. Humphreys and Michael Mondello, "Intercollegiate Athletic Success and Donations at NCAA Division I Institutions," *Journal of Sport Management* 21: 2 (April 2007).

10. Jonathan Meer and Harvey S. Rosen, *The Impact of Athletic Performance on Alumni Giving: An Analysis of Micro Data, Working Paper No. 13937* (Cambridge, Mass.: National Bureau of Economic Research, April 2008).

11. Soebbing, B. P., & Washington, M., "Leadership Succession and Organizational Performance: Football Coaches and Organizational Issues, *Journal of Sport Management* (In Press).

12. "PMorgan Paid Dimon $20.8 million in 2010." Dealbook. New York Times, April 7, 2011.

13. "JPMorgan Chase Reports Fourth-Quarter 2010 Net Income of $4.8 Billion, up 47% over Prior Year, on Revenue of $26.7 Billion; $1.12 Earnings Per Share." Business Wire. January 14, 2011.

14. "Texas leads nation in total revenue, football revenue for 2007-08." Street and Smith's Sports Business Journal. June 2009.

15. "Texas Gives Mack Brown Raise, Extension." By Jim Vertuno. The Associated Press. August 28, 2007.

16. Brown, R.W., "An Estimate of the Rent Generated by a Premium College Football Player," *Economic Inquiry*, 31(1993): 671–684.

CHAPTER 7

1. R. Hyatt, "Barriers To Persistence among African American Intercollegiate Athletes: A Literature Review of Non-Cognitive Variables," *College Student Journal* 37:2 (2003): 260.

2. Sports Litigation Alert Archives, April 7, 2006, Richard Sheinis, Esq.

3. "NBA Defends Age Limit Policy in Letter" Associated Press, July 21, 2009.

4. "Stern Wants NBA Age Limit Raised to 20," ESPN.com News Services, April 13, 2005.

5. Tim Sullivan, "One-and-done Basketball Sham Is Legally a Shame," *The San Diego Union Tribune*, April 23, 2008.

6. http://www.bohnbooks.com/pdf/grange-excerpt.pdf, accessed March 10, 2011.

7. http://www.bohnbooks.com/pdf/grange-excerpt.pdf, accessed March 10, 2011.

8. "Harold 'Red' Grange – Turns Heads by Turning Pro." http://sports.jrank .org/pages/1742/Grange-Harold-Red-Turns-Heads-by-Turning-Pro.html

9. *The Story of Pro Football*. Published by Howard Roberts (1953).

10. Bob Carroll, *The Grange War* (1926).

11. "Pipeline to the Pros." NFL Players' Association presentation. 2006.

12. "Pipeline to the Pros."

13. "Pipeline to the Pros."

14. http://en.wikipedia.org/wiki/Maurice_Clarett, accessed March 14, 2011.

15. http://en.wikipedia.org/wiki/Maurice_Clarett, accessed March 14, 2011.

16. Mike Freeman, "Citing Antitrust, Clarett Sues N.F.L. To Enter Its Draft," *New York Times*, September 24, 2003.

17. "Suit Claims NFL Rules Restrain Amateurs," Associated Press, September 24, 2003.

18. "NFL Plans To Appeal Ruling," Associated Press, February 6, 2004

19. *Clarett v. National Football League*, 306 F. Supp. 2d 379 (S.D.N.Y. 2004).

20. "Wide Receiver Mike Williams Decides to Leave USC Early and Apply For NFL Draft," Pac-10 News, February 25, 2004.

21. "Mike Williams to Leave USC Early."

22. "Mike Williams to Leave USC Early."

23. "Mike Williams to Leave USC Early."

24. "Mike Williams to Leave USC Early."

25. USC Trojans Official Athletic Site, accessed March 14, 2011, www.usctrojans.com

26. USCTrojans.com.

27. USCTrojans.com.

28. University of Southern California; Professional Sports Counseling Panel (PSCP) Program and Services, accessed March 12, 2011 http://www.usctrojans.com/genrel/usc-compliance- pscp.html.

29. Gary Klein, "Williams Hires Florida Agent," *Los Angeles Times*, February 27, 2004.

30. Mark Maske, "Denied NCAA Bid, Williams Considers Options," *Washington Post*, August 27, 2004.

31. Mike Fish, "Making a Reinstatement," *Sports Illustrated*, June 8, 2004.

32. "Making a Reinstatement."

33. "NCAA Turns Down Williams' Reinstatement Bid," Associated Press, August 26, 2004.

34. Please see John J. Miller's *The Big Scrum: How Teddy Roosevelt Saved Football* (Harper, 2011) which chronicles the president's efforts to save college football through the creation of the NCAA.

35. D1 Manual, Supra note 8.

36. Id., Supra note 8, Article 14, Eligibility.

37. NCAA Division I Manual at 12.01.2.

38. NCAA Division I Manual at 12.02.3.

39. Division I Manual, Supra note 8, Bylaw 12.1.2.

40. Division I Manual, Supra note 8. Bylaw 12.1.2.1.

41. Darren Rovell, "Williams Marketing Deals Now in Limbo," *ESPN.com*, April 20, 2004.

42. Mark Maske, "Denied NCAA Bid, Williams Considers Options," *The Washington Post*, August 27, 2004.

43. NFL CBA, Supra note 10, Article XVI, Section 2 (b).

44. See generally the NFL CBA, Supra note 10.

45. Robert Ruxin, *An Athlete's Guide to Agents*, 4th ed. (Jones and Bartlett., 2003).

46. Chris Low, "Alabama's Smith Expected to be first-round pick," January 3, 2009, accessed March 12, 2009, http://sports.espn.go.com/ncf/news/story?id=3808765.

47. Libby Sander, "Game Over for 3 UNC Football Players Who Accepted Agents' Gifts," October 11, 2010, accessed March 12, 2009, http://chronicle.com/blogs/players/game-over-for-3-unc-football-players-who-accepted-agents-gifts/27557.

48. Sports Litigation Alert, accessed on March 14, 2011, http://www.hackneypublications.com/sla/archive/001111.php.

49. Glenn M. Wong, Warren K. Zola, & Chris Deubert, "Going Pro in Sports: Providing Guidance to Student-Athletes in a Complicated Legal & Regulatory Environment," *Cardozo Arts & Entertainment Law Journal* 201:28 (3).

50. Division I Manual, Supra note 8, Bylaw 12.3.4. NCAA Regulations Related to Agents and Other Amateurism Provisions, 639 Practicing Law Institute Understanding Business & Legal Aspects of the Sports Industry 155 (February 2001).

51. Division I Manual, Supra note 8, Bylaw 12.3.4

52. Division I Manual, Supra note 8, Bylaw 12.3.4.2.

53. Division I Manual, Supra note 8, Bylaw 12.3.4.2.

54. Division I Manual, Supra note 8, Bylaw 12.3.4

55. Libby Sander, "NCAA Considers a National Pro-Sports Counseling Panel," *The Chronicle of Higher Education*, October 19, 2010.

56. Taken in part from a letter written by Rachel Newman Baker, director of Agent, Amateurism, and Gambling of the NCAA.

57. DI Manual, Supra note 8, Bylaw 12.2.4.2.3.

58. See generally Wong and Deubert supra.

59. See generally Wong and Deubert supra.

60. See generally Wong and Deubert supra.

61. See generally Wong and Deubert supra at 488. Permanent total disability typically requires that the athlete be completely unable to perform his or her profession or sport for an entire twelve-month period after the initial injury.

62. Id. citing NCAA ESDI Program, Supra n. 61.

63. See Wong & Deubert, Supra note 61 at 507.

64. See Wong & Deubert, Supra note 61 at 507.

65. See Wong & Deubert, Supra note 61 at 507.

66. See Wong & Deubert, Supra note 61 at 507.

### CHAPTER 8

1. College Football Historical Society Newsletter, Volume XI, Number II, February 1998.

2. College Football Historical Society Newsletter, February 1998.

3. The Churchill Center and Museum at the Churchill War Rooms, London (www.winstonchurchill.org)

4. Tiger Ellison, *Run and Shoot Offense: The Now Attack* (Tiger Ellison, 1965).

5. Carolyn J. Ellison, *Coach the Kid, Build the Boy, and Mold the Man: The Legacy of Run and Shoot Football* (Xlibris Corp, 2007).

### CHAPTER 9

1. "Top 100 Prospects are No Lock for the NFL." By David Biderman. *Wall Street Journal*. April 27, 2010.

2. Biderman, "Top 100 Prospects are No Lock for the NFL."

3. Ekman, Paul. *Telling Lies*. New York: Norton, 1992.

4. Ames [Iowa] Straw Poll, August 2007; New Hampshire primary campaigning, January 2008.

5. Nationwide Insurance, 2005; Taco John's, 2007.

6. Philadelphia Literacy Initiative, 2009.

7. Prostaff, 2006; WBEB, 2009 and 2011.

8. Gladwell, Malcolm. *Blink*. New York: Little, Brown, 2005.

9. Gladwell, Malcolm. *Blink*.

10. Mahrabian, Albert. *Silent Messages*. Belmont, CA: Wadsworth, 1981.

11. Banich, Marie T. *Cognitive Neuroscience and Neuropsychology*. Boston: Houghton Mifflin, 2004.

12. "Darwin at the Zoo." By Jonathan Weiner. *Scientific American*. December 2006.

13. "Facial Behavior in Child Development." By Harriet Oster and Paul Ekman. Minnesota Symposia on Child Psychology, Volume 11.

14. Howard, Pierce J. *The Owner's Manual for the Brain*. Atlanta: Bard, 2000.

15. Zaltman, Gerald. *How Customers Think*. Boston: Harvard Business Press, 2003.

16. Ekman, Paul and Wallace Friesen. *Manual for the Facial Action Coding System*. San Francisco: Human Interaction Laboratory, 1978.

17. Salter, Chuck. "What LeBron James and the Miami Heat Teach Us about Teamwork." *Fast Company*, April 20, 2011.

CPSIA information can be obtained at www.ICGtesting.com
Printed in the USA
LVOW01s1251310813

350424LV00016B/787/P